Emotion and Its Relationship to Acceptance, Food Choice, and Consumption

Emotion and Its Relationship to Acceptance, Food Choice, and Consumption

The New Perspective

Editors

Witoon Prinyawiwatkul
Adriano Gomes da Cruz

MDPI • Basel • Beijing • Wuhan • Barcelona • Belgrade • Manchester • Tokyo • Cluj • Tianjin

Editors
Witoon Prinyawiwatkul
Louisiana State University
USA

Adriano Gomes da Cruz
Federal Institute of Rio de Janeiro (IFRJ)
Brazil

Editorial Office
MDPI
St. Alban-Anlage 66
4052 Basel, Switzerland

This is a reprint of articles from the Special Issue published online in the open access journal *Foods* (ISSN 2304-8158) (available at: https://www.mdpi.com/journal/foods/special_issues/Emotion_Acceptance_Food_choice_Consumption).

For citation purposes, cite each article independently as indicated on the article page online and as indicated below:

LastName, A.A.; LastName, B.B.; LastName, C.C. Article Title. *Journal Name* **Year**, *Volume Number*, Page Range.

ISBN 978-3-0365-0370-7 (Hbk)
ISBN 978-3-0365-0371-4 (PDF)

© 2021 by the authors. Articles in this book are Open Access and distributed under the Creative Commons Attribution (CC BY) license, which allows users to download, copy and build upon published articles, as long as the author and publisher are properly credited, which ensures maximum dissemination and a wider impact of our publications.

The book as a whole is distributed by MDPI under the terms and conditions of the Creative Commons license CC BY-NC-ND.

Contents

About the Editors vii

Witoon Prinyawiwatkul
Relationships between Emotion, Acceptance, Food Choice, and Consumption:
Some New Perspectives
Reprinted from: *Foods* **2020**, *9*, 1573, doi:10.3390/foods9111573 1

Pitchayapat Chonpracha, Ryan Ardoin, Yupeng Gao, Pamarin Waimaleongora-ek, Georgianna Tuuri and Witoon Prinyawiwatkul
Effects of Intrinsic and Extrinsic Visual Cues on Consumer Emotion and Purchase Intent:
A Case of Ready-to-Eat Salad
Reprinted from: *Foods* **2020**, *9*, 396, doi:10.3390/foods9040396 5

Mădălina Iuga, Víctor D. Ávila Akerberg, Tanya M. González Martínez and Silvia Mironeasa
Consumer Preferences and Sensory Profile Related to the Physico-Chemical Properties and
Texture of Different Maize Tortillas Types
Reprinted from: *Foods* **2019**, *8*, 533, doi:10.3390/foods8110533 21

Héctor Hugo Pérez-Villarreal, María Pilar Martínez-Ruiz and Alicia Izquierdo-Yusta
Testing Model of Purchase Intention for Fast Food in Mexico: How do Consumers React to
Food Values, Positive Anticipated Emotions, Attitude toward the Brand, and Attitude toward
Eating Hamburgers?
Reprinted from: *Foods* **2019**, *8*, 369, doi:10.3390/foods8090369 39

Serafín J. Cruces-Montes, Ana Merchán-Clavellino, Antonio Romero-Moreno and Alberto Paramio
Perception of the Attributes of Sherry Wine and Its Consumption in Young People in the South
of Spain
Reprinted from: *Foods* **2020**, *9*, 417, doi:10.3390/foods9040417 57

Ana Merchán-Clavellino, María Pilar Salguero-Alcañiz, Rocío Guil and Jose Ramón Alameda-Bailén
Impulsivity, Emotional Intelligence, and Alcohol Consumption in Young People:
A Mediation Analysis
Reprinted from: *Foods* **2020**, *9*, 71, doi:10.3390/foods9010071 69

Giulia Mascarello, Anna Pinto, Valentina Rizzoli, Barbara Tiozzo, Stefania Crovato and Licia Ravarotto
Ethnic Food Consumption in Italy: The Role of Food Neophobia and Openness to
Different Cultures
Reprinted from: *Foods* **2020**, *9*, 112, doi:10.3390/foods9020112 83

Cen Song, Chunyu Guo, Kyle Hunt and Jun Zhuang
An Analysis of Public Opinions Regarding Take-Away Food Safety: A 2015–2018 Case Study
on Sina Weibo
Reprinted from: *Foods* **2020**, *9*, 511, doi:10.3390/foods9040511 97

About the Editors

Witoon Prinyawiwatkul holds a PhD in Food Science from the University of Georgia, USA. He is currently the Horace J. Davis Endowed Professor of Food Science at Louisiana State University, Agricultural Center, Louisiana, USA. His research is predominantly focused on sensory science and consumer research, in addition to added-value and healtheir product development. He also oversees the Sensory Services Lab http://nfs.lsu.edu/sensory/index.htm#p6. Along with his active collaborations with researchers worldwide, he has published 220 refereed articles (with a h-index of 45 and an i10-index of 103), is an author/co-author of 1 book and 5 book chapters, and has delivered 346 professional scientific presentations. His publications have been cited nearly 6700 times with 794, 304, 286, 198, and 189 citations for the top five articles (based on Google Scholar as of December 2, 2020; https://scholar.google.com/citations?hl=en&user=_Wv_dYoAAAAJ). He is a fellow of IFT (Institute of Food Technologists, USA). He has served as the scientific associate Editor/Editorial Board Member for several prestigious journals, including *Foods*.

Adriano Gomes da Cruz holds a PhD in Food Technology from the Faculty of Food Engineering, State University of Campinas. He is also an associate professor within the Department of Food at the Federal Institute of Education, Science and Technology of Rio de Janeiro (IFRJ). He has experience in teaching and professional experience in food science and technology, with an emphasis on dairy science and technology, in addition to sensory and consumer science.

Editorial

Relationships between Emotion, Acceptance, Food Choice, and Consumption: Some New Perspectives

Witoon Prinyawiwatkul

School of Nutrition and Food Sciences, Louisiana State University Agricultural Center, Baton Rouge, LA 70803, USA; wprinya@lsu.edu

Received: 26 October 2020; Accepted: 29 October 2020; Published: 29 October 2020

Abstract: Food is more than just a source of nutrients—it also provides basic pleasure as well as aesthetic experiences. A number of studies have reported that acceptance, food choice, and consumption are affected by a large number of factors, including both intrinsic and extrinsic factors and cues, as well as consumer characteristics. Food-elicited emotions are becoming a critical component in designing products that meet consumers' needs and expectations. Several studies have reported emotional responses to food and their relationships to product acceptability, preference, and choice. This Special Issue brings together a small range of studies with a diversity of approaches that provide good examples of the complex and multidisciplinary nature of the subject matter.

Keywords: food-evoked emotions; sensory liking; consumer acceptance; purchase intent; food choice; food intake and consumption

---

Introduction

Modern consumers are becoming ever-more health conscious and more educated about what constitutes their foods. Many consumers want healthier and safer versions of retailed food products. These consumers are concerned about the health benefits or risks associated with food consumption. Globalization has enabled consumers to be exposed to various cuisines which can be readily available to them. With the world population increasing rapidly, alternative food sources and mass food production will be needed to support sustainability and safety. The questions are: "Would consumers be willing to consume this? How do they feel about the food they eat? Do they like and will they purchase it?" Based on many studies, acceptance, food choice, and consumption are affected by a large number of factors, including both intrinsic and extrinsic factors and cues, as well as consumer characteristics.

It is known that food elicits emotion. Measuring food-evoked emotions is topical in sensory and consumer sciences. Emotions are becoming a critical component in designing products that meet consumers' needs and expectations. Emotional profiles may effectively differentiate products with similar sensory characteristics and hedonic ratings, hence, they may provide additional information that goes beyond traditional hedonic ratings, and provide more insight toward food choice. Several studies have reported emotional responses to food, and their relationship to product acceptability and purchase intent. Appropriate health benefit information has also been reported to impact emotion, purchase decisions and food choices. Human senses and cues play an instrumental role in food choice and intake, emotion and product acceptance, hence, understanding their roles and importance is critical.

This Special Issue of Foods aimed to present both original and cutting-edge research contributing to a deeper understanding of relationships between food-evoked emotion, food choice, acceptance, and consumption.

Consumers use various intrinsic and extrinsic informational cues to form impressions about the quality of food products and to make subsequent purchase and consumption decisions. One study utilized a multifaceted approach to develop an emotional and wellness profile associated with ready-to-eat (RTE) salads [1]. Several emotional terms were proven to distinguish among RTE salad samples, depending on the prominent visual cues presented to consumers. The effects of both intrinsic and extrinsic visual cues on emotions and the liking of RTE salads were evident. The authors concluded that liking intrinsic visual characteristics of salads may moderate the effects of extrinsic cues. Providing additional product information, such as naming or information on packaging, may help reinforce positive tendencies towards making healthy food choices and purchasing intentions.

Maize tortilla is known to be a staple food in Mexico. Contemporary commercial-scale production of tortillas makes use of instant maize flours and specialized machines, which leads to drastic changes in sensory characteristics. One study was performed to investigate consumer preference and choices related to tortillas; comparing artisanal hand-made ones vs. those produced mechanically [2]. The authors reported that the sensory profile of the artisanal ones was better and more nutritious compared to the others. Differences between women's and men's preferences and purchase decisions were observed; men considered taste, while women considered the maize type as a critical factor. Consumers' choices for tortilla are important for producers, so the results of this study may help tortilla producers to better understand some quality characteristics of their products that affected consumer preferences. Alternate research has investigated the hamburger. One study connected the rationale (food values) and positive anticipated emotions to different attitudes in order to predict purchase intent of hamburgers [3]. The authors attempted to identify which emotions, food values and types of attitudes significantly and positively influenced purchase intent. They concluded that the positive anticipated emotion (contentment, excited and satisfied) positively influenced attitudes toward the brand, attitude toward eating, and intention to buy a hamburger at a fast-food restaurant.

There are two studies in this Special Issue that are related to alcohol and wine consumption. Only a few studies have been devoted to address the impact of both intrinsic (taste, aroma, flavor, etc.) and extrinsic (brand, labelling, price, etc.) factors in conjunction with consumer characteristics and attitudes on preference, choice and consumption of wine. One study was performed to analyze preferences of sherry wines as influenced by gender, knowledge, and interest in wine, particularly among young consumers between 18 and 30 years old [4]. The authors concluded that there was a relationship between prior knowledge of and interest in wine culture and wine consumption in young adults. The findings would allow wine producers to have a better idea of young consumer perceptions towards wine, and how to promote a non-abusive consumption of wine among young adults. Contrarily, another study was devoted to alcohol consumption in young people, which is a public health problem [5]. From a psychological point of view, personality variables are clearly associated with alcohol consumption. The authors stated that no data have been found regarding the relationship between emotional intelligence (EI, the ability to perceive, evaluate and express emotions accurately), impulsivity, and alcohol consumption. They concluded that young people with a low level of EI tended to be more impulsive and had poor handling of their emotions, leading to a possible increased risk of alcohol consumption. The findings demonstrated some variables that could prevent alcohol consumption in young people.

In another study, the relationships among ethnic food consumption, food neophobia, consumers' openness to different cultures, and consumer sociodemographic characteristics were evaluated using an online survey with Italian consumers [6]. The authors concluded that consumers with food neophobia would not consume ethnic food, while those with openness to different cultures would. Some sociodemographic variables associated with food neophobia included gender, age, education, marital status (with or without children), and income. The findings from this study may be useful in promoting a diversity of healthy ethnic diets.

The last study utilized massive online textual data to evaluate public opinions on the safety of take-out foods in China between 2015–2018 [7]. The collected data were mined and analyzed using a dictionary-based emotional analysis of text, followed by emotional time series analysis to reveal emotional trends and tendencies. The authors concluded that during this four-years period, the trends of topics/discussions, which carried positive and negative emotions, on take-away food safety were similar, although the number of positive posts about food safety were much higher than the negative posts. The findings would offer insights for government and industry stakeholders as to how to promote safety of take-away food.

The editor hopes that the readers will find this Special Issue insightful, interesting and useful for future research. The diversity of both the content and the methodologies presented in this Special Issue should inspire and encourage future exploration of multidisciplinary research collaboration, which would lead to a better understanding of the complex relationships between emotion, acceptance, choice, and consumption of food.

Funding: This research received no external funding.

Conflicts of Interest: The author declares no conflict of interest.

References

1. Chonpracha, P.; Ardoin, R.; Gao, Y.; Waimaleongora-ek, P.; Tuuri, G.; Prinyawiwatkul, W. Effects of Intrinsic and Extrinsic Visual Cues on Consumer Emotion and Purchase Intent: A Case of Ready-to-Eat Salad. *Foods* **2020**, *9*, 396. [CrossRef] [PubMed]
2. Iuga, M.; Ávila Akerberg, V.D.; González Martínez, T.M.; Mironeasa, S. Consumer Preferences and Sensory Profile Related to the Physico-Chemical Properties and Texture of Different Maize Tortillas Types. *Foods* **2019**, *8*, 533. [CrossRef] [PubMed]
3. Pérez-Villarreal, H.H.; Martínez-Ruiz, M.P.; Izquierdo-Yusta, A. Testing Model of Purchase Intention for Fast Food in Mexico: How do Consumers React to Food Values, Positive Anticipated Emotions, Attitude toward the Brand, and Attitude toward Eating Hamburgers? *Foods* **2019**, *8*, 369. [CrossRef] [PubMed]
4. Cruces-Montes, S.J.; Merchán-Clavellino, A.; Romero-Moreno, A.; Paramio, A. Perception of the Attributes of Sherry Wine and Its Consumption in Young People in the South of Spain. *Foods* **2020**, *9*, 417. [CrossRef] [PubMed]
5. Merchán-Clavellino, A.; Salguero-Alcañiz, M.P.; Guil, R.; Alameda-Bailén, J.R. Impulsivity, Emotional Intelligence, and Alcohol Consumption in Young People: A Mediation Analysis. *Foods* **2020**, *9*, 71. [CrossRef] [PubMed]
6. Mascarello, G.; Pinto, A.; Rizzoli, V.; Tiozzo, B.; Crovato, S.; Ravarotto, L. Ethnic Food Consumption in Italy: The Role of Food Neophobia and Openness to Different Cultures. *Foods* **2020**, *9*, 112. [CrossRef] [PubMed]
7. Song, C.; Guo, C.; Hunt, K.; Zhuang, J. An Analysis of Public Opinions Regarding Take-Away Food Safety: A 2015–2018 Case Study on Sina Weibo. *Foods* **2020**, *9*, 511. [CrossRef] [PubMed]

Publisher's Note: MDPI stays neutral with regard to jurisdictional claims in published maps and institutional affiliations.

© 2020 by the author. Licensee MDPI, Basel, Switzerland. This article is an open access article distributed under the terms and conditions of the Creative Commons Attribution (CC BY) license (http://creativecommons.org/licenses/by/4.0/).

Article

Effects of Intrinsic and Extrinsic Visual Cues on Consumer Emotion and Purchase Intent: A Case of Ready-to-Eat Salad

Pitchayapat Chonpracha [1], Ryan Ardoin [1], Yupeng Gao [1], Pamarin Waimaleongora-ek [2], Georgianna Tuuri [1] and Witoon Prinyawiwatkul [1,*]

[1] School of Nutrition and Food Sciences, Louisiana State University, Agricultural Center, Baton Rouge, LA 70803, USA; pitchayapat_chonpracha@hotmail.com (P.C.); rardoi7@lsu.edu (R.A.); ygao19@lsu.edu (Y.G.); gtuuri@agcenter.lsu.edu (G.T.)

[2] Institute of Nutrition, Mahidol University, Phutthamonthon Rd., Salaya, Phutthamonthon, Nakhon Pathom 73170, Thailand; pamarin.wai@mahidol.ac.th

* Correspondence: wprinya@lsu.edu

Received: 27 February 2020; Accepted: 30 March 2020; Published: 31 March 2020

Abstract: With increasing demand for ready-to-eat (RTE) fresh vegetables, it is important to understand how visual information cues, both intrinsic and extrinsic, affect consumer perception of these products. This study developed an emotional and wellness lexicon related to RTE salads. Subsequent questionnaires with images of salads were used to quantify consumer (N = 150) emotional and hedonic perceptions related to green color shade, shape/size of pieces, multicolor scheme, product name, and packaging. The different visual cues significantly impacted emotions and their intensities. Qualitatively, feelings of health and wellness predominated across salad samples. Negative emotions were more influenced by size of piece and green-color (intrinsic), while positive emotions were influenced by viewing salads of multiple colors (intrinsic) and packaging (extrinsic). Pale green salads were generally less liked than darker green ones. Values, in one case, ranged from 4.39 to 7.28 (on a 9-point hedonic scale), but naming the product ("iceberg lettuce") did raise the lowest score to 5.75. The addition of vegetables with orange and purple colors to the salad mix had a positive impact on the perception of pale green salads. This study demonstrated that intrinsic and extrinsic visual cues significantly influenced consumer emotions, hedonic perception and purchase intent of RTE salads, but the effects of extrinsic cues were generally less prominent.

Keywords: consumer perception; emotion; purchase intent; salads; visual cues

1. Introduction

Consumers use various intrinsic and extrinsic informational cues to form impressions about the quality of food products and to make subsequent purchase and consumption decisions. Intrinsic attributes are inherent to the product itself and cannot be manipulated without affecting its physical properties, such as appearance, taste and texture. In contrast, extrinsic sources of information are related to the product but are not physically a part of it, such as labeling, packaging, marketing information, or situational contexts [1,2]. In the product development process, both intrinsic and extrinsic cues can be directed toward generating positive sensory expectations, which can then dictate judgments of experienced quality upon consumption [3].

Sight is usually the first sense connected to our evaluation of foods [4]. While taste is reported to have the greatest influence on food choice [5], visual information is typically processed prior to food entering the mouth [6] and can even influence flavor perception [7]. These visual cues are not limited to intrinsic characteristics of the product itself (e.g., portion size, shape, color), but also pertain to extrinsic characteristics such as food packaging [4]. In addition to packaging design (e.g., color scheme, transparency/opacity, pictures), written information presented thereupon can also affect perceived value and expected outcomes, including how the product will be liked [8,9]. Ultimately, visual cues can be very impactful and influence consumer sensory expectations, hedonic evaluations, and emotions associated with food products and the overall eating experience [10–14].

Evaluating food-evoked emotions has recently gained interest in the fields of sensory and consumer research [15]. Emotional data have demonstrated added value, compared to traditional liking scores alone, in discriminating products, predicting food choice, and determining purchase intent. Furthermore, consumer emotional profiles are differentially affected by intrinsic and extrinsic product characteristics [10]. Visually, for example, food color intensity (intrinsic) and exposure to packaging (extrinsic) [16] have been shown to affect consumer product-related emotions and product liking [16,17]. Various methods for assessing food–elicited emotions have been employed [15], and the current study combined a few of these techniques to obtain emotional profiles for ready-to-eat salads based on visual evaluation.

The benefits of convenience and portability have driven the growing market for ready-to-eat (RTE) food products [18]. The demand for fresh–cut or minimally processed vegetable salads has also risen worldwide due to changes in demographics, lifestyles, and eating habits [19]. Thus, the hypothesis of this study was that visual intrinsic (green color shade, single vs. multiple vegetable colors, and size/shape of pieces) and extrinsic (product name and packaging) cues of RTE salads would affect consumer emotion expression (terms and their intensities), liking and purchase intent. The research experiment was divided into two main parts: (i) to develop an emotion lexicon related to RTE salads using the individual sample description technique and online questionnaire, and (ii) to investigate the effects of the above-mentioned intrinsic and extrinsic visual cues on consumer liking, emotion, and purchase intent of RTE salads. Data should shed light on salient emotions related to RTE salads, and guide methods to effectively employ visual cues in enhancing perceived product quality.

2. Materials and Methods

2.1. Development of Emotion Lexicon Related to Ready-To-Eat (RTE) Salads

Twelve RTE salads were purchased (from local supermarkets in Baton Rouge, LA, USA.) for evaluation. Selection was based on vegetable variety (e.g., iceberg lettuce, green cabbage, romaine lettuce, spring mix, and spinach), convenience orientation (complete salad kit with and without dressing), and packaging (elastic plastic bag and solid plastic container). The salads were stored under refrigeration (3–5 °C) one day before visual evaluations.

Twenty-three consumers (Figure 1) who frequently purchased or consumed RTE salads (at least twice a week) were recruited to participate in the session. Emotion terminology was generated using a modified individual sample description technique [20]. Consumers were presented with the entire set of 12 salad samples at once but asked to evaluate them one at a time and write down perceived emotions associated with each salad. The typical total evaluation time was approximately 30–35 min (modified from [20]).

Figure 1. A consumer performing the modified individual sample description technique [20] with RTE salads.

The selection of emotion descriptors began with sorting of terms within each salad. Terms with similar meaning were grouped together, and the most representative term from each group was chosen based on frequency of usage, and redundancies were eliminated. For example, if "safe" occurred more often than "secure" in relation to a salad sample, "safe" was retained. Then, emotion terms were pooled across all salad samples, and the same grouping and selection/elimination procedure was employed. This process yielded a list of 35 emotions pertaining to the RTE salads (Table 1).

Table 1. Emotion terms (35) elicited by ready-to-eat (RTE) salads, as generated by the modified individual sample description technique [20].

Emotion Terms		
Accomplished (+)	Excited (+)	Peaceful * (+)
Bored * (-)	Feel different (N)	Pleasant * (+)
Calm * (+)	Feel healthy (+)	Pleased * (+)
Comfortable (+)	Feel special (+)	Refreshing (+)
Confident (+)	Feel wellness (+)	Safe * (+)
Creative (+)	Fullness (+)	Satisfied * (+)
Curious (+)	Guilty * (-)	Steady * (+)
Dangerous (-)	Happy * (+)	Trust (+)
Desired (+)	Interested * (+)	Unique (+)
Disappointed (-)	Joyful *(+)	Warm * (+)
Discouraged (-)	Mad (-)	Worried * (-)
Disgusted * (-)	Nostalgic * (+)	

* indicates 16 terms shared with the *EsSense Profile*™ [21]. ( ) indicates the emotion status; + = positive emotion, - = negative emotion, N = neutral.

These 35 terms were combined with those from the EsSense Profile™ [21], an existing set of 39 common food-evoked emotions. A resulting list of 58 emotion terms was obtained after consolidating 16 duplicate terms (Table 2). In order to further identify those emotion terms most relevant to RTE salads, an online survey (Qualtrics, Provo, UT, USA.) was developed, and completed by an additional 118 consumers (consuming salads at least twice a week). This online survey presented consumers with photographs of RTE salads and asked them to select, in a check-all-that-apply (CATA) format, emotion terms (from a list of 58 terms) associated with the salads. The most relevant emotion terms, based on a selection rate of at least 30%, were chosen for rating measurement in the subsequent consumer study.

Table 2. Percentage of emotion terms (58) elicited by ready-to-eat (RTE) salads and mentioned by consumers (N = 118).

Emotion Terms	Percentage	Emotion Terms	Percentage	Emotion Terms	Percentage
Feel healthy	79%	Loving	15%	Glad	4%
Feel wellness *	58%	Peaceful	15%	Affectionate	4%
Safe	45%	Joyful	14%	Darling	3%
Satisfied	44%	Bored	14%	Disgusted	3%
Active	39%	Calm	14%	Merry	3%
Good	37%	Understanding	13%	Tender	2%
Happy	31%	Accomplished	11%	Tame	2%
Interested	31%	Excited	10%	Nostalgic	1%
Refreshing	30%	Feel different	8%	Polite	1%
Pleased	28%	Free	8%	Dangerous	
Trust	27%	Mild	1%	Mad	1%
Confident	25%	Unique	7%	Quiet	1%
Desired	25%	Eager	6%	Wild	1%
Energetic	25%	Curious	6%	Aggressive	0%
Comfortable	24%	Disappointed	6%	Creative	0%
Feel special	23%	Guilty	5%	Discouraged	0%
Good-natured	22%	Adventurous	5%	Fullness	0%
Pleasant	22%	Enthusiastic	5%	Steady	0%
Friendly	21%	Warm	4%		
Worried	18%	Whole	4%		

* Also referred to as "engaging in a wellness lifestyle".

2.2. The Impact of Visual Cues on Consumer Liking, Emotions and Purchase Intent

2.2.1. Visual Cues Tested in a Consumer Study

Photographs of RTE salads were captured, uploaded in an online questionnaire, and presented as the visual cues for the consumer study. These photograph images were employed as surrogates for fresh salads to maintain visual consistency [22] and to mitigate effects of sensory attributes other than appearance. The four visual cues of interest were: shade of green color, shape/size of vegetable pieces, single color or multicolor salad, and packaging (with or without) (see Table 3). The green color varied in visual green color shade to an extent deemed obvious to the normal human eye. From lightest to darkest green, the images depicted: square-cut iceberg lettuce (Sample A), shredded iceberg lettuce (Sample B), romaine lettuce (Sample C), or spinach (Sample D). The shape/size component was based on cut of the iceberg lettuce: square cut, considered large (square-L), or shredded, considered small (shredded-S). Additionally, the impact of product name (named or unnamed) was evaluated within these factors. Single-color salads consisted of lettuce only, and multicolor salad contained lettuce, shredded carrots (orange hue), and shredded red cabbage (purple hue). Multicolor salads were presented with and without their respective package. The visual effects of packaging presentation and multicolor were compared between pale green (PG; iceberg and romaine lettuce mix) and dark green (DG; romaine lettuce and spinach) salads.

Table 3. Salad images used to determine visual cue effects.

	Visual Attribute	Ready-to-Eat (RTE) Salad Samples			
Unnamed	Lightness/Darkness	Sample A	Sample B	Sample C	Sample D
	Shape/Size	Square-L		Shredded-S	
Named	Lightness/Darkness	Iceberg Lettuce	Iceberg Lettuce	Romaine Lettuce	Spinach
	Shape/Size	Square Iceberg lettuce		Shredded Iceberg lettuce	
Unnamed	Pale green (PG)	Single-color	Multicolor	Multicolor with Package	
	Dark green (DG)				

2.2.2. Consumer Study

Consumers were recruited from the Louisiana State University (LSU; Baton Rouge, LA, USA.) campus to participate in this study, which was approved by the LSU Agricultural Center Institutional Review Board (IRB HE#18-22). Selection criteria were that participants were regular salad consumers (at least twice per week) and over 18 years of age. Consumers (N = 150) completed the three questionnaires in 3 consecutive days. Using Compusense five® Software (Compusense Inc., Ontario, Canada), online questionnaires were administered in partitioned booths under cool white lighting. Images of salads (Table 3) were presented in a randomized order. On day 1, the first questionnaire evaluated liking (a 9-point hedonic scale; 1 = dislike extremely, 5 = neither like nor dislike, 9 = like extremely) of green color and liking of size and cut for unnamed ready-to-eat salads. Each hedonic question was followed by a rating of emotions (a 5-point intensity scale; 1 = not at all, 2 = slightly, 3 = moderately, 4 = very much, 5 = extremely [21]; see justification for emotion term inclusion in Section 3.1). From each product image, purchase intent (PI) of the 'actual product' was evaluated on a 'Yes'/'No' scale. On day 2, the second questionnaire was administered with the only difference being that salads were named (i.e., "[square/shredded] iceberg lettuce," "romaine lettuce," or "spinach"). On day 3, the third questionnaire evaluated effects of single color, multicolor, and multicolor with packaging on liking of green color, liking of overall appearance, emotions, and PI for both PG and DG salads.

2.2.3. Statistical Analysis

Analysis of variance (ANOVA with the Tukey's HSD post-hoc test) and the Student's t-test were used to determine whether mean liking and emotional ratings were significantly different at $\alpha = 0.05$. In order to identify significant predictors for purchase intent, Logistic Regression Analysis (LRA) was used to model purchase intent as a function of liking and/or emotion intensity. These data were analyzed with SAS® software (version 9.4, 2003). Correlation between emotion profiles and visual cues (green color, shape/size, multicolor and package) was demonstrated via a bi-plot by Principal Component Analysis (PCA). Emotion-driven green color liking scores were modeled using Partial Least Squares Regressions (PLSR), in which the standardized regression coefficient was used to further identify which emotions influenced liking scores. These analyses were carried out using XLSTAT® software (Addinsoft Inc., 2015).

3. Results and Discussion

3.1. Development of Emotion Lexicon Related to Ready-To-Eat (RTE) Salads

Although the modified individual sample description technique [20] facilitated reporting of both positive and negative emotions, RTE salads seemed to elicit more positive than negative feelings (Table 1). The tendency for consumers to report more positive than negative associations with foods, or "hedonic asymmetry," [23] has been previously reported and was not unexpected. In the present study, 26 of the 35 emotions identified from the individual sample description approach were considered positive, eight were negative, and the one remaining response "feel different" was neutral.

Specifically, the term "feel healthy" was repeatedly mentioned across samples. The idea of healthiness is often associated with the feelings of wellness, which is of interest to product developers. Wellness has been used to describe a subjective, multidimensional aspect of health, viewed with positive valence [15]. While the scientific literature has attempted to distinguish between the two concepts, it is not necessarily assumed that these differences are realized by all consumers, and for the purpose of this qualitative assessment the terms were considered separately (Table 1).

From the online CATA survey including 58 emotions (Table 2), nine were selected by at least 30% of the 118 participating consumers and used for further measurement in the subsequent consumer study. They were, in order of selection frequency: feel healthy, feel wellness, safe, satisfied, active, good, happy, interested, and refreshing. The terms "feel healthy" (79%) and "feel wellness" (58%) were the two most common responses and the only two reported by over half of the participants. Previous research of implicit color associations and emotional responses suggested that green color could elicit "energized" feeling [24], and using only food images (photographs), as in the present work, researchers demonstrated consumer capacity to experience "desire" for the actual product [22,25]. Therefore, these two emotions were included. Despite the hedonic asymmetry suggested from our emotion screening, the negative emotions "bored," "disgusted," "guilty," and "worried" were also included based on their significant impact (typically negative) on purchase intent for various products with health benefits [26–28]. Although not reaching the 30% selection rate from the online questionnaire, the feeling "special" was also included due to its prominence in the open-ended individual sample description session. Accounting for these additional feelings would help depict a more comprehensive consumer perceptions related to RTE salads. As such, these seven additional emotion terms were incorporated for rating; hence, a total of 16 terms used for the subsequent consumer study.

3.2. The Effect of Visual Cues on Consumer Liking of Ready-To-Eat (RTE) Salads

Liking of "green color" and liking of "size of the cut pieces" were analyzed separately, based on combinations of green color shade and naming, or shape/size of pieces and naming, respectively (Table 4). Shade of green color had a significant ($p < 0.05$) impact on hedonic scores independent of whether names were presented with the images. For unnamed samples, the two darkest salads (Sample C and Sample D) were liked most in terms of green color ($p < 0.05$), with mean scores of 7.28 and 7.09, respectively. In practical terms, these mean ratings, above "like moderately," for darker green salads indicated substantial hedonic superiority compared to Sample B (below the "like slightly" criterion) and the most pale Sample A, which was scored on the negative, or "dislike," side of the scale (mean of 4.39). More intense green color may have implied greater freshness [29].

Table 4. Mean liking scores of green color and size of ready-to-eat (RTE) salads.

Visual Cue Factors	Product Naming	RTE Salads *			
		Sample A	Sample B	Sample C	Sample D
Green color	No	4.39 c	5.40 b	7.28 a	7.09 a
	Yes	5.75 b	6.00 b	7.28 a	6.52 a,b
	p-value	0.000 **	0.07	0.961	0.074
		Square-L	Shredded-S		
Size	No	4.96 ns	5.36 ns	ND	ND
	Yes	5.27 ns	5.76 ns	ND	ND
	p-value	0.382	0.178		

* Sample A—Square Iceberg; Sample B—Shredded Iceberg; Sample C—Romaine; Sample D—Spinach; Square-L—square-cut iceberg lettuce (large piece); Shredded-S—shredded iceberg lettuce (small piece). a, b, c indicated significant differences of mean scores in each row ($p < 0.05$). ns indicated no significant differences of mean scores ($p > 0.05$). ** indicated significant differences of mean scores in each column using the Student's t-test. ND not determined.

When salads were named, the darker "romaine" salad scored significantly higher (7.28) than both of the pale "iceberg lettuce" samples (5.75 and 6.0, Table 4). The only statistically significant ($p < 0.05$) effect of naming, however, was observed when comparing Sample A (iceberg lettuce but unnamed) with "iceberg lettuce" (named). Perception of this pale green color, which was "disliked" at face value, was boosted by identification of the vegetable (increase from 4.39 to 5.75). The effect of green color shade was slightly less pronounced when salads were named, but the darker green shades still clearly predominated in terms of hedonic judgments.

When provided information about the salad constituent (iceberg lettuce, romaine lettuce, or spinach), consumers' attentions may have turned to recollections of recent eating experiences and/or expectations of how the food would make them feel [30]. By calling upon these higher-level cognitive processes after product information was disclosed, green color cues may have subsequently become less salient in consumer evaluations. Additionally, consumers' levels of familiarity with the salad samples (once the identity was made known) may have influenced the importance of extrinsic information on value judgments [31].

On the other hand, no statistically significant differences in size/cut liking between Square-L and Shredded-S salads were observed, whether or not they were identified as iceberg lettuce (Table 4). Liking of size of piece was, however, directionally higher for Shredded-S than Square-L salads (mean differences of 0.40 (unnamed) and 0.49 (named)) on the 9-point hedonic scale). With other food products, such as cut/sliced meats [32], small/large snack foods [33], and shaped pasta [34], consumer perceptions were largely influenced by size and shape. Based on the present results, it seems that the cut and size of iceberg lettuce was less influential to liking than the green color shade and product identification (naming) among adult regular salad consumers. However, to influence children's consumption of vegetables, shape has shown to be important [35].

When evaluating pictures of single-color salads (green lettuce only), multicolor salads (lettuce, carrots, and red cabbage), and multicolor salads with package (see Table 3 for images), only the phrase "ready-to-eat salad" was used to describe the products. Liking of green color and overall appearance was measured, for both pale green (PG) and dark green (DG) lettuce variations (Table 5). With PG lettuce, liking of green color was significantly higher ($p < 0.05$ statistically; >1-point increase practically) for multicolor (with and without packaging) than single color salads; liking of overall appearance was higher for multicolor PG salad than both the single color and packaged items. This suggests that for pale green colored salads, such as those made with iceberg lettuce, color addition (here, orange and purple) had a positive visual impact on consumers. It has been suggested that, when balanced appropriately within the presentation, a variety of colors enhanced the attractiveness of a dish, in the same way it did with artwork [36].

Table 5. Liking scores of overall appearance and liking scores of green color for ready-to-eat (RTE) salads with a single color, multicolor and package.

Visual Cue Factors	Liking of Green Color			Liking of Overall Appearance		
	PG *	DG *	p Value	PG	DG	p Value
Single color	5.49 b	6.92 ns	<0.0001 **	5.28 b	6.39 ns	0.001 **
Multicolor	6.65 a	6.93 ns	0.293	6.51 a	6.56 ns	0.829
Package	6.37 a	7.10 ns	0.029 **	6.24 b	6.68 ns	0.078

* PG: pale green lettuce, DG: dark green lettuce. (see Table 3 for images). a, b, c: indicated significant differences of mean scores in each column ($p < 0.05$). ns indicated no significant differences of mean scores ($p > 0.05$). ** indicated significant differences of mean scores in each row using the Student's t-test.

Consistent with the previously discussed results comparing four shades of green salad (Table 4), single color DG salads were liked more ($p < 0.05$) in terms of green color and overall appearance than single color PG versions (Table 5). This was also the case for green color liking when packaging was included in the image. Differences in liking were minimized between multicolor PG and DG salads, suggesting that including vegetables with a variety of colors increased the salad's appeal. In other studies, vegetables with higher chroma and vivid colors have been positively associated with freshness and quality, compared to dull colored vegetables [37–39].

For DG salads, directional but insignificant increases in both visual liking dimensions were observed (from single color, to multicolor, to multicolor with package). Overall, it may become more difficult to achieve statistical improvement in liking scores for DG than PG salads. Our evidence suggested visual appeal of DG salad varieties relies more on their intrinsic green color than extrinsic cues. Furthermore, sensitivity to detect differences is often reduced for highly acceptable products using the 9-point hedonic scale [40]. In this study, dark green salad varieties generally received relatively high liking scores, approaching or exceeding the "like moderately" mark.

3.3. The Effect of Visual Cues on Consumer Emotions of Ready-To-Eat (RTE) Salads

Different shades of green color were not only important to visual liking, but also significantly ($p < 0.05$) affected consumer emotional reactions to images of salads presented without (Figure 2a) and with product name (the extrinsic information) (Figure 2b). Overall, darker green salads (samples C and D) elicited higher intensities of positive emotions (ranging from 2.20 to 3.88 on a 5-point intensity scale) than pale green salads (samples A and B, ranging from 1.56–2.95). Accordingly, the opposite was observed for negative emotions, with paler green salads generating scores ranging from 1.36 to 2.37 versus 1.13 to 1.69 for darker green. Eight of the measured emotions (active, bored, energetic, feel wellness, good, healthy, interested, and satisfied) showed statistically significant differences among salad samples. In fact, a difference of >0.3 units (meaning increased positive feelings and decreased negative ones) in the mean emotional intensity scores was observed between dark green and pale green samples across all eight emotion terms. Based on the current scale, these changes in effect can also be considered practically significant [41].

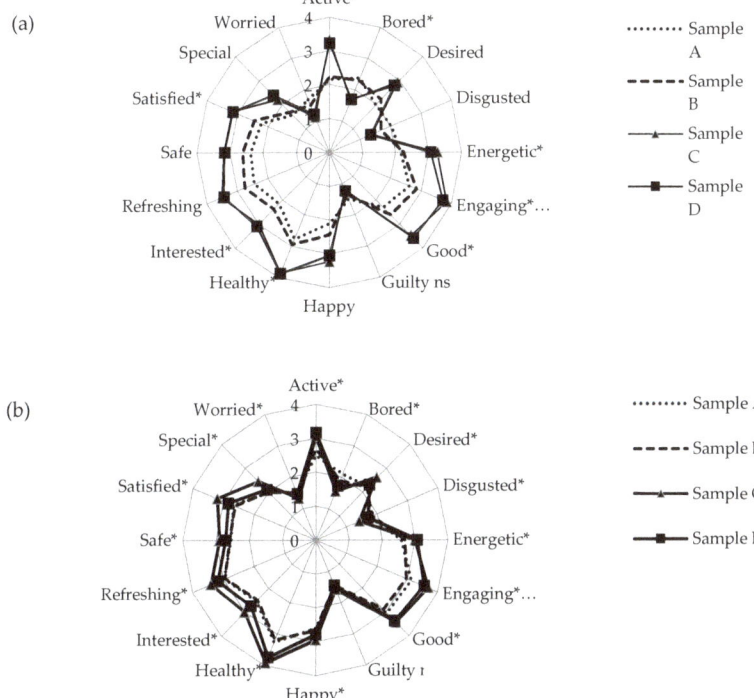

Figure 2. Mean emotion scores elicited by green color cues: (**a**) without product name and (**b**) with product name. * indicates significant difference among mean emotion scores ($p < 0.05$). Refer to Table 3 for sample (A–D) image and description.

As previously mentioned, and substantiated in the current study, green color may be associated with memories and expectations about healthy foods, thereby influencing liking and emotions [16]. Interestingly, only consumers' "guilty" feelings did not distinguish ($p > 0.05$) among salad samples (scores ranging between 1.20 and 1.50), although they did in similarly designed investigations of different product-types [17,27,28]. Perhaps the nature of the sample, green salads in this case, and their evocation of health and wellness overrode any expectations of guilt associated with consumption.

Presentation of salad name clearly affected emotional profiles (Figure 2a vs. Figure 2b), particularly for Sample A/iceberg lettuce (Figure 2b). Intensities of positive emotions (energetic, happy, healthy, interested, refreshing, satisfied and special) were all significantly higher for the named product-image. On the other hand, there was no effect on negative emotion intensity. As with liking scores, identifying the salad constituent by name may have elicited more specific memories and experienced emotions than the more general "ready-to-eat salad" label. For example, if experience dictated that iceberg lettuce is always pale, confirmed expectations may lead to more positive reactions. Previous research suggested that product naming had more impact on dieters than non-dieters [42], implying that health-conscious eaters were more sensitive to this external cue. In the present study, all participating consumers reported consuming salad at least twice per week (based on our initial screening), perhaps lending to the positive emotional effect of naming information.

Comparing emotions related to size/shape of iceberg lettuce pieces (without inclusion of salad name), only healthy and wellness feelings proved to be significantly different ($p < 0.05$, Figure 3) between Square-L and Shredded-S salads, with the larger square-cut (Square-L) salads yielding higher intensity scores. When the vegetable name was given (iceberg lettuce), these two emotional intensities increased ($p < 0.05$). The same mechanism suggested above, for color-elicited emotions, is suspected.

To formally differentiate between "health" and "wellness" is beyond the scope of this study and is an issue that is not fully resolved in the literature. However, health is sometimes viewed as a more objective measure of physical well-being, while wellness incorporates physical, emotional, and spiritual aspects [15]. In the present context of self-reported emotions, both are considered innately subjective, and it is not expected that consumers adhered to such formal definitions.

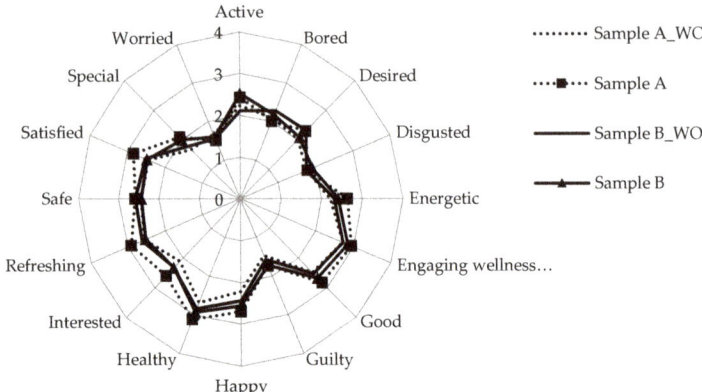

Figure 3. Mean emotion scores elicited by salad size, without (WO) and with product name. Refer to Table 3 for sample (A and B) image and description.

Consumer emotions showed a similar trend to those of liking of overall appearance and green color as affected by monochromatic salads versus multicolor salads with and without package. Significant effects of multicolor and package on consumer emotions were observed for PG colored salads ($p < 0.05$) (Figure 4a) but not for DG salads (Figure 4b). Notably, the feeling "special" showed a mean increase of >0.4 units with addition of vegetables with orange and purple hues and package depiction, compared to the single-color PG sample. The single pale color also induced significantly more boredom (higher "bored" intensity) than its multicolor counterparts. Indeed, a meal consisting of a single color or only white foods was perceived as boring by some consumers [43]. As with liking scores, the high intrinsic acceptability of green color shade for DG salads may have left little room for further increasing emotional intensities from added color components or the package cue. It was suggested elsewhere [44] that intrinsic product characteristics are more associated with emotions than packaging, as was also observed here.

Figure 4. Mean emotion scores elicited by visual cues: single color, multicolor and package for (**a**) pale green color salad and (**b**) darker green color salad. * indicates significant difference among mean emotion scores ($p < 0.05$). Refer to Table 3 for sample image and description

3.4. Correlation between Emotional Profiles and Visual Cues of Ready-To-Eat (RTE) Salads

Figure 5 shows the PCA bi-plot depicting correlations between the four visual cues (green color, size, multicolor and package) and emotion. Results indicated that the visual cues significantly influenced the emotion ratings, as both PC components can explain the variance up to 95.34%. The differences between positive and negative emotions were heavily seen in the first PC dimension, which accounted for 67.46% of the total variance. In the first dimension, negative emotions were on the left while positive ones on the right. The green color effect was correlated with the emotion "bored." Conversely, most of the positive emotion terms were characterized by the multicolor and package cues. The second dimension accounted for 27.88% of the total variance. It can also be seen that the rest of the negative emotions (disgusted, guilty, and worried) were loaded on this dimension. These negative emotions were generally associated with the cut size of salads.

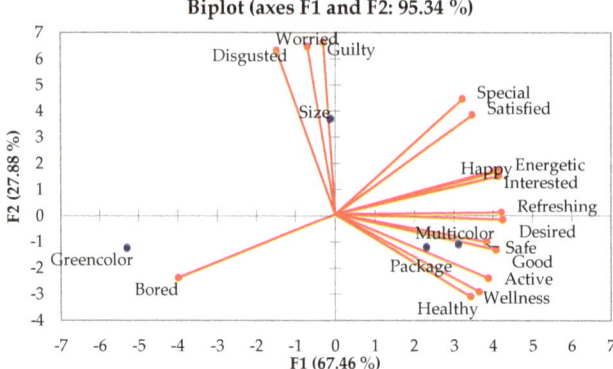

Figure 5. A PCA-biplot of emotion terms elicited by four visual cues (green color, size, multicolor and package) of ready-to-eat (RTE) salads.

3.5. Correlation between Emotions and Consumer Liking of Green Color of Ready-To-Eat (RTE) Salads

Figure 6 shows correlations between emotional attributes evoked by green color cues and liking of green color of salads at a confidence interval 95% using PLRS. It was observed that consumer liking scores for green color salads were driven by the positive emotions. The standardized regression coefficients loaded across all variables were 0.033 to 0.097. The emotion "special" showed the highest standardized regression coefficient value, whereas the term "safe" showed the lowest value. This implied that feeling "special" largely influenced liking scores of green color salads. In contrast, the negative emotions (bored, disgusted, and worried) contributed to decreased liking of green color of salads. As expected, the term "bored" with a standardized regression coefficient of −1.06 was an influential emotion associated with negative liking. Indeed, the liking score would decrease if consumers rated those negative terms with higher scores. Interestingly, the term "guilty" was positively correlated with green color liking scores. It is possible that consumers consciously considered health benefits of salad consumption and thus, would not feel guilty about consuming these products, even the pale green versions. Consequently, this term was positively correlated with green color of salads and did not decrease the liking scores.

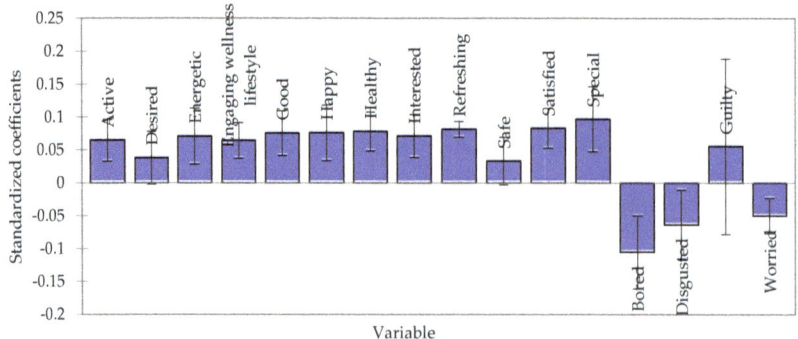

Figure 6. Correlations between emotional attributes evoked by green color cues and the liking of green color based on the partial least squares regression analysis (PLSR).

3.6. The Effect of Visual Cues on Purchase Intent (PI) of Ready-To-Eat (RTE) Salads

The odds of positive PI ("Yes" response) were modeled separately based on liking and emotion scores for each of the four visual cues (green color, size, multicolor and package) (Table 6). A simple model using liking alone as a predictor showed a significant positive effect on PI ($p < 0.05$) from liking of size, multicolor and package. A one unit increased (on a 9–point hedonic scale) was associated with an increase in PI odds of 52%, 168%, and 171%, respectively. However, any effect of green color liking did not meet the criterion for significance ($p = 0.5255$).

Table 6. Predicting purchase intent of the ready-to-eat (RTE) salads by sensory visual cues.

Variables Used in Model	Sensory Visual Cues Effects							
	Green Color		Size		Multicolor		Package	
	p-Value	OR ˆ	p-Value	OR	p-Value	OR	p-Value	OR
Liking only								
Liking	0.5255	0.933	0.0076	1.521	<0.0001	2.681	<0.0001	2.711
Emotions only								
Active	0.023	3.652	0.955	1.030	0.050	2.523	0.035	5.028
Desired	0.185	0.430	0.536	0.794	0.468	1.441	0.094	3.274
Energetic	0.730	1.243	0.599	1.319	0.090	0.360	0.753	0.805
Wellness	0.354	0.464	0.120	0.389	0.426	1.400	0.188	0.320
Good	0.348	2.324	0.096	2.883	0.171	0.440	0.214	3.411
Happy	0.908	1.079	0.874	0.913	0.347	1.767	0.029	0.130
Healthy	0.054	3.869	0.672	1.213	0.174	0.451	0.043	5.047
Interested	0.520	0.601	0.629	0.780	0.744	0.831	0.220	2.541
Refreshing	0.789	0.838	0.041	2.751	0.091	2.822	0.178	0.349
Safe	0.049	0.299	0.749	1.136	0.118	0.497	0.056	0.280
Satisfied	0.049	4.265	0.541	0.740	0.064	2.996	0.074	5.002
Special	0.637	0.721	0.500	1.401	0.691	1.191	0.620	1.462
Bored	0.565	0.832	0.214	0.566	0.488	0.766	0.095	0.481
Disgusted	0.034	0.148	0.555	1.337	0.034	0.219	0.951	1.062
Guilty	0.216	0.394	0.866	1.081	0.462	1.626	0.913	0.909
Worried	0.014	1.646	0.346	0.619	0.836	1.142	0.138	0.183
Liking and emotions								
Liking	0.280	1.256	0.222	1.354	0.009	2.994	0.026	7.686
Active	0.016	4.735	0.943	0.962	0.050	2.685	0.022	13.732
Desired	0.200	0.433	0.490	0.771	0.935	1.044	0.102	4.055
Energetic	0.914	1.071	0.700	1.230	0.480	0.611	0.903	0.897
Wellness	0.325	0.440	0.105	0.362	0.693	1.203	0.249	0.204
Good	0.358	2.291	0.113	2.817	0.090	0.329	0.431	2.495
Happy	0.927	1.063	0.814	0.869	0.943	0.951	0.045	0.097
Healthy	0.043	4.291	0.469	1.428	0.565	0.677	0.042	7.597
Interested	0.790	0.799	0.786	0.868	0.835	1.129	0.144	7.635
Refreshing	0.796	0.843	0.047	2.711	0.210	2.426	0.097	0.134
Safe	0.031	0.250	0.603	1.233	0.130	0.477	0.043	0.096
Satisfied	0.050	4.359	0.360	0.622	0.090	3.113	0.108	13.822
Special	0.480	0.603	0.553	1.357	0.641	0.788	0.466	0.472
Bored	0.695	0.879	0.272	0.592	0.684	1.213	0.847	1.154
Disgusted	0.023	0.123	0.385	1.589	0.070	0.215	0.145	8.596
Guilty	0.205	0.381	0.673	1.232	0.316	1.979	0.198	0.224
Worried	0.010	1.654	0.261	0.543	0.926	0.937	0.066	0.051

ˆ OR = odds ratio.

When considering the nine emotional intensities as predictors of PI in a model, the impact of individual emotions depended on the eliciting condition under investigation. Results showed that increasing positive emotions would increase odds of positive PI, and more intense negative emotions would have the opposite effect (Table 6). The emotion "active" showed the most consistent significance for three of four visual cues (except shape/size), with each one-unit increase raising predicted PI odds by 2.5 to 5 times. The "disgusted" emotion scores for green color and multicolor would reduce PI odds by 85% and 78%, respectively, and a one-unit increase in "healthy" score was associated with a 3.8 to 5 times predicted rise in PI odds.

When including both liking and emotion in the model, green color and multicolor eliciting conditions became more significant predictors ($p < 0.05$). Further model selection techniques should be employed to obtain the most practical models. These results do, however, demonstrate the importance of the visual experience in food choice and purchase intent, influenced by both intrinsic and extrinsic information sources.

4. Conclusions

A multifaceted approach to qualitative lexicon development, as it pertains to the appearance of food products, may enhance the quality of consumer emotional profile data. The present combination of methods narrowed the most relevant emotions associated with RTE salads down from a list of 58 to 16 terms. Of these, several proved to distinguish among salad samples, depending on the prominent visual cues presented to consumers. Given the observed perceptions of RTE salads, future studies should elucidate between the product-evoked feelings of "healthy" vs. "wellness." The effects of both intrinsic and extrinsic visual cues on emotion and liking were evident; however, color may be more important to positive product perceptions of salad than size of the salad pieces. The intrinsic value of a darker green color-shade invoked greater impressions of hedonic and emotional benefits for the salad consumers, repressing the potential for feelings of guilt and even overriding the marked improvement in consumer liking obtained by adding color variety to pale monochromatic salads. Our results suggested that liking of intrinsic visual characteristics of salads may moderate the effects of extrinsic cues. Providing additional product information such as naming or information on packaging may help reinforce positive tendencies toward making healthy food choices and purchase intent.

Author Contributions: Conceptualization: P.C., R.A., Y.G., P.W., G.T. and W.P.; Performing the research work: P.C., R.A. and Y.G.; Data analysis and interpretation: P.C., R.A., Y.G. and P.W.; Writing—original draft preparation: P.C., R.A. and Y.G.; Writing—review and editing: P.W., G.T. and W.P.; Supervision: G.T. and W.P.; Project administration and resource/funding acquisition: W.P. All authors have read and agreed to the published version of the manuscript.

Funding: This work was partially supported by the USDA National Institute of Food and Agriculture Hatch project (accession number 1006697; LAB94291) and the LSU AgCenter.

Acknowledgments: The authors would like to acknowledge Ashley Gutierrez, the lab manager, for facilitating the use of the LSU AgCenter Sensory Services Lab for the entire study.

Conflicts of Interest: The authors declare no conflict of interest. The funders had no role in the design of the study; in the collection, analyses, or interpretation of data; in the writing of the manuscript, or in the decision to publish the results.

References

1. Olson, J.C.; Jacoby, J. Cue Utilization in the Quality Perception Process. In Proceedings of the Third Annual Conference of the Association for Consumer Research, Chicago, IL, USA, 3–5 November 1972; pp. 167–179.
2. Piqueras–Fiszman, B.; Spence, C. Sensory expectations based on product–extrinsic food cues: An interdisciplinary review of the empirical evidence and theoretical accounts. *Food Qual. Prefer.* **2015**, *40*, 165–179. [CrossRef]
3. Acebrón, B.L.; Dopico, C.D. The importance of intrinsic and extrinsic cues to expected and experienced quality: An empirical application for beef. *Food Qual. Prefer.* **2000**, *11*, 229–238. [CrossRef]
4. Wadhera, D.; Capaldi–Phillips, E.D. A review of visual cues associated with food on food acceptance and consumption. *Eat. Behav.* **2014**, *15*, 132–143. [CrossRef] [PubMed]
5. Glanz, K.; Basil, M.; Maibach, E.; Goldberg, J.; Snyder, D. Why Americans eat what they do: Taste, nutrition, cost, convenience, and weight control concerns as influences on food consumption. *J. Am. Diet. Assoc.* **1998**, *98*, 1118–1126. [CrossRef]
6. Zellner, A.D. Effect of Visual Cues on Sensory and Hedonic Evaluation of Food. In *Nutrition and Sensation*; Hirsch, A.R., Ed.; CRC Press: New York, NY, USA, 2015; pp. 159–171.
7. Shankar, M.U.; Levitan, C.A.; Prescott, J.; Spence, C. The influence of color and label information on flavor perception. *Chemosens. Percept.* **2009**, *2*, 53–58. [CrossRef]
8. Burger, K.S.; Cornier, M.A.; Ingebrigtsen, J.; Johnson, S.L. Assessing Food Appeal and Desire to Eat: The Effect of Portion Size & Energy Density. *Int. J. Behav. Nutr. Phys. Act.* **2011**, *8*, 101.
9. Apaolaza, V.; Hartmann, P.; Echebarria, C.; Barrutia, J.M. Organic label's halo effect on sensory and hedonic experience of wine: A pilot study. *J. Sens. Stud.* **2017**, *32*, 1–12. [CrossRef]

10. Gutjar, S.; Dalenberg, J.R.; de Graaf, C.; de Wijk, R.A.; Palascha, A.; Renken, R.J.; Jager, G. What reported food–evoked emotions may add: A model to predict consumer food choices. *Food Qual. Prefer.* **2015**, *45*, 140–148. [CrossRef]
11. Kostyra, E.; Wasiak–Zys, G.; Rambuszek, M.; Waszkiewicz–Robak, B. Determining the sensory characteristics, associated emotions and degree of liking of the visual attributes of smoked ham. A multifaceted study. *Food Sci. Technol.* **2016**, *65*, 246–253. [CrossRef]
12. Schifferstein, H.N.J.; Desmet, P.M.A. Hedonic asymmetry in emotional responses to consumer products. *Food Qual. Prefer.* **2010**, *21*, 1100–1104. [CrossRef]
13. Hurling, R.; Shepherd, R. Eating with your eyes: Effect of appearance on expectations of liking. *Appetite* **2003**, *41*, 167–174. [CrossRef]
14. Zhang, B.; Seo, H.S. Visual attention toward food–item images can vary as a function of background saliency and culture: An eye–tracking study. *Food Qual. Prefer.* **2015**, *41*, 172–179. [CrossRef]
15. Meiselman, H.L. A review of the current state of emotion research in product development. *Food Res. Int.* **2015**, *76*, 192–199. [CrossRef]
16. Wardy, W.; Chonpracha, P.; Chokumnoyporn, N.; Sriwattana, S.; Prinyawiwatkul, W.; Jirangrat, W. Influence of Package Visual Cues of Sweeteners on the Sensory-Emotional Profiles of Their Products. *J. Food Sci.* **2017**, *82*, 500–508. [CrossRef]
17. Sukkwai, S.; Kijroongrojana, K.; Chonpracha, P.; Pujols, K.D.; Alonso-Marenco, J.R.; Ardoin, R.; Prinyawiwatkul, W. Effects of colorant concentration and 'natural colour' or 'sodium content' claim on saltiness perception, consumer liking and emotion, and purchase intent of dipping sauces. *Int. J. Food Sci. Technol.* **2018**, *53*, 1246–1254. [CrossRef]
18. Stratakos, A.C.; Koidis, A. Suitability, efficiency and microbiological safety of novel physical technologies for the processing of ready–to–eat meals, meats and pumpable products. *Int. J. Food Sci. Technol.* **2015**, *50*, 1283–1302. [CrossRef]
19. Zhang, J.; Yuan, L.; Liu, W.; Lin, Q.; Wang, Z.; Guan, W. Effects of UV-C on antioxidant capacity, antioxidant enzyme activity and color of fresh–cut red cabbage during storage. *Int. J. Food Sci. Technol.* **2017**, *52*, 626–634. [CrossRef]
20. Fiszman, S.; Salgado, N.; Orrego, C.E.; Ares, G. Comparison of methods for generating sensory vocabulary with consumers: A case study with two types of satiating foods. *Food Qual. Pref.* **2015**, *44*, 111–118. [CrossRef]
21. King, S.C.; Meiselman, H.L. Development of a method to measure consumer emotions associated with foods. *Food Qual. Prefer.* **2010**, *21*, 168–177. [CrossRef]
22. Maughan, C.; Chambers, E.; Sandria, I.V. A procedure for validating the use of photographs as surrogates for samples sin sensory measurement of appearance: An example with color of cooked turkey patties. *J. Sens. Stud.* **2016**, *31*, 507–513. [CrossRef]
23. Desmet, P.M.; Schifferstein, H.N. Sources of positive and negative emotions in food experience. *Appetite* **2008**, *50*, 290–301. [CrossRef] [PubMed]
24. Gilbert, N.A.; Fridlund, J.A.; Lucchina, A.L. The color of emotion: A metric for implicit color associations. *Food Qual. Prefer.* **2016**, *52*, 203–210. [CrossRef]
25. Barthomeuf, L.; Rousset, S.; Droit–Volet, S. Emotion and food. Do the emotions expressed on other people's faces affect the desire to eat liked and disliked food products? *Appetite* **2009**, *52*, 27–33. [CrossRef] [PubMed]
26. Poonnakasem, N.; Pujols, K.D.; Chaiwanichsiri, S.; Laohasongkram, K.; Prinyawiwatkul, W. Different oils and health benefit statements affect physicochemical properties, consumer liking, emotion, and purchase intent: A case of sponge cake. *J. Food Sci.* **2016**, *81*, 165–173. [CrossRef] [PubMed]
27. Carabante, K.M.; Ardoin, R.; Scaglia, G.; Malekian, F.; Khachaturyan, M.; Janes, M.E.; Prinyawiwatkul, W. Consumer Acceptance, Emotional Response, and Purchase Intent of Rib-Eye Steaks from Grass-Fed Steers, and Effects of Health Benefit Information on Consumer Perception. *J. Food Sci.* **2018**, *83*, 2560–2570. [CrossRef]
28. Pujols, K.D.; Ardoin, R.; Chaiya, B.; Tuuri, G.; Prinyawiwatkul, W. Low-sodium roasted peanuts: Effects of salt mixtures (NaCl, KCl and glycine) on consumer perception and purchase intent. *Int. J. Food Sci. Technol.* **2019**, *54*, 2754–2762. [CrossRef]
29. Lee, S.M.; Lee, K.T.; Lee, S.H.; Song, J.K. Origin of human colour preference for food. *J. Food Eng.* **2013**, *119*, 508–515. [CrossRef]
30. Higgs, S. Cognitive processing of food rewards. *Appetite* **2016**, *104*, 10–17. [CrossRef]

31. Borgogno, M.; Favotto, S.; Corazzin, M.; Cardello, A.V.; Piasentier, E. The role of product familiarity and consumer involvement on liking and perceptions of fresh meat. *Food Qual. Prefer.* **2015**, *44*, 139–147. [CrossRef]
32. Reisfelt, H.H.; Gabrielsen, G.; Aaslyng, M.D.; Bjerre, M.S.; Møller, P. Consumer preferences for visually presented meals. *J. Sens. Stud.* **2009**, *24*, 182–203. [CrossRef]
33. Weijzen, P.L.G.; Liem, D.G.; Zandstra, E.H.; de Graaf, C. Sensory specific satiety and intake: The difference between nibble– and bar–size snacks. *Appetite* **2008**, *50*, 435–442. [CrossRef] [PubMed]
34. Rolls, B.J.; Rowe, E.A.; Rolls, E.T. How sensory properties of foods affect human feeding behavior. *Physiol. Behav.* **1982**, *29*, 409–417. [CrossRef]
35. Olsen, A.; Ritz, C.; Kramer, L.; Møller, P. Serving styles of raw snack vegetables. What do children want? *Appetite* **2012**, *59*, 556–562. [CrossRef] [PubMed]
36. Zellner, D.A.; Lankford, M.; Ambrose, L.; Locher, P. Art on the plate: Effect of balance and color on attractiveness of, willingness to try and liking for food. *Food Qual. Prefer.* **2010**, *21*, 575–578. [CrossRef]
37. Jantathai, S.; Sungsri–in, M.; Mukprasirt, A.; Duerrschmid, K. Sensory expectations and perceptions of Austrian and Thai consumers: A case study with six colored Thai desserts. *Food Res. Int.* **2014**, *64*, 65–73. [CrossRef]
38. Schloss, K.B.; Poggesi, R.M.; Palmer, S.E. Effects of university affiliation and "school spirit" on color preferences: Berkeley versus Stanford. *Psychon. Bull. Rev.* **2012**, *18*, 498–504. [CrossRef]
39. Manninen, H.; Paakki, M.; Hopia, A.; Franzarn, R. Measuring the green color of vegetables from digital images using image analysis. *Food Sci. Technol.* **2015**, *63*, 1184–1190. [CrossRef]
40. da Silva, A.N.; dos Santos Navarro, R.D.C.; Ferreira, M.A.M.; Minim, V.P.R.; da Costa, T.D.M.T.; Perez, R. Performance of hedonic scales in sensory acceptability of strawberry yogurt. *Food Qual. Prefer.* **2013**, *30*, 9–21. [CrossRef]
41. King, S.C.; Meiselman, H.L.; Carr, B.T. Measuring emotions associated with foods: Important elements of questionnaire and test design. *Food Qual. Prefer.* **2013**, *28*, 8–16. [CrossRef]
42. Irmak, C.; Vallen, B.; Robinson, S.R. The Impact of Product Name on Dieters' and Non dieters' Food Evaluations and Consumption. *J. Consum. Res.* **2011**, *38*, 390–405. [CrossRef]
43. Hutchings, J.B. *Expectations and the Food Industry: The Impact of Color and Appearance*; Kluwer Academic/Plenum Publishers: New York, NY, USA, 2003; pp. 141–175.
44. Ng, M.; Chaya, C.; Hort, J. The influence of sensory and packaging cues on both liking and emotional, abstract and functional conceptualizations. *Food Qual. Prefer.* **2013**, *29*, 146–156. [CrossRef]

© 2020 by the authors. Licensee MDPI, Basel, Switzerland. This article is an open access article distributed under the terms and conditions of the Creative Commons Attribution (CC BY) license (http://creativecommons.org/licenses/by/4.0/).

Article

Consumer Preferences and Sensory Profile Related to the Physico-Chemical Properties and Texture of Different Maize Tortillas Types

Mădălina Iuga [1], Víctor D. Ávila Akerberg [2,*], Tanya M. González Martínez [2] and Silvia Mironeasa [1,*]

[1] Faculty of Food Engineering, Stefan cel Mare University of Suceava, 13, Universității Street, C.P. 720229 Suceava, Romania; iugamada@yahoo.com
[2] Instituto de Ciencias Agropecuarias y Rurales, Universidad Autónoma del Estado de México, Campus Universitario "El Cerrillo", A.P. 435, Toluca, Estado de México C.P. 50200, Mexico; tanyamgm@gmail.com
* Correspondence: vicaviak@gmail.com (V.D.Á.A.); silviam@fia.usv.ro (S.M.)

Received: 26 September 2019; Accepted: 29 October 2019; Published: 31 October 2019

Abstract: Maize tortilla is a basic food in Mexico, and, lately, the food industry has tried to make the manufacturing process easier by using instant flours and specialized machines. The purpose of this study was to investigate consumers' behaviors related to tortillas and to evaluate the sensory, textural, and physico-chemical parameters of tortillas from the Tlazala region, Mexico. The sensory profile revealed that the artisanal ones had better parameters in terms of smell, taste, and appearance compared to the others. These results are consistent with consumers' preferences for tortillas made of maize grain instead of industrial corn flour. The sensory parameters and the physico-chemical and texture profile parameters varied with the maize type and manufacturing process. Our findings showed that the artisanal hand-made ones were more nutritious, followed by those mechanically made using maize grain, and finally by those mechanically made from industrialized corn flour. The results of this study may help processors to better understand the parameters of their products and people's preferences.

Keywords: maize tortilla; consumer behavior; sensory profile; texture; physico-chemical parameters

1. Introduction

Maize is one of the most cultivated crops in America, Europe, and Asia, being largely consumed in Latin America. Maize is a key element in the Mesoamerican diet; however, only in Mexico is it mainly consumed in the shape of "tortilla"—a flat 12 to 18 cm disc made of nixtamalized maize flour, cooked over a hot comal or skillet [1]. Maize tortilla is one of the most popular foods in Mexico, and it is strongly related to the Mexican identity and considered a cultural heritage. It presents very different organoleptic parameters among Mexican territories, with the average daily consumption per capita being 180 g in urban areas and 300 g in rural zones of the country [2]. The materials used to obtain maize-based products, the processes, and equipment influence the nutritional value via loss of components [3]. Nixtamalization, a word coming from the indigenous Nahuatl linguistic root nixtli—meaning ashes or lime—and tamalli, a maize dough, is an ancient treatment (since 400–500 a. c.) used for maize grains. It involves grains boiling in approximately 5% lime water (calcium hydroxide) which enhances maize quality by softening the pericarp of the seed while increasing protein quality and the availability of niacin and calcium [4]. This treatment also promotes flavor development and improves tortillas' consistency, while reducing the effects of fumosin, aflatoxin, deoxynivalenol, and zearalenone, all major contaminants of maize [4].

Tortillas are unfermented flat maize breads, with a soft, flexible, and easy to fold and roll structure and of various colors, depending on the flour and maize source [5]. In Mexico, there are more than 52 species and more than 350 cultivars/colors per species; they are called natives and are cultivated in traditional peasant farming systems, such as the cornfield, as well as genetically improved maize hybrids cultivated in intensive production systems with less costs [6,7]. Today, most of the commercial maize products consumed in Mexico are obtained from industrially grown maize imported from the United States, but in the center of Mexico native maize is still consumed. The quality differences among the tortillas on the market appear due to the fact that some artisanal tortillerias incorporate industrial maize flour gradually [6,8]. The traditional method of tortilla making involves maize grain nixtamalization to obtain the nixtamalized maize dough; however, nowadays, this procedure has been replaced by industrial nixtamalized maize flour [9]. Maize tortillas are a good source of proteins, providing important caloric intake. Taking into consideration peoples from Africa and Latin America, maize consumption is between 15% and 56% [10]. The chemical and physical parameters of nixtamalized maize and flour tortillas are influenced by the grain's properties. The conditions of the nixtamalization process and the milling method also play an important role [10,11].

In rural households, the perception of quality, which is considered as "a good tortilla", is closely related to the artisanal process, which also includes cooking in a wood-burning stove and clay dish [12]. Consumers' preferences regarding tortillas depend on the region of the country [13]. In urban areas, tortillas of industrial origin are more readily accepted, while in rural areas, artisanal manufacturing, still dominated by women, is preferred [14,15]. Nowadays, traditional tortillas handmade by women tend to be replaced by the use of electric machines and gas combustion [16].

People's choices regarding tortilla products is important for producers, especially from the product quality enhancement point of view. In rural areas, traditional agricultural practices registered substantial changes, mainly due to the free-trade policies which caused an increase in imported crops [17]. A commercial-scale production of tortillas implies changes to the traditional processes which lead to products with different sensory parameters. Some studies revealed that tortilla purchase intent is influenced by appearance, textural properties, and taste [18]. Industrialized tortillas, sold in self-service stores and mechanized tortillerias, tend to be much thinner, become hard quickly, and have a slightly sweet taste of maize which is almost imperceptible, while a lime flavor predominates [6]. These industrial tortillas are made with flours from large business monopolies, with imported maize that, due to the fact of their practicality, accessibility, shelf-life, and price, displace the original meaning of freshly made tortillas with their market model. Food perception and choices are different between women and men as a result of distinct energy needs, depending on their activities. Men consume foods with a higher energy density, while women prefer diets rich in vegetables, fruits, and fibers [19]. Regarding eating styles, men take bigger food bites and eat faster than women. Different food preferences among the two groups are related to the response at stimuli, such as visual image, gustatory information, emotions, hormonal changes, and weight status [19].

Tortilla quality can be evaluated by many methods, including sensory and objective methods. Many studies have been conducted to evaluate tortillas from different maize sources [9,10,20–22]. The mechanical textural properties of tortillas can be evaluated by elongation tests with the results depending on the product freshness and flour composition [9]. The color properties of the final product depend on the nixtamalization process with the intensity being related to the content of carotenoids and flavonoids and to Maillard reactions [23]. Tortilla sensory evaluation can bring information about acceptance, appearance, smell, taste, and textural properties. Bejosano et al. [22] revealed that sensory parameters and textural parameters evaluated by subjective and objective methods changed with time and presented significant correlations. The color, odor, flavor, shelf-life, and textural properties of nixtamalized tortillas are strongly influenced by lime concentration [23].

The aim of this study was to investigate the preferences related to tortillas and to evaluate the sensory, texture, and physico-chemical parameters of three types of maize tortillas among consumers from a small rural mountain village, Tlazala, Municipality of Isidro Fabela, which has experienced a rapid urbanization process over the last two decades due to the fact of its proximity to Mexico City's Metropolitan Area. To this purpose, a questionnaire was applied and tortillas from different markets in Tlazala and from different maize sources were evaluated by determining the sensory profiles, texture parameters, color, chemical composition, and water absorption indexes. To our knowledge, no study has been performed on the quality of tortilla products from Tlazala, Mexico. Furthermore, this study focused on not only consumers' behavior and sensory perceptions, but also on product parameters and their interactions.

2. Materials and Methods

2.1. Consumers Preferences

Consumers' behavior were evaluated by applying a questionnaire to 60 randomly selected tortilla consumers out of approximately 2000 habitants, of which 30 were women and 30 men, in Tlazala village, Mexico. People on the street in Tlazala's center were asked to complete the questionnaire by choosing the answer from a given list. The collection period was between 25 January and 10 March 2019, and the working language was Spanish. The participants' ages varied between 14 and 75 years old and they had different jobs. The questionnaire was divided into two sections: the first one regarding purchases and preferences and the second regarding purchase decision factors related to tortillas (Table 1). The hypothesis was that tortilla consumers' preferences and purchase decisions depend on gender.

Table 1. Questionnaire items that consumers could choose.

Section	Dimension	Items
Purchase and preferences	Tortilla type preference	I prefer tortillas made of maize. I prefer tortillas made of industrial flour. I prefer tortillas made of mix of maize and industrial flour.
	Tortillas type purchase	I buy tortillas made of maize. I buy tortillas made of industrial flour. I buy tortillas made of mix of maize and industrial flour.
	Consumption frequency	I consume tortillas daily. I consume tortillas every 2–3 days. I consume tortillas weekly. I consume tortillas monthly. I never consume tortillas.
	Consumption quantity	I consume 1 or 2 tortillas a day. I consume between 3 and 5 tortillas a day. I consume between 6 and 10 tortillas a day. I consume more than 10 tortillas a day.
	Time of highest consumption	I consume tortillas the most at breakfast. I consume tortillas the most at lunch. I consume tortillas the most at dinner. I consume tortillas the most at snack.
	Purchase frequency	I buy tortillas daily. I buy tortillas every 2–3 days. I buy tortillas weekly. I buy tortillas monthly. I never buy tortillas.
	Purchase quantity	0.5 to 3 kg (open question)
	Family size	My family size is of 1 or 2 persons. My family size is of 3 or 4 persons. My family size is of 5 or 6 persons. My family size is of more than 7 persons.

Table 1. *Cont.*

Section	Dimension	Items
Purchase and preferences	Purchase place	I usually buy tortillas from supermarket. I usually buy tortillas from shop. I usually buy tortillas from tortillerías. I usually buy tortillas from particular houses. I make tortillas home.
	Color preference	I prefer white tortillas. I prefer yellow tortillas. I prefer blue tortillas. It does not matter.
	Tortilla color type purchase	I buy white tortillas. I buy yellow tortillas. I buy blue tortillas. It does not matter.
	Reason for color tortillas purchase	They are the most popular. I like them. It is nearby my house.
Factors influencing the purchase decision		Maize origin Maize type Tortillas manufacture type Tortillas appearance Price Taste Shelf-life

2.2. Materials

Eight tortillas samples were acquired from markets in the Tlazala region, Mexico. Six samples were obtained from specialized shops called "tortillerías" where tortillas are mechanically made on-site using machines, and two were completely hand-made, also known as "artisanal tortillas". There were two samples of tortillas made of industrial maize flour (TMN1 and TMN2); two made of nixtamalized maize at the same place of production (TMZ1 and TMZ2); and two samples in which 50% of nixtamalized maize was substituted with industrialized maize flour (TMX1 and TMX2). For the TMZ1 tortillas, maize from the north region of Mexico was used (perhaps from Sinaloa, a region that uses technological packages for hybrid and transgenic maize massive cultivation), while the TMZ2 were made of maize from the central region of the country (Hidalgo) and a tortilla preservative was added. One of the artisanal tortillas contained a small quantity of wheat flour (TA1) and was baked on a gas cooker, while the other one (TA2) was made only of maize from the same region, Tlazala, in a traditional way using firewood. The samples were kept in paper and polyethylene bags at 4 °C until the experiments were performed. The samples were dried at 55 °C for 24 h and grounded in a Tomas Willy mill with a 0.84 mm sieve. The dried sample flours were kept in glass containers until analysis were performed.

2.3. Sensory and Subjective Textural Parameters

The sensory profile of fresh tortillas samples was performed following an adaptation of the lexicon and parameters assessed by Bejosano et al. [22], with the participation of nine semi-trained gastronomy specialists with prior training, with at least 3 replications, in 3 sessions of approximately 40 min, using a 15 point scale to value the intensity of each attribute. Parameters evaluated included color uniformity, surface uniformity, moisture, opacity, maize smell, lime smell, fermented smell, acid taste, salted taste, sweet taste, lime taste, roughness, elasticity, hardness, masticability, moisture absorption, and tooth packing (Table 2). The subjective textural parameters were evaluated according to the method described by Meilgaard, Vance Civille, and Carr [24] with some modifications. The descriptive spectrum method with references points was used, the scale and the anchors being adapted for the tortilla product characterization. Panelists were provided with one coded sample of tortilla once, on the same day the tortillas were made. A randomized block design was used to arrange the serving order of tortillas and the samples were distributed into individual plates. Drinking water and apple pieces were used to cleanse the mouth between samples.

Roughness is defined as the amount of irregularities, protrusions, grains, or bumps which appear on the surface of the product [24]. Elasticity shows the degree to which the sample returns to its original shape at partial compression without breaking [22]. Hardness is the force applied to achieve a given deformation [22,24]. The moisture absorption refers to the amount of saliva absorbed by the sample during the chew down [24]. Tooth packing is a measure of the degree to which the sample sticks on the surface of teeth [24]. The rollability test was performed by rolling the sample around a 13 mm diameter dowel and the breakings were evaluated using a 15 points scale [22].

Table 2. Sensory analysis and subjective textural characteristics scores [22,24].

Name	Score Sheet for Descriptive Analysis of Tortilla Samples
Color uniformity	1 = nothing uniform, 15 = very uniform
Surface uniformity	1 = nothing uniform, 15 = very uniform
Moisture	1 = nothing moist, 15 = very moist
Opacity	1 = translucent, 7 = a little opaque, 15 = very opaque
Maize smell	1 = nothing intense, 15 = very intense
Lime smell	1 = nothing intense, 15 = very intense
Fermented smell	1 = nothing intense, 15 = very intense
Acid taste	1 = nothing acid, 15 = very acid (2 = mineral water, 7.5 = orange juice, 15 = lime)
Salted taste	1 = nothing salted, 15 = very salted (8 = crackers, 13 = potato chips)
Sweet taste	1 = nothing sweet, 15 = very sweet (6 = orange juice, 9 = cola juice)
Lime taste	1 = nothing intense, 15 = very intense
Roughness	1 = nothing rough, 15 = very rough (1 = gelatin, 5 = orange peel, 8 = potato chips, 12 = hard granola bar)
Rollability	1 = nothing rollable, 15 = it rolls without breaking (1 = breaks along the axis, 7 = it breaks on both sides, 11 = it breaks on one side)
Elasticity	1 = nothing elastic, 15 = very elastic (1 = cheese cream, 5 = sausage, 9.5 = marshmallow, 15 = gelatin)
Hardness	1 = soft, 15 = hard (1 = cheese cream, 4.5 = cheese, 6 = olive, 9 = peanuts, 11 = almonds)
Masticability	1 = nothing chewable, 15 = very chewable
Moisture absorption	1 = it does not absorb water, 15 = it absorbs a large quantity of water (1 = candy, 7.5 = popcorn, 10 = potato chips, 15 = biscuits)
Tooth packing	1 = nothing sticky, 2 = very sticky (1 = carrot, 9 = cheese, 15 = gummy candy)

2.4. Chemical, Physical, and Objective Textural Parameters

The proximate composition of the tortilla samples was achieved according to the USA Association of Official Analytical Chemists methods [25]. Moisture content was assessed by sample drying at 105 °C for 24 h (method 925.098), ash content by incineration at 550 °C (method 923.03), fat content by Soxhlet extraction in petroleum ether (method 920.39C), and proteins content (N × 6.25) by the Kjeldahl method. Neutral detergent fibers (FNDs) and acid detergent fibers (FADs) were determined according to the filter bag method using an ANKOM 200 fibers analyzer [26]. Total carbohydrate content was calculated by difference. Water absorption and soluble solids indexes were evaluated according to the method described by Serena-Saldivar [27]. All measurements were performed in triplicate.

The color profile (L^*, a^*, and b^*) of fresh tortilla samples at room temperature was measured using a Konica Minolta Chroma Meter CR-410 and the hue angle (H^*) and chroma (C^*) were calculated [28]. Three measurements points for three fresh tortillas samples of each type were performed.

Tortillas tensile strength at break and breaking distance was estimated according to the method described by Vaca-Garcia et al. [9] using a TA-TX Plus Texture Analyser (Stable Micro Systems, Godalming, United Kingdom). Circular sample pieces of 6.5 cm diameter were held by two metallic plates with a circular perforation of 2.54 cm diameter, and a spherical probe of 0.635 cm (PO25S) diameter moved through the circular perforation at a rate of 10 mm s^{-1} until the sample broke. The breaking distance and the tensile strength at break were recorded. Nine measurements for each fresh sample were performed.

2.5. Statistical Analysis

The statistical software SPSS version 13.0.0 for Windows (SPSS, Chicago, IL, USA) was used for the treatment of data and statistical tests. Results were reported as mean value ± standard deviation. Analysis of variance (ANOVA) was performed to determine differences between means by using Tukey's test at a 95% confidence level. Statistically significant differences were considered at $p < 0.05$. Correlation coefficients (r) were determined by Pearson correlation matrix method. Principal component analysis (PCA) was carried out in order to evaluate the relationships among the studied variables and to visualize the similarities between these. Non-parametric Mann–Whitney tests were applied in order to identify the statistical differences ($p < 0.05$) among women and men in relation to the variables referring to tortilla preferences, purchase, consumption quantity, family size, purchase reasons, and purchase decision factors.

3. Results

3.1. Consumers Preferences

In this study, all participants who completed the questionnaire were tortilla consumers, the mean age being 37 years. The first part of the questionnaire contained information about preferences and purchase, while the second part was about factors influencing the purchase decision. Regarding maize type, 90% of women and men preferred tortillas made of nixtamalized maize in the purchase place, while only 63.33% of women and 73.33% of men buy it near the market which offers mostly machine tortillas made of industrialized maize flour or mixes of maize and industrialized flour. More than 90% of women and men reported consuming tortillas on a daily basis, mostly at lunch, with the majority of women consuming less than 5, while the men consumed more than 6 per day. More than 70% of the women and men buy tortillas every day, the quantity depending on the family size. Eighty percent of women and 90% of men buy tortillas from tortillerías, mostly the white variety, women because they are more common and men because they like them more. However, women reported to prefer blue tortillas, while men preferred the white ones. Regarding the factors that influence the purchase decision, the women thought that the most important was maize type, followed by maize origin, manufacturing, taste, shelf-life, appearance, and, lastly, price. Conversely, men considered taste to be the most important factor, followed by maize type, maize origin, manufacturing, price, appearance, and finally shelf-life.

To highlight the relationship among the 12 components explored in relation to the consumers' preferences and purchase decision, a multivariate analysis was performed using PCA as an extraction method [29]. For the first part of the questionnaire, regarding preferences and purchase reasons, eight of the components were omitted from the results of the commonalities. Four components (Table 3) contributed the most and explained 71.44% of the total variance of the model. The first component (reason for color tortilla purchase) explained 29.66% of the total variance, the second one (tortilla type purchase) explained 17.48%, the third one (family size) 13.12%, and the last one (purchase place) explained 11.17%. For the second part, even if seven components were generated, only the first four satisfied the selection criteria (eigenvalue = 1), contributing mostly (80.63%) to the explained variance of the analyzed data (Table 3). The first component (maize origin) explained 27.921% of the total variance, the second one (maize type) 20.90%, the third one (tortilla manufacture type) 16.719%, and the last one (appearance) 15.09%.

Table 3. PCA with the correspondent eigenvalues and the percentages of variance explained.

Component	Name	Eigenvalues	Total Explained Variance	
			% of Variance	% Accumulated
Purchase and preferences				
Component 1	Reason for color tortilla purchase	2.67	29.66	29.66
Component 2	Tortillas type purchase	1.57	17.48	47.15
Component 3	Family size	1.18	13.12	60.27
Component 4	Purchase place	1.00	11.17	71.44
Factors influencing purchase decision				
Component 1	Maize origin	1.95	27.92	27.92
Component 2	Maize type	1.46	20.90	48.82
Component 3	Tortillas manufacture type	1.17	16.71	65.54
Component 4	Tortillas appearance	1.05	15.09	80.63

To see if there were differences between the female and male group preferences and purchase decisions, the Mann–Whitney test was applied. According to the results presented in Table 4, the favorite tortillas and the tortillas that women purchase did not differ significantly ($p > 0.05$) from those ones of the men. Also, the consumption frequency did not differ significantly ($p > 0.05$) among groups. There were significant differences ($p < 0.01$) at the medium effect size ($r = 0.37$) regarding the consumption quantity, U = 263.50, z = −2.88. The time of highest consumption differed among groups, U = 377.00, z = 2.25, $p < 0.05$. The effect size ($r = 0.29$) corresponded to a low to medium effect of the gender variable on the time of highest consumption, according to the Cohen [30] criteria. The purchase frequency and quantity, family size, purchase place, favorite color of tortillas, the actual color of purchased tortillas, and the reason for color purchase did not differ significantly ($p > 0.05$) between the female and male groups. Small-to-medium effects sizes were recorded for all factors.

According to the results presented in Table 4, there were no significant differences ($p > 0.05$) between the factors that influences women's and men's purchase decisions. There were weak effect sizes in all cases ($r < 0.30$).

Table 4. Mann–Whitney test results for the female and male group comparison regarding tortilla preferences and purchase decision.

Factor	Median	Range	Minimum	Maximum	U	z	r	Significance
Purchase and preferences								
Favorite tortillas	1.00	2.00	1.00	3.00	448.50	−0.04	0.01	0.96
Purchased tortillas	1.00	2.00	1.00	3.00	411.50	−0.69	0.09	0.48
Consumption frequency	1.00	1.00	1.00	2.00	435.00	−0.58	0.07	0.55
Consumption quantity	3.00	3.00	1.00	4.00	263.50	−2.88	0.37	0.00
Time of highest consumption	2.00	2.00	1.00	3.00	377.00	−2.25	0.29	0.02
Purchase frequency	1.00	4.00	1.00	5.00	439.00	−0.20	0.02	0.83
Purchase quantity	3.00	6.00	1.00	7.00	411.50	−0.61	0.08	0.53
Family size	2.00	3.00	1.00	4.00	434.00	−0.25	0.03	0.80
Purchase place	3.00	4.00	1.00	5.00	377.00	−1.741	0.22	0.08
Color of favorite tortilla	3.00	6.00	1.00	7.00	355.50	−1.43	0.18	0.15
Color of tortilla purchase	2.00	6.00	1.00	7.00	417.50	−0.51	0.06	0.60
Reason of color tortilla purchase	2.00	3.00	1.00	4.00	422.50	−0.43	0.05	0.66

Table 4. Cont.

Factor	Median	Range	Minimum	Maximum	U	z	r	Significance
Factors influencing purchase decision								
Price	6.00	6.00	1.00	7.00	367.00	−1.29	0.16	0.19
Taste	3.00	6.00	1.00	7.00	331.00	−1.80	0.23	0.07
Tortillas manufacture	4.00	6.00	1.00	7.00	401.50	−0.72	0.09	0.46
Tortillas appearance	5.00	6.00	1.00	7.00	435.00	−0.22	0.02	0.82
Shelf-life	5.00	6.00	1.00	7.00	352.00	−1.47	0.19	0.13
Maize type	3.00	6.00	1.00	7.00	397.00	−0.79	0.10	0.42
Maize origin	3.00	6.00	1.00	7.00	420.00	−0.45	0.05	0.65

U: Mann–Whitney; z: z score; r: the effect size; median: measure of the central tendency of the two groups; range: median dispersion.

3.2. Sensory, Texture Profile, and Physico-Chemical Parameters of Tortillas

The sensory parameters of the tortilla samples are presented in Table 5. Artisanal tortillas did not have as much of a uniform color and surface as the industrial ones due to the manufacturing process [31]. Higher moisture perception and opacity were recorded for the artisanal samples.

The smell of maize was more present in the artisanal (TA1 and TA2) and maize tortillas (TMZ1 and TMZ2), while the smell of lime was more intense for the tortillas containing industrialized maize flour. The taste of ferment and acid was not so present in any sample. The salted taste was due to the presence of natural salts in maize grains because no salt is added in the manufacturing process. A sweet taste was more pronounced in the artisanal tortillas, while the taste of lime was stronger in the industrialized samples.

The texture parameters of the tortillas evaluated using the subjective methods are showed in Table 5. According to the obtained results, the artisanal tortilla TA1 was the roughest, while the maize tortilla TMZ2 was the softer. All samples had good rollability, the less rollable being the mix tortilla TMX1. The most elastic were the artisanal TA1 and the industrialized flour tortilla TMN1. The maize tortilla TMZ1 was the hardest, while the less one was made of industrialized flour (TMN2). Good masticability values were obtained for the artisanal and the industrial flour samples. No significant differences ($p > 0.05$) were recorded between samples regarding the moisture absorption and tooth packing parameters.

The color of food products influences consumers preferences and can be expressed as lightness (L^*), hue angle (H^*), and color saturation index (chroma) [27,32,33]. According to the results presented in Table 6, the values of lightness of the artisanal tortillas samples were lower than those of the industrialized ones. Significant differences ($p < 0.05$) in the hue angle were recorded between the artisanal and the machine-made tortillas, the highest values being for TA1 and TA2. Great saturation indexes (chroma) were recorded for the samples containing industrialized maize flour, while for the maize tortillas the values were lower.

The texture profile parameters of the tortillas achieved using the instrumental method (Table 5) depended on the maize type and manufacturing process. Higher tensile strength at break values was obtained for artisanal samples, while the mix sample TMX1 had the lower value. The breaking distance was significantly higher ($p < 0.05$) for the artisanal tortillas than for the industrial ones.

The chemical parameters of the tortilla samples are presented in Table 7. The artisanal tortillas had the higher proteins contents compared to the industrial ones. The lipids contents varied in function of the maize origin and manufacturing process, the higher value being recorded for TMX1 sample made of industrial flour and nixtamalized maize, while the maize tortilla TMZ2 had the lower lipid content. Artisanal tortillas samples proved to have higher carbohydrates content, while the industrialized ones made with machines (TMN) had the lower content.

Table 5. Sensory and subjective textural parameters of tortilla samples.

Sensory Characteristic	TMX1	TMX2	TMZ1	TMZ2	TMN1	TMN2	TA1	TA2
Color uniformity	12.00 ± 1.39 bc	10.77 ± 1.38 bc	10.77 ± 1.71 bc	9.66 ± 2.54 b	10.88 ± 1.52 bc	12.22 ± 0.57 c	6.11 ± 1.63 a	5.66 ± 2.87 a
Surface uniformity	9.44 ± 2.22 abc	8.00 ± 2.23 ab	10.55 ± 1.77 bc	11.77 ± 1.82 c	11.77 ± 1.67 c	9.44 ± 2.22 abc	6.55 ± 2.87 a	7.55 ± 2.85 ab
Moisture	7.33 ± 2.57 a	6.33 ± 1.98 a	6.22 ± 2.73 a	8.11 ± 2.26 a	8.00 ± 2.16 a	8.22 ± 1.49 a	9.33 ± 3.27 a	8.11 ± 2.30 a
Opacity	7.66 ± 1.25 ab	9.11 ± 2.08 bc	8.88 ± 2.19 bc	6.00 ± 2.36 a	7.77 ± 2.57 ab	9.22 ± 1.70 bc	11.88 ± 1.34 c	9.77 ± 1.57 bc
Maize smell	6.33 ± 2.69 ab	4.88 ± 3.49 a	7.33 ± 3.14 ab	8.55 ± 2.58 ab	7.66 ± 2.14 ab	5.77 ± 3.03 ab	10.00 ± 2.50 b	8.88 ± 3.38 ab
Lime smell	8.00 ± 3.67 bc	8.66 ± 3.55 c	5.77 ± 4.03 abc	3.55 ± 2.14 ab	9.89 ± 2.81 c	8.89 ± 3.26 c	4.33 ± 3.03 c	3.55 ± 2.13 a
Fermented smell	3.22 ± 1.11 a	3.00 ± 2.57 a	4.22 ± 1.67 a	3.66 ± 1.25 a	4.00 ± 2.93 a	4.55 ± 2.60 a	3.44 ± 1.27 a	2.11 ± 1.21 a
Acid taste	2.55 ± 1.13 a	4.00 ± 2.07 a	2.66 ± 1.61 a	2.89 ± 1.70 a	1.89 ± 0.78 a	3.66 ± 2.69 a	2.66 ± 1.86 a	2.33 ± 1.46 a
Salted taste	2.66 ± 0.97 a	3.44 ± 2.11 a	3.33 ± 1.82 a	3.66 ± 1.13 a	2.44 ± 0.97 a	3.22 ± 0.81 a	3.55 ± 1.27 a	2.78 ± 1.13 a
Sweet taste	4.00 ± 1.57 abc	1.67 ± 0.53 a	3.44 ± 0.81 ab	3.78 ± 1.27 abc	3.89 ± 1.39 abc	2.44 ± 1.13 a	5.44 ± 2.26 bc	5.44 ± 1.27 c
Lime taste	5.89 ± 3.28 ab	11.11 ± 2.87 c	5.11 ± 2.22 ab	4.55 ± 2.03 ab	8.11 ± 4.02 bc	8.78 ± 2.92 bc	3.78 ± 2.38 a	3.44 ± 1.95 a
Roughness	5.00 ± 1.06 ab	5.39 ± 1.01 ab	4.94 ± 2.14 ab	2.55 ± 0.37 a	4.55 ± 0.48 ab	5.22 ± 1.52 ab	5.83 ± 3.65 b	4.11 ± 1.86 ab
Rollability	10.44 ± 3.82 a	13.11 ± 1.70 a	11.89 ± 1.70 a	12.55 ± 1.27 a	12.22 ± 4.48 a	13.89 ± 1.57 a	14.11 ± 0.78 a	11.55 ± 1.60 a
Elasticity	5.78 ± 1.79 a	6.55 ± 1.73 a	6.89 ± 1.15 a	5.00 ± 1.41 a	7.05 ± 2.49 a	6.44 ± 1.13 a	7.89 ± 3.43 a	5.33 ± 2.38 a
Hardness	3.89 ± 0.95 a	5.89 ± 1.98 a	7.33 ± 4.25 a	3.78 ± 1.11 a	4.05 ± 0.83 a	3.66 ± 0.75 a	5.33 ± 1.49 a	4.11 ± 1.29 a
Masticability	7.55 ± 4.11 a	7.77 ± 3.59 a	8.89 ± 2.21 a	10.77 ± 2.21 a	10.11 ± 2.07 a	10.44 ± 1.70 a	9.66 ± 2.70 a	10.11 ± 2.92 a
Moisture absorption	8.55 ± 2.76 a	11.11 ± 1.57 a	10.77 ± 1.77 a	9.11 ± 2.60 a	8.20 ± 3.26 a	9.66 ± 3.31 a	11.11 ± 2.81 a	9.55 ± 2.00 a
Tooth packing	6.00 ± 3.49 a	8.22 ± 4.37 a	8.78 ± 3.14 a	7.44 ± 2.13 a	6.89 ± 3.43 a	7.33 ± 3.43 a	9.44 ± 3.09 a	7.89 ± 2.60 a

TMX: tortillas from maize grains and industrialized corn flour; TMZ: tortillas from locally grinded and nixtamalized maize grains only; TMN: tortillas from industrialized maize flour; TA: artisanal hand-made tortillas. The results are reported as the mean of at least three replications. Means with the same letters in the same row are not significantly different (Tukey $p < 0.05$).

Table 6. Color and mechanical texture parameters of tortillas samples.

Sample	L*	H*	C*	Tensile Strength at Break (N)	Breaking Distance (mm)
TMX1	69.94 ± 0.81 de	92.92 ± 0.85 ab	19.95 ± 0.31 e	438.33 ± 59.99 a	6.79 ± 0.31 a
TMX2	67.87 ± 0.65 c	91.60 ± 0.73 a	19.64 ± 0.56 e	684.71 ± 86.13 bcd	7.39 ± 0.27 a
TMZ1	71.16 ± 0.86 b	92.69 ± 1.17 ab	15.30 ± 0.61 c	713.26 ± 56.61 cd	7.53 ± 0.39 d
TMZ2	68.11 ± 0.98 c	95.19 ± 1.81 c	12.75 ± 0.77 a	571.15 ± 70.61 abc	6.61 ± 0.40 a
TMN1	68.85 ± 0.68 cd	91.96 ± 1.13 a	20.06 ± 0.60 e	551.29 ± 78.17 ab	6.61 ± 0.40 a
TMN2	71.07 ± 0.89 ef	93.97 ± 0.63 bc	19.83 ± 0.30 e	457.88 ± 67.31 a	6.79 ± 0.92 a
TA1	58.09 ± 0.77 a	266.18 ± 1.94 d	16.71 ± 0.69 d	1064.75 ± 71.46 e	11.34 ± 0.93 c
TA2	61.49 ± 0.88 b	268.45 ± 0.92 e	13.69 ± 0.69 b	725.37 ± 45.38 d	9.24 ± 0.30 b

TMX: tortillas from maize grains and industrialized corn flour; TMZ: tortillas from grinded and nixtamalized maize grains only; TMN: tortillas from industrialized maize flour; TA: artisanal hand-made tortillas; L^*: luminosity; H^*: hue angle; C^*: chroma. The results are reported as the means of nine replications. Means with the same letters in the same column are not significantly different (Tukey $p < 0.05$).

The neutral detergent fibers (FND) included cellulose, hemicelluloses, and lignin [34] and had the greatest values for the mixed tortilla TMX1 (made of maize grains and industrialized corn flour) and the artisanal one which contained maize and wheat (TA1). The acid detergent fiber (FAD) included cellulose and lignin [33] and presented higher values for the artisanal tortillas than for the industrial ones (Table 7). Samples containing industrialized corn flour (TMX and TMN) presented higher values of ash contents than the other ones. Artisanal tortillas had a lower water content than samples made in tortillerías shops. The artisanal tortilla TA1 had the higher water absorption index (WAI) value, while TA2 had the lowest water absorption index. Lower water soluble solids index (WSI) values were recorded for the tortilla made of local maize only (TMZ1), followed by the industrialized ones (TMN1 and TMN2), while the artisanal (TA2) had a high-water soluble solids index.

3.3. Multivariate Analysis

The multivariate analysis showed many effects compared to ANOVA because it takes into consideration the correlations among the dependent variables [35]. The relationships between physical (L^*, a^*, b^*, C^*, H^*-color parameters, tensile strength, breaking distance) and textural parameters (hardness, roughness, elasticity, masticability, tooth packing, rollability) and the results of the sensory testing of the tortilla samples analyzed (opacity, surface uniformity and color uniformity) are shown in Figure 1a. The first two principal components explain 55.17% of the total variance (PC1 = 38.18% and PC2 = 16.98%). For the first principal component PC1, a good correlation was obtained between luminosity and color uniformity evaluated by sensory analysis ($r = 0.78$), between hue angle and a^* parameter ($r = 0.82$) and between tensile strength and breaking distance ($r = 0.87$), the correlation coefficients being significant at 0.01 level. The first principal component PC1 was associated with tensile strength, breaking distance, color parameters, a^*, and hue angle. The PC1 underlines the opposition between color uniformity and hue angle. As for the second principal component PC2, b^*, and C^* parameters were opposed to opacity characteristic. The PCA loadings showed, along PC2, a close association between roughness and elasticity, which reflects the highly significant correlation coefficient ($r = 0.44$, $p < 0.01$). These variables indicate a strong correlation with this component that can be described as a function of the sensory parameters which have an important role in assessment of tortilla samples. The second component PC2 distinguished the roughness and surface uniformity which were opposed. Significant indirect correlations were obtained between roughness and surface uniformity ($r = -0.46$, $p < 0.01$). Regarding PC2, the roughness, elasticity, opacity, tooth packing, braking distance, tensile strength, and hue angle were placed in the left of the graph which shows that these contribute to a larger extent to the evaluation of tortilla samples in comparison with the parameters on the right.

Table 7. Chemical parameters of tortilla samples expressed as g/100 g.

Sample	Proteins	Lipids	Carbohydrates	FND	FAD	Ash	Moisture	WAI	WSI
TMX1	7.51 ± 0.01 [a]	1.43 ± 0.00 [d]	37.22 ± 0.68 [c]	33.95 ± 0.53 [g]	0.60 ± 0.25 [ab]	2.16 ± 0.13 [c]	51.57 ± 0.65 [d]	4.00 ± 0.16 [ab]	2.80 ± 0.29 [ab]
TMX2	7.66 ± 0.02 [ab]	1.12 ± 0.01 [bc]	39.57 ± 0.83 [d]	17.31 ± 0.61 [e]	0.76 ± 0.34 [ab]	3.34 ± 0.04 [e]	47.94 ± 0.87 [bc]	3.91 ± 0.02 [ab]	2.72 ± 0.35 [ab]
TMZ1	7.84 ± 0.01 [bc]	1.14 ± 0.03 [bc]	41.06 ± 0.04 [e]	15.44 ± 0.54 [cd]	0.75 ± 0.09 [ab]	1.28 ± 0.08 [a]	48.52 ± 0.25 [c]	4.18 ± 0.13 [bc]	2.07 ± 0.39 [a]
TMZ2	8.04 ± 0.01 [cd]	0.73 ± 0.02 [a]	38.59 ± 0.51 [d]	16.20 ± 0.54 [d]	0.54 ± 0.18 [a]	1.54 ± 0.03 [b]	50.99 ± 0.39 [d]	4.06 ± 0.05 [ab]	3.61 ± 0.25 [c]
TMN1	7.65 ± 0.21 [ab]	1.20 ± 0.16 [c]	34.20 ± 0.66 [b]	14.24 ± 0.51 [b]	1.01 ± 0.15 [ab]	2.51 ± 0.04 [d]	54.22 ± 0.58 [e]	3.98 ± 0.08 [ab]	2.76 ± 0.13 [ab]
TMN2	8.09 ± 0.09 [d]	1.02 ± 0.05 [b]	32.44 ± 0.82 [a]	14.83 ± 0.26 [bc]	0.73 ± 0.14 [ab]	2.58 ± 0.02 [d]	55.57 ± 0.85 [e]	4.19 ± 0.07 [bc]	2.36 ± 0.05 [a]
TA1	9.33 ± 0.15 [e]	1.13 ± 0.01 [bc]	41.65 ± 0.48 [e]	22.65 ± 0.37 [f]	1.82 ± 0.18 [c]	1.55 ± 0.08 [b]	46.49 ± 0.28 [b]	4.46 ± 0.01 [c]	3.35 ± 0.27 [bc]
TA2	9.52 ± 0.09 [e]	1.09 ± 0.00 [bc]	43.94 ± 0.48 [f]	8.31 ± 0.44 [a]	1.07 ± 0.39 [b]	1.41 ± 0.04 [ab]	43.71 ± 0.61 [a]	3.80 ± 0.44 [a]	5.14 ± 0.34 [d]

TMX: tortillas from maize grains and industrialized corn flour; TMZ: tortillas from locally grinded and nixtamalized maize grains only; TMN: tortillas from industrialized maize flour; TA: artisanal hand-made tortillas; FND: neutral detergent fibers; FAD: acid detergent fibers; WAI: water absorption index; WSI: water soluble solids index. The results are reported as the means of at least three replications. Means showing the same letters in the same column are not significantly different (Tukey $p < 0.05$).

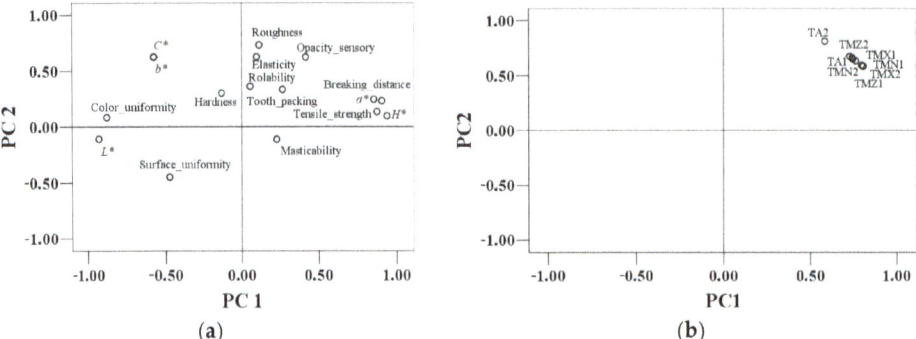

Figure 1. Principal component analysis: distribution of the physical (L^*, a^*, b^*, C^*, H^*-color parameters, tensile strength, breaking distance), textural (hardness, roughness, elasticity, masticability, tooth packing, rollability), and sensory parameters (opacity, surface uniformity, color uniformity) analyzed (**a**). Distribution of tortillas samples (TMX—tortillas from maize grains and industrialized corn flour; TMZ—tortillas from locally grinded and nixtamalized maize grains only; TMN—tortillas from industrialized maize flour; and TA—artisanal hand-made tortillas) in the function of the analyzed parameters (**b**).

The distribution of all tortilla samples in the function of the physical, textural, and sensory analyzed parameters is presented in Figure 1b. The first two principal components explain 98.87% of the total variance (PC1 = 97.93% and PC2 = 0.93%). There were strong significant correlations at 0.01 levels among all the tortilla samples evaluated. Clustering of the samples TMZ1, TMZ2, TMX1, TMX2, TMN1, TMN2, and TA1 can be interpreted as an indication of similarity between the interrelated physical, textural, and sensory parameters. Based on the bi-plot of the principal component scores, the artisanal TA2 sample appeared quite distinct from all the other samples (Figure 1b), suggesting its differences among the evaluated parameters.

In Figure 2a, the PCA loadings of the chemical (moisture, ash, proteins, lipids, neutral detergent fiber (FND), acid detergent fiber (FAD), carbohydrates, water absorption index (WAI), water soluble solids index (WSI)) and sensory parameters (moisture absorption, acid taste, lime taste, lime smell, fermented smell, moisture sensory, salted taste, sweet taste, maize smell) are presented. A value of 41.53% of the total variance was explained by the first two principal components (PC1 = 29.04% and PC2 = 12.48%). There were statistically significant correlations ($p < 0.01$) between neutral detergent fibers (FNDs) and lipids ($r = 0.55$), maize smell and salted taste ($r = 0.45$) and water absorption index (WAI) ($r = 0.34$), and carbohydrates and water soluble solids index (WSI) ($r = 0.57$). The first principal component was associated with protein content, sweet taste, WSI, and carbohydrates, while the second one was associated with fermented smell, WAI, and lime smell. Along the PC1 axis, the ash content and moisture measured chemically was opposed to proteins content, WSI, and carbohydrates. The PC2 distinguished between moisture absorption and WAI with the latter showing a positive effect on the fermented smell. From the PCA bi-plot in Figure 2a, the correlations between the results of the chemical and sensory evaluation for the tortillas samples are observed.

The scores were also denoted for each tortilla sample and grouped corresponding to their manufacturing process type (Figure 2b). The first two principal components explain 93.66% of the total variance (PC1 = 90.04% and PC2 = 3.62%). Samples grouping (Figure 2b) shows that, probably, the processing method did not remarkably influence the tortilla quality considered from the point of view of the sensory and chemical parameters. The TA1 sample was visibly differentiated from the others, a fact that may be attributed to the use of an amount of wheat flour in the formulation recipe, the ingredients used being a critical factor that affects tortilla quality [36]. Apart of TA1, two more sample groups can be distinguished. The first one included the samples made of only of maize grains (TMZ1, TMZ2m and TA1), while the second one comprised the samples with industrial flour (TMX1,

TMX2, TMN1, and TMN2). Regarding PC2, the WAI, FAD, fermented smell, sweet taste, salted taste, maize smell and the moisture sensory evaluated are placed on the left of the graph which shows that these contributed to a larger extent at the evaluation of tortillas samples in comparison with the parameters on the right. There were strong correlations among all tortillas samples made with industrialized corn flour, either alone (TMN) or mixed with local maize flour (TMX) (Figure 2b), between TMX2 and TMX1 ($r = 0.86$), TMX2 and TMN2 ($r = 0.87$), and TMX1 and TMN2 ($r = 0.85$) at the 0.01 significance level. However, artisanal TA1 was strongly correlated with tortillas made from locally grinded and nixtamalized maize grains TMZ2 ($r = 0.93$) and TMZ1 ($r = 0.93$) at the 0.01 significance level and was characterized by high WAI.

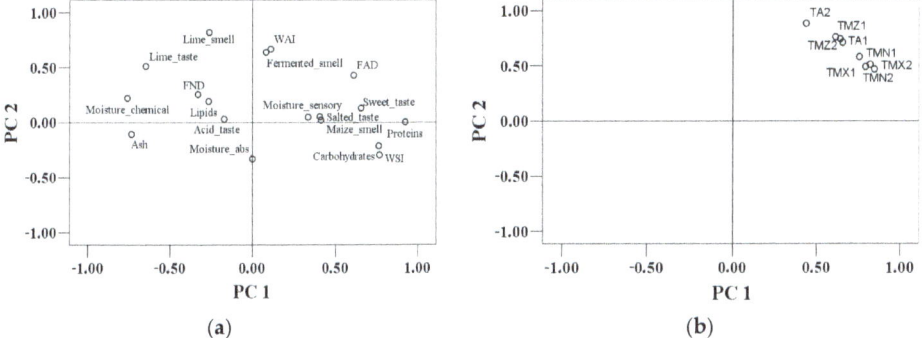

Figure 2. Principal component analysis: distribution of chemical (moisture, ash, proteins, lipids, neutral detergent fiber (FND), acid detergent fiber (FAD), carbohydrates, water absorption index (WAI), water soluble solids index (WSI)) and sensory (moisture absorption, acid taste, lime taste, lime smell, fermented smell, moisture sensory, salted taste, sweet taste, maize smell) analyzed parameters (**a**). Distribution of tortillas samples (TMX—tortillas from maize grains and industrialized corn flour; TMZ—tortillas from locally grinded and nixtamalized maize grains only; TMN—tortillas from industrialized maize flour; and TA—artisanal hand-made tortillas) in the function of the analyzed parameters (**b**).

4. Discussion

The hypothesis that there are differences between women's and men's preferences and purchase decisions was confirmed by the results obtained for the factors affecting the purchase decision; men considered taste as the most important fact while, for women the maize type was essential. Another study mentioned that food choice is a complex process which depends on gender influences [37]. Significant differences ($p < 0.01$) among the two groups were obtained for the consumption quantity and time of highest consumption of tortillas which is due to the distinct energy needs between women and men [19]. Women are reported to be the main decision-makers for food purchase [38] and household economics, trying to offer pragmatic responses when spending on food for their families, as it is for the purchase of tortillas. Several studies revealed that the nutritional value of the product is an important factor that affects consumer's behavior [38–42]. Our results showed that women consume less than 5 pieces of tortillas daily, while men consume more than 6, and this is in accordance with the findings reported by Cárdenas-Marcelo et al. [15] which stated that women consume approximately seven tortillas daily and men nine. Our study revealed that 80% of women and 90% of men buy tortillas from tortillerías, while Cárdenas-Marcelo et al. [15] reported that only 16% of women and 9% of men buy them from such places. These differences may be due to the fact that our study was performed in the center of the village of Tlazala which is close to the urban area of Mexico City, while their study was conducted in a local market where artisanal products are sold, in the State of Mexico. The most important factors that influence consumers from Tlazala tortillas selection were the maize type, origin, manufacture, and taste. The reasons for their choices were related to the preference or to the product availability which implies the proximity of their houses and the variety of products, a fact also confirmed by other studies [38,43,44].

Characteristics such as taste, smell, appearance, and texture of food products have a determinant role when a person decides to buy and consume an item [45]. The obtained results showed higher scores for the sensory parameters such as moisture, opacity, maize smell, and sweet taste, and lower scores for lime taste and the smell of the artisanal and maize made tortillas which are in agreement with the results for the consumers' preferences. Similar findings were reported by Méndez-Albores et al. [31] for maize tortillas with different nixtamalization processes when panelists detected the lime smell and taste at 0.50% (w/w) lime used. According to the texture parameters scores, the artisanal tortilla TA1 roughness was appreciated with 5.83 points and the elasticity with 7.89, being higher compared to most of the industrial ones studied. All the samples presented high scores for rollability and masticability, while the hardness varied from 3.66 for TMN2 made of industrial flour to 7.33 for the TMZ2 industrially made of maize grains. These results are near to those obtained by Bejosano et al. [22] for wheat flour tortillas which had a rollability score of 15.00, elasticity of 11.10, and hardness of 6.50, measured using a 15 points scale. Méndez-Albores et al. [31] reported roughness scores between 4.77 and 4.90, rollability between 4.19 and 4.51, tooth packing between 4.87 and 4.90 for maize tortillas evaluated using a 10 point scale. The relationship between the sensory profile of food products and consumers' behavior has been previously described in the literature [46–48].

Higher nutritional value and satisfactory texture parameters obtained for the tortillas made of maize grains instead of industrial flour sustain the preferences of consumers for this kind of product. Genetic and environmental conditions affect both the chemical and physical parameters of maize grains and, thus, the tortillas quality [42]. The textural properties are determined by the competition of starch, proteins, and fibers for water, influencing the starch matrix formation and starch grain hydration and plasticization. Thus, the chemical composition of tortillas is responsible for the textural property changes [10]. The chemical and physical parameters of tortillas depend on the maize variety, nixtamalization, and manufacturing process. Our results showed a lower lightness value for the artisanal tortillas, in agreement with the findings reported by Khan et al. [32] for traditional and machine tortillas. The hue angle of the artisanal tortillas was higher than 266, while the industrial ones varied from 91.92 to 95.19. Our results showed higher values than those by Vasquez-Carrillo et al. [33] for industrial tortillas which presented values between 70.00 and 82.90, probably due to the maize type and manufacturing process. The tensile strength at the highest break value (1064.75 N) for the artisanal tortilla TA1 compared to the industrial ones was in agreement with that obtained by Vaca-García et al. [9] which showed a value of 1684.00 N for the maize tortilla. The artisanal tortillas had the highest protein content of 9.33 g/100 g for TA1 and 9.52 g/100 g for TA2, the results being in agreement with those obtained by Valderrama-Bravo et al. [10] for tortillas from different maize genotypes which presented values higher than 11 g/100 g. The lipid contents of the studied tortillas were lower than those reported by Valderrama-Bravo et al. [10] and can be due to the fat hydrolysis in alkaline solution and solubilization during the nixtamalization process [33]. The artisanal tortilla TA2 had the lowest water absorption index. As water content influences texture, lower values lead to harder and brittle tortillas which cannot support a stew portion on top of it, which is the most common way to consume tortillas in Mexico [33]. The artisanal tortillas presented the highest fiber and lower ash contents which are in agreement with Valderrama-Bravo et al.'s [10] previous study. Therefore, our results highlighted that the chemical composition of the artisanal tortillas recommend them as being more nutritious compared to the industrial ones.

This study underlines the properties of some tortilla types and people's preferences from a specific region in Mexico. However, it may represent a starting point for future investigations regarding the relationships between tortilla quality and consumer behavior.

5. Conclusions

The industrialization of the food sector leads to product changes. Tortillas parameters and consumers' behavior knowledge is important for all implied actors, from consumer to producer. Consumers' preferences for artisanal maize tortillas instead of industrialized maize flour were supported by the quality parameters of these products. The artisanal tortillas stand out from the industrial ones by higher nutritional value and proper sensory parameters. Tortillas made of maize processed in a mechanized way had satisfactory physical, chemical, and sensory parameters compared to those made of industrialized flour and, thus, can be considered as an intermediate choice between the artisanal and industrialized ones. In Tlazala, no significant differences were found between women's and men's behavior regarding tortilla choice, except for purchase decision factors. Women agreed that the most important aspect was the maize type, while men were more interested in the product's taste. People search for healthy and convenient products with good parameters, and producers should be focused on product quality improvement and consumer need satisfaction.

Author Contributions: Conceptualization, M.I., V.D.Á.A., T.M.G.M. and S.M.; Methodology, M.I., V.D.Á.A. and T.M.G.M.; Software, M.I. and S.M., Validation, M.I., V.D.Á.A., T.M.G.M. and S.M.; Formal analysis, M.I., V.D.Á.A., T.M.G.M. and S.M.; Investigation, M.I.; Resources, V.D.Á.A.; Data curation, V.D.Á.A., T.M.G.M. and S.M.; Writing—original draft preparation, M.I.; Writing—review and editing, T.M.G.M., V.D.Á.A., and S.M.; Visualization, V.D.Á.A., T.M.G.M. and S.M.; Supervision, T.M.G.M., V.D.Á.A., and S.M.; Project administration, V.D.Á.A. and S.M.; Funding acquisition, S.M.

Funding: This work was supported from contract no. 18PFE/16.10.2018 funded by Ministry of Research and Innovation within Program 1—Development of national research and development system, Subprogram 1.2—Institutional Performance—RDI excellence funding projects.

Acknowledgments: This work was made under an Erasmus+ scholarship. We would like to thank Francisco Herrera Tapia, director of ICAR-UAEM, and Marlín Pérez Suárez, research professor, and the laboratory responsible for ICAR-UAEM for supporting this research, Laura Edith Martínez Contreras and María de Lourdes Maya Salazar, technicians at ICAR-UAEM laboratories, for the analysis methodology and equipment use assistance, Aurelio Dominguez-Lopez and Jesús Castillón Jardón, research professors at UAEM, for approving the use of the equipment, Baciliza Quintero Salazar, research professor at UAEM, for supporting and advising the sensory analysis methodology, and Ivonne Vizcarra Bordi, research professor at ICAR-UAEM, for the careful revision.

Conflicts of Interest: The authors declare no conflict of interest.

References

1. Rodríguez Calderón, T.J.; Chávez Mejía, M.C.; Thomé Ortiz, H.; Miranda Román, G. Production and consumption of tortillas as a cultural heritage of San Pedro del Rosal, Mexico. *Región Y Sociedad* **2017**, *29*, 155–179.
2. Novelo, V.; García, A. La tortilla: Alimento, trabajo y tecnología. In *Complementos del Seminario de Problemas Científicos y Filosóficos*; Universidad Nacional Autónoma de México: Mexico City, Mexico, 1987.
3. Gwirtz, A.J.; Garcia-Casal, M.N. Processing maize flour and corn meal food products. *Ann. N. Y. Acad. Sci.* **2014**, *1312*, 66–75. [CrossRef] [PubMed]
4. Bourges, H.; Lehrer, S. *Assessment of Human Health Effects in Maize and Biodiversity: The Effects of Transgenic Maize in MEXICO*; Commission for Environmental Cooperation: Montreal, QC, Canada, 2004. Available online: http://www3.cec.org/islandora/en/item/2152-maize-and-biodiversity-effects-transgenic-maize-in-mexico-key-findings-and-en.pdf (accessed on 25 September 2019).
5. Pourafshar, S.; Rosentrater, K.A.; Krishnan, P.G. Changes in chemical and physical properties of Latin American wheat flour based tortillas substituted with different levels of distillers dried grains with solubles (DDGS). *J. Food Sci. Technol.* **2015**, *52*, 5243–5249. [CrossRef] [PubMed]
6. Vizcarra Bordi, I. *Volteando la Tortilla*; Juan Pablos Editores: Mexcio City, Mexico, 2018.
7. Isakson, R. Between the Market and the Milpa: Market Engagements, Peasant Livelihood Strategies, and the On-Farm Conservation of Crop Genetic Diversity in the Guatemalan Highlands. Ph.D. Thesis, University of Massachusetts Amherst, Amherst, MA, USA, 2007.
8. Sain, G.; Amaya, N.; Trejos, R. *Maize Situation in Latin America: Outlook and Investment Opportunities*; Inter-American Institute for Cooperation on Agriculture: San José, Costa Rica, 2014.

9. Vaca-García, V.M.; Martínez-Rueda, C.G.; Mariezcurrena-Berasain, M.D.; Domínguez-López, A. Functional properties of tortillas with triticale flour as a partial substitute of nixtamalized corn flour. *LWT-Food Sci. Technol.* **2011**, *44*, 1383–1387. [CrossRef]
10. Valderrama-Bravo, C.; Domínguez-Pacheco, A.; Hernández-Aguilar, C.; Zepeda-Bautista, R.; del Real-López, A.; Pahua-Ramos, M.E.; Arellano-Vázquez, J.L.; Moreno-Martínez, E. Physical and chemical characterization of masa and tortillas from parental lines, crosses, and one hybrid. *Int. Agrophys.* **2017**, *31*, 129–138. [CrossRef]
11. Vizcarra Bordi, I. *Entre el taco Mazahua y el Mundo. La Comida de las Relaciones de Poder, Resistencia e Identidades*; Universidad Autónoma del Estado de México: Toluca, Mexico, 2002.
12. Appendini, K.; Quijada, M.G. Consumption strategies in Mexican rural households: Pursuing food security with quality. *Agric. Hum. Values* **2016**, *33*, 439–454. [CrossRef]
13. La percepción del consumidor de tortillas. Available online: https://www.jornada.com.mx/2018/02/17/cam-tortillas.html (accessed on 17 February 2018).
14. Ortega, T. Género, Soberanía Alimentaria y Agrobiodiversidad: La Unión de Palmeadoras de la Heroica Ciudad se Tlaxiaco, Oaxaca. Ph.D. Thesis, Colegio de Postgraduados, Motnecillo, Texcoco, Mexico, 2018.
15. Cárdenas Marcelo, A.L.; Vizcarra Bordi, I.; Espinoza-Ortega, A.; Espinosa Calderón, A. Artisanal Mazahua Tortillas and Native Maize Biodiversity. Reflexion from the Ecofeminism of Subsistence. *Sociedad Y Ambiente* **2019**, *7*, 265–291. [CrossRef]
16. Torres-Salcido, G. De la producción de maíz al consumo social de tortilla. In *Políticas de Producción y Abastecimiento Urbano*; Universidad Nacional Autónoma de México: Mexico City, Mexico, 2009.
17. Arabi, M. *Linking Tortilla Price Policies to Household Food Consumption and Child Nutritional Intake: Potential Outcomes of Globalization in Rural Mexico*; Faculty of the Graduate School of Cornell University: New York, NY, USA, 2010.
18. Herrera-Corredor, J.A.; Saidu, J.E.; Khachatryan, A.; Prinyawiwatkul, W.; Carballo-Carballo, A.; Zepeda-Bautista, R. Identifying drivers for consumer acceptance and purchase intent of corn tortilla. *J. Food Sci.* **2007**, *72*, 727–731. [CrossRef]
19. Chao, A.M.; Loughead, J.; Bakizada, Z.M.; Hopkins, C.M.; Geliebter, A.; Gur, R.C.; Wadden, T.A. Sex/gender differences in neural correlates of food stimuli: A systematic review of functional neuroimaging studies. *Obes. Rev.* **2017**, *18*, 687–699. [CrossRef]
20. Rangel Meza, E.; Muñoz Orozco, A.; Vázquez Carrillo, G.; Cuevas Sánchez, J.; Merino Castillo, J.; Miranda Colín, S. Nixtamalización, elaboración y calidad de tortilla de maíces de ecatlán, Puebla, México. *Agrociencia* **2004**, *38*, 53–61.
21. Figueroa Cardenas, J.D.; Acero Godínez, M.G.; Vasco Méndez, N.L.; Lozano Guzman, A.; Flores Acosta, L.M.; González-Hernández, J. Fortification and evaluation of nixtamal tortillas. *Arch. Latinoam. Nutr.* **2001**, *51*, 293–302. [PubMed]
22. Bejosano, F.P.; Joseph, S.; Lopez, M.L.; Kelekci, N.N.; Waniska, R.D. Rheological a sensory evaluation of wheat flour tortillas during storage. *Cereal Chem.* **2016**, *82*, 256–263. [CrossRef]
23. Méndez-Albores, A.; Martínez-Morquecho, R.A.; Moreno-Martínez, E.; Vázquez-Durán, A. Technological properties of maize tortillas produced by microwave nixtamalization with variable alkalinity. *Afr. J. Biotechnol.* **2012**, *11*, 15178–15187.
24. Morten Meilgaard, D.S.; Gail Vance Civille, B.S.; Thomas Carr, M.S. *Sensory Evaluation Techniques*, 4th ed.; Taylor & Francis: Boca Raton, FL, USA, 2007; p. 448.
25. Association of Official Analytical Chemists (AOAC). *Official Methods of Analysis of the AOAC*, 16th ed.; Association of Official Analytical Chemists: Washington, DC, USA, 1999.
26. Ankom Anal Methods. Available online: https://www.ankom.com/analytical-methods-support/fiber-analyzer-a200 (accessed on 2 April 2019).
27. Serena-Saldivar, O. *Cereal Grains Laboratory Reference and Procedures Manual*; CRC PRESS Taylor & Francisc Group: Boca Raton, FL, USA, 2012.
28. Hernández-Martínez, V.; Salinas-Moreno, Y.; Ramírez-Díaz, J.L.; Vásquez-Carrillo, G.; Domínguez-López, A.; Ramírez-Romero, A.G. Color, Phenolic composition and antioxidant activity of blue tortillas from Mexican maize races. *CYTA J. Food* **2016**, *14*, 473–481. [CrossRef]
29. Espinoza-Ortega, A.; Martínez-García, C.G.; Thomé-Ortiz, H.; Vizcarra-Bordi, I. Motives for food choice of consumers in Central México. *Br. Food J.* **2016**, *118*, 2744–2760. [CrossRef]

30. Cohen, J. *Statistical Power Analysis for the Behavioral Sciences*, 2nd ed.; Lawrence Erlbaum Associate: Mahwah, NJ, USA, 1988.
31. Méndez-Albores, A.; Zamora-Rodríguez, D.; Arámbula-Villa, G.; Vásquez-Durán, A.; Moreno-Martínez, E. Impact of different alkaline-heating processes on technological and nutritional properties of maize tortillas. *J. Food Nutr. Res.* **2012**, *53*, 60–70.
32. Khan, M.N.; Des Rosiers, M.C.; Rooney, L.W.; Morgan, R.G.; Sweat, V.E. Corn tortillas: Evaluation of corn cooking procedures. *Cereal Chem.* **1982**, *59*, 279–284.
33. Vázquez-Carrillo, G.; García-Lara, S.; Salinas-Moreno, Y.; Bergvinson, D.J.; Palacios-Rojas, N. Grain and Tortilla Quality in Landraces and Improved Maize Grown in the Highlands of Mexico. *Plant Foods Hum. Nutr.* **2017**, *66*, 203–208. [CrossRef]
34. Van Soest, P.J.; Robertson, J.B.; Lewis, B.A. Carbohydrate methodology, metabolism and nutritional implications in dairy cattle. *J. Dairy Sci.* **1991**, *74*, 3583–3597. [CrossRef]
35. Field, A. *Discovering Statistics Using IBM SPSS Statistics*; SAGE Publications: Thousand Oaks, CA, USA, 2013.
36. Rooney, L.W.; Serena-Saldivar, S.O. *Tortillas Wheat Flour and Corn Products*; AACC International: St Paul, MN, USA, 2015.
37. Woodhall-Melnik, J.; Matheson, F. More than convenience: The role of habitus in understanding the food choices of fast food workers. *Work Employ. Soc.* **2016**, *31*, 800–815. [CrossRef]
38. Escobar-López, S.Y.; Espinoza-Ortega, A.; Vizcarra-Bordi, I.; Thomé-Ortiz, H. The consumer of food products in organic markets of central Mexico. *Br. Food J.* **2017**, *119*, 558–574. [CrossRef]
39. Lee, H.J.; Yun, Z.S. Consumers' perceptions of organic food attributes and cognitive and affective attitudes as determinants of their purchase intentions toward organic food. *Food Qual. Prefer.* **2015**, *39*, 259–267. [CrossRef]
40. Aschemann-Witzel, J.; Maroscheck, N.; Hamm, U. Are organic consumers preferring or avoiding foods with nutrition and health claims? *Food Qual. Prefer.* **2013**, *30*, 68–76. [CrossRef]
41. Pérez-Villarreal, H.H.; Martínez-Ruiz, M.P.; Izquierdo-Yusta, A. Testing Model of Purchase Intention for Fast Food in Mexico: How do Consumers React to Food Values, Positive Anticipated Emotions, Attitude toward the Brand, and Attitude toward Eating Hamburgers? *Foods* **2019**, *8*, 369. [CrossRef]
42. Vázquez-Carrillo, M.G.; Santiago-Ramos, D.; Salinas-Moreno, Y.; López-Cruz, J.; Ybarra-Moncada, M.C.; Ortega-Corona, A. Oil content in maize (*Zea mays* L.) genotypes and its relationship with quality and texture of tortilla. *Agrociencia* **2011**, *48*, 159–172.
43. Lim, W.M.; Yong, J.L.S.; Suryadi, K. Consumers' perceived value and willingness to purchase organic food. *J. Glob. Mark.* **2014**, *27*, 298–307. [CrossRef]
44. Hjelmar, U. Consumers' purchase of organic food products. A matter of convenience and reflexive practices. *Appetite* **2011**, *56*, 336–344. [CrossRef]
45. Pollard, J.; Kirk, S.L.; Cade, J.E. Factors affecting food choice in relation to fruit and vegetable intake: A review. *Nutr. Res. Rev.* **2002**, *15*, 373–387. [CrossRef]
46. Steptoe, A.; Pollard, T.M.; Wardle, J. Development of a measure of the motives underlying the selection of food: The food choice questionnaire. *Appetite* **1995**, *25*, 267–284. [CrossRef]
47. Eertmans, A.; Victoir, A.; Vansant, G.; Van den Bergh, O. Food-related personality traits, food choice motives and food intake: Mediator and moderator relationships. *Food Qual. Prefer.* **2005**, *16*, 714–726. [CrossRef]
48. Baudry, J.; Péneau, S.; Allès, B.; Touvier, M.; Hercberg, S.; Galan, P.; Amiot, M.J.; Lairon, D.; Mejean, C.; Kesse-Guyot, E. Food choice motives when purchasing in organic and conventional consumer clusters: Focus on sustainable concerns (The NutriNet-Santé Cohort Study). *Nutrients* **2017**, *9*, 88. [CrossRef] [PubMed]

© 2019 by the authors. Licensee MDPI, Basel, Switzerland. This article is an open access article distributed under the terms and conditions of the Creative Commons Attribution (CC BY) license (http://creativecommons.org/licenses/by/4.0/).

Article

Testing Model of Purchase Intention for Fast Food in Mexico: How do Consumers React to Food Values, Positive Anticipated Emotions, Attitude toward the Brand, and Attitude toward Eating Hamburgers?

Héctor Hugo Pérez-Villarreal [1,2,*], María Pilar Martínez-Ruiz [1] and Alicia Izquierdo-Yusta [3]

1. Faculty of Economics and Business Studies, University of Castilla-La Mancha, 02071 Albacete, Spain
2. Engineering and Business Postgraduate Center, Popular Autonomous University of Puebla State, 72410 Puebla, Mexico
3. Faculty of Economics and Business Studies, University of Burgos, 09001 Burgos, Spain
* Correspondence: hectorhugo.perez@upaep.mx

Received: 13 July 2019; Accepted: 21 August 2019; Published: 27 August 2019

Abstract: This research investigated the effect of the food values, positive anticipated emotions, attitude toward the brand, and attitude toward eating a hamburger on purchase intention in fast-food restaurants in Mexico conjointly. The purpose of this study was to discover which variables influenced the consumer´s intention to buy. Data was collected from a survey of 512 Mexicans fast-food consumers. Structural equation modeling was used to test the hypothesized associations. The results showed that food values and positive anticipated emotions absolutely impact the attitude toward the brand, which impacts the purchase intention of the Mexican consumers. Nonetheless, the positive anticipated emotions impact stronger than food values, and the best way to get a purchase intention is toward the attitude of the brand rather than attitude toward eating a hamburger. The authors discussed inferences and suggestions for consumer approaches.

Keywords: food values; positive anticipated emotions; attitude toward the brand; attitude toward eating a hamburger; purchase intention

1. Introduction

Food choice decisions are complicated when every day the consumers make a lot of decisions about one excellent fast food [1]. Over the past few years, some studies have had a primordial objective to explain how interaction facts affect purchase intention through theory planned behavior (TPB) [2–4]. However, none focused on the food values, especially when the research was about food choice and positive anticipated emotions like a central variable in the model. Based on a dataset of 1169 abstracts of marketing from 2005 to 2014, Barahona et al. (2018) [5] explained that one crucial dimension for researchers is emotional marketing. Topics such as evaluation, experience, message, people, emotional, goal, and hedonic are the keywords for studies in this field. Therefore, this research was based on the purpose of explaining the purchase intention in four main premises. First, fast food consumption has a purchase intention by the attitude toward the brand into the means of an emotional need according to a physiological desire [6–8]. Second, the consumers' emotions influence the purchase intention [9]. Third, what is the role of food values on attitude toward the brand and attitude toward eating a hamburger [10]? Fourth, what is more essential to predict the purchase intention: attitude toward the brand or attitude toward eating a hamburger [11]?

Through this research, a model with these variables was proposed because there is a synergistic effect between them. The approach rests with the effects of food values and positive early emotions directed towards the form of the attitude as a predecessor of the purchase intention [12–14]. This model was designed from the separation of attitudes: one directed towards the act of eating and another towards the brand. The application covers the principle on attitudes directed towards the product and another towards the brand. Thus, this model is the first that uses the rational and emotional part of consumption and separates the attitude of eating from the attitude towards the brand. In this case, the model provides information on the importance of the product and the brand and towards launch, modifications and valuations of products and brands. The consumer's decisions are based on some level of rational or emotional effect [15,16].

This study forms the rational (food values) and emotional (positive anticipated emotions) parts to connect them with different attitudes to predict purchase intention. Consequently, it used these two attitudes roles, eating versus brand, to test the relationship to purchase intention. The importance of the study is to predict the purchase intention and to know the consumers' behavior choices with a hamburger. If the calculations, weights, loadings, etc. contribute to explaining more of the purchase intention, it should make an important and significant contribution to academic literature. This is because it gives off too many forms to investigates and implement strategies in fast-food restaurants, knowing the protrusion factors in the model.

For these reasons, it is intended to identify which emotions, food values and types of attitudes impact significantly and positively on the purchase intention. Through these findings, marketing strategies can be formulated and it is possible to know what the most convenient way for this field is. The objective of the present study was to explicitly test the purchase intention toward attitudes, food values and positive anticipated emotions. The study built a model on purchase intention research by examining the consumer before the purchase decision. Also, this study emphasized the meaning of the role of attitudes (eating hamburger and brand) on purchase intentions of fast food consumers. Finally, the study tested and confirmed the hypotheses planted in this research.

1.1. Attitudes in Consumer Behavior

Attitude toward something is an antecedent of intention, but it is also the degree to which an individual has a favorable or unfavorable evaluation or appraisal of the behavior to any purchase situation [17]. Some research has also highlighted the role of purchase intention and the attitude impact [18]. On the other hand, the attitude that is formed in the first stage is formed of the decision process of purchase in the consumer (recognition of the need/problem). Some studies proved that the attitude directly affects the consumer's buying behavior [19–21]. This attitude is influenced by elements such as information, nature of the product, social media, ads and other behavioral factors. In the context of food consumption, the role of attitudes is at the top for research in consumer behavior. Thus, some consumers have attitudes toward eating hamburgers and others have attitudes toward the brand. This is because they keep both positive and negative evaluations, such as purchases intentions, purchases and repurchases [22]. However, in marketing as a discipline, the gap is different between attitude toward eating a hamburger and attitude toward the brand.

Attitudes toward eating hamburgers play a significant role in understanding consumer behavior. These attitudes can be decision-making components for the choice and intention to eat some food [23,24]. Once consumers recognize their need for food, they enter into a stage of searching and evaluating the alternatives [25]. It is at this stage, where people positively or negatively value the desired behavior without implying the degree of eating habits or the level of hunger [26]. Hence, the attitude of eating evaluates the favorable or unfavorable predisposition towards the act of eating any food [17]. Rezai et al. (2017) [27] pointed to a direct relationship between attitudes towards eating foods that generate a healthy benefit and the intention to buy. For this reason, it is vital to know one's attitude towards the act of eating as a central point towards the intention to buy.

On the other side, attitudes are cognitions and can sometimes be directed towards the brand [28]. So it is necessary to comment that attitudes towards the brand can generate a behavioral intent and the same behavior of the consumer's final purchase [29]. Therefore, attitudes towards the brand mean that consumers adopt or reject conduct based on experiences, personal recommendations and media exposure, as well as other media that use the brand and may have a point of contact with the consumer [30]. Hence, attitudes towards the brand have become one of the intangible components valued by consumers because when choosing the behavior, they do it more for the brand than for the product. Similarly, the attitude towards the brand makes consumers acquire feelings of security, confidence, convenience, and credibility among others, so for them, it is easier to recognize and choose the purchase [31]. Thus, the literature agrees that attitude towards the brand is the highest point through which the consumer disseminates the choice.

1.2. Purchase Intention

Assael (1998) [32] called purchase intention the conduct that seeks in response to an object and is before the purchase. Subsequently, Zhang et al. (2018) [33] approved the relationship between attitudes and purchase intention. Phau and Teah (2009) [34] demonstrated that when the consumer has a strong positive attitude, there is a higer intention to buy.

Rezai et al. (2017) [27] pointed out the importance of determining the intention to purchase functional products from examining the factors involved in the purchase decision process. For example, Jahn, Tsalis, and L'hteenm-ki (2019) [35] indicated that the general attitude towards products has a direct effect towards the intention to purchase, as long as the people are in a condition of suitability and knowledge of the problem. Asif et al. (2018) [36] pointed out that it is possible to find differences in intent to buy from one country to another, but they agreed that attitude and health awareness are the best predictors of the intention to buy in organic foods. Some studies pointed to some additional variables to the TPB including moral attitude and healthy awareness towards purchasing intent in organic foods [37]. Consequently, it is possible to include other variables in the purchase intention by extending the TPB. On the other hand, another study pointed to the involvement towards the consumption of products, price sensitivity and moderation of the effect of the identity of the local product towards the intention of purchase [38].

Chiu, Hsieh, and Kuo (2012) [39] and Diallo (2012) [40] underlined aspects about the probability to buy, not before the consumer formed an attitude and experience of the past. Now, as the intention is testified to be a significant factor of buying, it was thus, hypothesized that:

Hypothesis 1 (H1). *Attitude toward the brand will positively influence intention to buy.*

Hypothesis 2 (H2). *Attitude toward eating hamburger will positively influence the intention to buy.*

1.3. Food Values

The situation of obtaining information on the attributes of the product has always been a relevant topic in food consumer research. Today, exotic consumption attributes, towards the ethics of consumption, healthy awareness, animal impact and organic food are topics of interest in knowing one's behavior [41–44]. According to Basha and Lal (2019) [45], the ratio of environmental concern, health and lifestyle, supporting local farmers, product quality, convenience, price, animal welfare, safety-trust, subjective norms, and attitude is valued. The food choice has been becoming an advantage to improve healthy and sustainable diets and to know the different roles of high and low involvement [46]. Nevertheless, Boer and Schösler (2016) [46] mentioned that the differences in the affinities could be predicted by food-related value motivation.

Sprotles and Kendall (1986) [47], through consumer styles inventory (CSI), claimed that consumers choose to make their purchase decision through eight basic styles: high quality, innovation, brand awareness, price, hedonism, confusion with other brands, impulsivity, and habit. Other studies emphasized product presentation, food safety, environmental impact, and ethical consumer identity [48]. Another study found that depending on the type of food (organic or conventional) used, the effect on the consumer perception component (e.g., healthy consciousness) differs [49].

When researches talk about the food attributes, it can be partial to the real concept because the food attributes can be an infinite number of characteristics, but only some of them are important for the moment of choice [50]. For this reason, the attributes of the product became the consumer's values regarding food. Some researchers affirmed that these values were influenced through many factors, which relate to personal values [1,51–53]. This means that food values are exercised by the consumer and not by the product itself. However, each attribute mentioned above falls within a factor of the 11 described by Lusk (2011) [54]. Thus, it is possible that each product, depending on belonging in the category, constitutes intra-group differences, but it is possible to categorize them in general forms.

Lusk and Briggeman (2009) [55] explored all the factors that integrated the attributes of food. After this plan, Lusk (2011) [54] opened wide 11 items to identify the food values scale. These items are (1) naturalness (the extent to which food is produced without modern technologies), (2) taste (the extent to which consumption of food is appealing to the senses), (3) price (the amount paid for food), (4) safety (the extent to which consumption of food will not cause illness), (5) convenience (the ease with which food is cooked and consumed), (6) nutrition (the amount and type of fat, protein, vitamins, etc.), (7) tradition (preserving traditional consumption patterns), (8) origin (where the agricultural commodities were grown), (9) fairness (the extent to which all parties involved in food production equally benefit), (10) appearance (the extent to which food looks appealing), and (11) environmental impact (the effect of food production on the environment).

Studies have shown that food values are essential to explain attitudes. For example, Manan (2016) [1] emphasized to know the attitudes through personal values, but the question is whether personal values are influenced by the food benefits, if that correct, then these affect attitude. In order, Lang and Lemmerer (2019) [53] demonstrated the relationships across personal values and attitudes toward local food, but they did not separate the attitude toward eating a hamburger or the attitude toward the brand. As a result, it is hypothesized that:

Hypothesis 3 (H3). *Food values will positively influence attitude toward the brand.*

Hypothesis 4 (H4). *Food values will positively influence attitude toward eating a hamburger.*

1.4. Anticipated Emotions

Some researchers have been in charge of framing emotions as a fundamental, principal axis and detonator of all purchasing behavior, this adding to the part of information processing and consumer action [56–62]. Although the entire chain of observation (cognitive, conative and affective), the trigger and the key factors of success cannot be established, some researchers have taken a part of the chain towards the effective and successful verification of the application of branding emotional, buyback, purchase decision, search, and evaluation of purchase alternatives [63–66].

Within the contributions of advertising, it is possible to highlight that the emotional contagion may have main effects on the physiological changes of the people [67]. In this study, the participants felt sadder when they saw a victim with a sad face, and their sadness emanated the effect on the expression of the emotion in the sympathy. The effects of contagion are automatic and not inferential but are diminished by deliberative thinking. On the other hand, Nielsen et al. (2010) [68] showed that the "pre-attention" processing of semantic information in non-focal announcement titles can provoke orientations towards attention responses. The same results were in foreseeable increases in the ad and knowledge of the brand. Equally, Teixeira et al. (2012) [59] showed that surprise and joy concentrate effective attention and retain the viewers with more time. However, the most important thing is the level of retention instead of the speed of surprise, and it affects the concentration of attention more. Therefore, speed influences the level of joy, which affects spectator retention. These three studies placed the emotional part as the main factor in their research with the impact on advertising. It could be specified that the authors discussed the implications of the use of emotional expressions, titles of advertisements, and consumer knowledge of the brand to promote emotions in the consumer and help the purchasing decision process.

However, the emotions are present throughout the process of consumer behavior, but it is vital to determine what the origin of this is. Pelsmaeker et al. (2017) [69] explained the relationship of emotions in the begging of the process of consumer intention, and they determined the relevance of applying an evaluation before recognizing the need. Emotions can indeed be positive and negative depending on the moment or value. However, some researchers in recent years were working only for positive emotions because only these matter. Wen, Hu and Kim (2018) [70] examined the effect of individual culture on positive emotions for the recommendation intention. Finally, positive emotions are the principal element to determine the satisfaction of the consumer [71].

Williams and Aaker (2002) [72] believed that when individuals are exposed to mixed emotions, they influenced the individual´s attitudes in general. They also demonstrated that the detonation of emotions with duality (e.g., sadness and happiness) is less prone to form an attitude towards their behavior. Haws and Winterich (2013) [73] described the factors to measure the attitude toward eating directly to these items: pleasure, enjoy, satisfied, and good taste. However, the consumer can have an attitude toward the brand and not for eating. That reason describes Aggarwal and Mcgill's (2012) [74] finding that what consumers like, think, admire, and fit in their life is a good positive attitude that helps to stimulate the intention. This study proposed two constructs, one for eating the hamburger and the other for the brand.

Thus, the following hypothesis can be derived:

Hypothesis 5 (H5). *Positive anticipated emotions will positively influence attitude toward the brand.*

Hypothesis 6 (H6). *Positive anticipated emotions will positively influence attitude toward eating a hamburger.*

Hypothesis 7 (H7). *Positive anticipated emotions will positively influence the intention to buy.*

Therefore, seven hypotheses were tested in this research and based on the discussion above (see Figure 1), and considers seven proposed effects: (1) attitude toward the brand on purchase intention, (2) attitude toward eating hamburger on purchase intention, (3) food values on attitude toward the brand, (4) food values on attitude toward eating hamburger, (5) positive anticipated emotions on attitude toward the brand, (6) positive anticipated emotions on attitude toward eating hamburger, and (7) positive anticipated emotions on purchase intention. Thus, all the effects correspond to a new model for understanding better the purchase intention in fast-food restaurants.

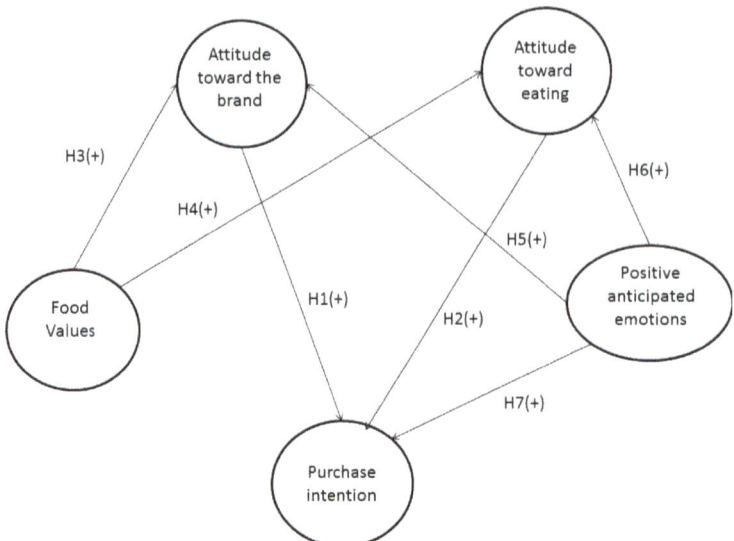

Figure 1. Model development.

2. Materials and Methods

This study utilized partial least squares-structural equation modelling (PLS-SEM) to examine the impact of the food values, emotions anticipated and attitudes on purchase intention (see Table 1 for technical details). The proposal was to estimate a model that includes a mix of factors and composites using the PLS algorithm procedure [75]. The idea was to maximize the explained variance of all dependent variables used in the research model. In this case, the research intent was to know the predictor variable and to identify possible drivers [76,77]. Therefore, the independent variables that the literature reports as important predecessors of purchase intention were also included.

Table 1. Technical Details.

Universe	Residents in Puebla State in México
Sample unit	People over 17 years old and buying fast food
Information collection method	Personal survey
Sample error	±4.335
Level of reliability	95%
Sample procedure	Probabilistic
Number surveyed	512 valid surveys
Period of information collection	January 26–May 23 (2018)
Language	Spanish

2.1. Data Collection

The data was collected from Puebla City in Mexico with a consumer survey of 512 participants. Participation was voluntary and all of them completed the questionnaire.

2.2. Statistics Analysis

The study used structural equation modeling (SEM) to test the conceptual model with SmartPLS 3.0 software. According to Streukekens and Leroi-Werelds (2016) [78], this study used partial least squares (PLS) with a 10,000 subsample bootstrapping procedure and the same software to know if the relationship was supported or not with the results. In the beginning, this model was composted from 34 items reduced to 28 items in five constructs. From there, no preliminary empirical parameters for this particular market were found.

2.3. Questionnaire Development

The questionnaire was constructed and divided into five sections: (a) food values, (b) positive and negative anticipated emotions, (c) attitude toward the brand, (d) attitude toward eating a hamburger, and (e) purchase intention (see Table 2). The first table shows the questionnaire section by source and the second explains details on how to measure each variable.

Table 2. Questionnaire sections.

Latent Variable	Observed Variables	Definition	Source
Food values are general food attributes that consumers believed were relatively more important when purchasing food	Appearance	Extent to which food looks appealing	Lusk (2011) [54]
	Convenience	Ease with which food is cooked and consumed	
	Environmental	Effect of food production on the environment	
	Fairness	The extent to which all parties involved in the production of the food equally benefit	
	Naturalness	Extent to which food is produced without modern technologies	
	Nutrition	Amount and type of fat, protein, vitamins, etc.	
	Origin	Where the agricultural commodities were grown	
	Price	The price that is paid for the food	
	Safety	Extent to which consumption of food will not cause illness	
	Taste	Extent to which consumption of the food is appealing to the senses	
	Tradition	Preserving traditional consumption patterns	
Positive and negative anticipated emotions	Contentment	If I can go to eat a hamburger in fast-food restaurants the next month, I feel contentment	Adapted from Bagozzi and Dholakia (2006) [79]
	Delighted	If I can go to eat a hamburger in fast-food restaurants the next month, I feel delighted	
	Excited	If I can go to eat a hamburger in fast-food restaurants the next month, I feel excited	
	Proud	If I can go to eat a hamburger in fast-food restaurants the next month, I feel proud	
	Satisfied	If I can go to eat a hamburger in fast-food restaurants the next month, I feel satisfied	
	Selfassured	If I can go to eat a hamburger in fast-food restaurants the next month, I feel self-assured	

Table 2. Cont.

Latent Variable	Observed Variables	Definition	Source
Attitude toward the brand (ATB)	ATB1	Like the brand	Aggarwal and McGill (2012) [74]
	ATB2	Admire the brand	
	ATB3	Fit in your life the brand	
Attitude toward eating a hamburger (ATEH)	ATEH1	Eating the hamburger would be pleasurable	Adapted from Haws and Winterich (2013) [73]
	ATEH2	I would enjoy eating the hamburger	
	ATEH3	If I eat a hamburger, it would be satisfying for me	
	ATEH4	If I eat a hamburger because of the good taste it has	
Purchase intention	PI1	You probably buy products in fast-food restaurants	Adapted from Chiu, Hsieh, and Kuo (2012) [39], Diallo (2012) [40]
	PI2	I would consider buying a product in fast-food restaurants if I need a product of this type	
	PI3	It is possible to buy a product in fast-food restaurants	
	PI5	The probability that you consider buying in fast-food restaurants is high	

The food values utilized a Likert scale 1–5 (1 = not at all important, to 5 = extremely important). The scale was adapted from 7 points to 5 points, because it was planned to explain each item as a formative construct. It is better to get an answer from the consumer on the assumption that some items do not have a relation with the construct. Positive and negative anticipated emotions applied a Likert scale 1–7 (1 = none, to 7 = severe). From the original items, it supported the positive emotions because the negatives did not have an impact and did not comply with the test of validity and reliability. It deleted the emotions for: glad, relief and happy for the reason to have multicollinearity and the VIF factor > 3.2. Also, it used the 7-point Likert scale as the author marked it. According to Becker and Ismail (2016) [80], it is possible to use different Likert scales within the same model. In the attitude toward the brand (ATB), it used a Likert scale 1–5, (1 = strongly disagree, to 5 = strongly agree). From the original contribution, it supported only the positive items because the weights were weak (item 4 "shame" and 5 "avoidance"). It changed the inverse items for the nature of the scale. For the attitude toward eating a hamburger (ATEH), it was handled with a Likert scale 1–5, (1 = strongly disagree, to 5 = strongly agree). These items were adapted to the specific product (in this case, hamburger). The variable purchase intention was measured by a Likert scale 1–5, (1 = strongly disagree, to 5 = strongly agree). PI4 was excluded because it had multicollinearity with PI3. The item was "I would buy in fast food restaurants next time".

All the constructs were reflective, not including food values. The construct formed the interpretations depending on the dependent variable. Hence, the formative indicators may show up as non-significant. Also, the indicators were correlated with other indicators in the model proposal [81]. Similarly, all the formative indicators required a census of all items for the construct because each one (it can be negative or positive) was formed into a complete variable. Even the negative influences on the consumer were one item that needed to be taken care of [82]. Finally, the overall fit of this model does not matter; the other covariances like the exogenous variables are outside the model proposal, and all the items are independent of themselves, according to Jarvis, MacKenzie and Podsakoff (2003) [82].

3. Results

The development model was constructed on an amalgamation of items, concepts, models, effects and principles about two parts: functional and emotional. This model was also composited about a series of research studies around four exceptional areas: (1) food values, (2) attitude toward the brand,

(3) attitude toward eating a hamburger, and (4) positive anticipated emotions. All were within the proposal to better explain the purchase intention in fast-food restaurants in Mexico.

To assess the goodness of model fit, the root mean square residual (SRMR) was utilized. According to Hu and Bentler (1998) [83] and Hu and Bentler (1999) [84], SRMR < 0.08 is a good fit for SRMR. This model has an SRMR = 0.049 < 0.08 SRMR criteria; these measures found that this model has a good fit with the parameters mentioned before. The normed fit index (NIF) results in values from 0 to 1, and the closer to 1, the better the fit [85]. In this model, the NIF was 0.899 and represented an acceptable fit.

To get confidence in this model, reliability and construct validity testing were carried out. Cronbach's alpha coefficient was accepted for all the constructs, having a value greater than 0.7 [86]. The rho_A value was reflected regularly if this index was larger than 0.7 [87]. The composite reliability (CR) values under 0.6 indicated a deficiency of internal consistency reliability [88]. The AVE of each construct was above the tolerability value 0.5 [89,90] (see Table 3).

Table 3. Validity Testing.

	Cronbach's Alpha Coefficient	rho_A	Composite Reliability (CR)	Average Variance Extracted (AVE)
Attitude toward eating a hamburger	0.847	0.862	0.897	0.687
Attitude toward the brand	0.822	0.836	0.893	0.736
Positive anticipated emotions	0.916	0.921	0.934	0.704
Purchase intention	0.895	0.896	0.927	0.760

As a final point, the discriminant validity of constructs showed the factor loading indicators on the assigned construct. Therefore, they had to be above all loading of other constructs (in the same column) with the condition that the cut-off value of factor loading was higher than 0.70 [89]. In addition, the model proved to have satisfactory reliability with convergent and discriminant validity. After this step, it was necessary to test the discriminant validity of constructs. According to Fornell and Larcker (1981) [89], with the correlation coefficient of the two dimensions less than the square root of the AVE, two dimensions were understood to have discriminant validity because of AVE > 0.5 (see Table 4).

Table 4. Association Testing.

	Attitude toward Eating a Hamburger	Attitude toward the Brand	Food Values	Positive Anticipated Emotions	Purchase Intention
Attitude toward eating a hamburger	0.829				
Attitude toward the brand	0.538	0.858			
Food values	0.431	0.444	Formative		
Positive anticipated emotions	0.482	0.544	0.401	0.839	
Purchase intention	0.537	0.665	0.407	0.544	0.872

The study confirmed the hypothesis with path coefficient, standard error, t-value, and p-value (see Table 5). It was concluded that all the hypotheses planted were supported and positive to predict the purchase intention with a high level, even though the study observed some differences about each association. The first force is the association between attitude toward the brand on purchase intention had the best path coefficient ($\beta = 0.447$). Moreover, the results showed that attitude toward eating a hamburger was also important to purchase intention ($\beta = 0.197$). However, the other association to predict purchase intention was throughout the positive anticipated emotions and for this model was ($\beta = 0.206$), more than attitude toward eating a hamburger.

Table 5. Hypothesis Testing and Path Coefficients.

		Beta	Standard Error	t-Value	p-Value	f^2	q^2	Supported
H1	Attitude toward the brand -> Purchase intention	0.447 ***	0.041	10.849	0.000	0.249	0.134	Yes
H2	Attitude toward eating a hamburger -> Purchase intention	0.197 ***	0.043	4.574	0.000	0.053	0.030	Yes
H3	Food values -> Attitude toward the brand	0.270 ***	0.042	6.447	0.000	0.095	0.050	Yes
H4	Food values -> Attitude toward eating a hamburger	0.284 ***	0.043	6.608	0.000	0.097	0.052	Yes
H5	Positive anticipated emotions -> Attitude toward the brand	0.436 ***	0.043	10.126	0.000	0.248	0.146	Yes
H6	Positive anticipated emotions -> Attitude toward eating a hamburger	0.368 ***	0.040	9.167	0.000	0.163	0.088	Yes
H7	Positive anticipated emotions -> Purchase intention	0.206 ***	0.050	4.129	0.000	0.057	0.030	Yes

Note: $n = 10,000$ subsamples; *** $p < 0.001$; R^2 (Attitude toward the brand = 0.357; Attitude toward eating = 0.300; Purchase intention = 0.515); q^2 = Predictive relevance calculated ((R-Sq included)-(Q-Sq excluded))/(1-R-Sq included).

The great force to constitute the attitude toward the brand was with the construct positive anticipated emotions ($\beta = 0.436$). Because, in comparison, the attitude toward eating a hamburger only has $\beta = 0.368$. Something relevant was the impact of food values to the attitudes, where it had some consideration to attitude toward eating a hamburger ($\beta = 0.270$), in contrast to the brand, where was higher ($\beta = 0.284$).

Some reflections about all the hypotheses proposed are the level of significance, where p-value <0.001 with the 99%; it means that these study results were statistically significant.

Also, the H5 line of positive anticipated emotions to attitude toward the brand ($\beta = 0.436$, $t = 10.126$, $p = < 0.001$) and the H1 line of attitude to purchase intention ($\beta = 0.447$, $t = 10.849$, $p = <0.001$) indicated an abundant positive effect to form the purchase intention; this was the best way to predict it. Table 5 shows that in all the relations, t-value ≥ 1.96 and p-value ≤ 0.05; thus, this model supported all the hypotheses with high path coefficients and t-values. Hence, outer model loadings were highly significant. In addition, f^2 was utilized to confirm the hypotheses null in the model and the outcomes supported each hypothesis but with different effects from weak <0.15 to large >0.15 [91]. All q2 are above zero, which supports the model presenting in Figure 2 [88].

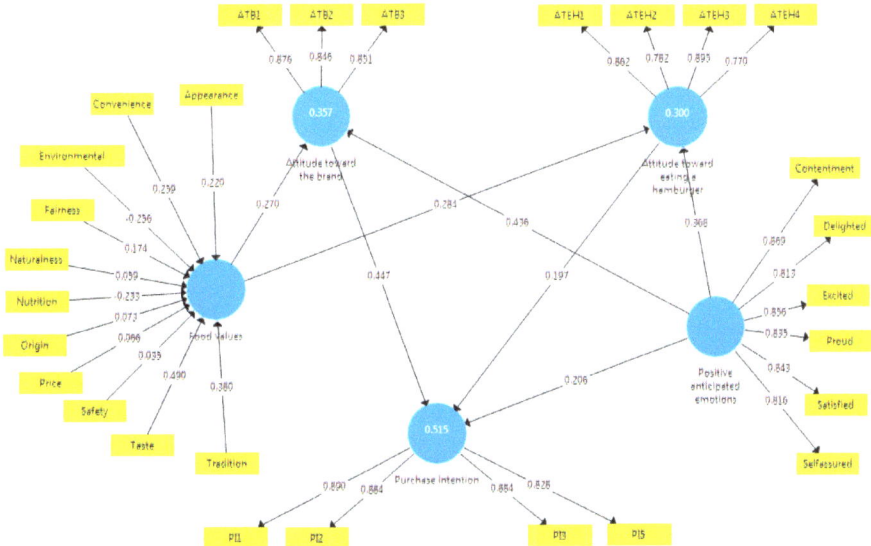

Figure 2. PLS analysis results.

Esposito et al. (2010) [92] stated that formative constructs need not be correlated between them. Also, the construct needs to be supported with the theory about food values. Similarly, the PLS algorithm produced loadings for reflective construct and weight for formative. Moreover, the study used the loadings and weights indicator for each construct by nature.

Figure 2 indicates the formative construct (food values), and inside the construct, the best items are taste and tradition (0.490; 0.380). On the other hand, the food values show negative loading with environment and nutrition (−0.256; −0.233). These facts do not have a position for the food value. Also, the model indicates that the emotions of contentment, excited and satisfied are the best loadings in the model (0.869, 0.856, 0.843).

It is distinguished that R^2 (ATEH) is 0.357 higher than ATB (0.300). Additionally, R^2 (PI) is 0.515, signifying that both attitudes toward eating and the brand plus positive anticipated emotions explain 51% of purchase intention. Even though R^2-ATEH and R^2-ATB are weak, the R^2-purchase intention is substantial [91].

4. Discussion

All the hypotheses proposed were supported and confirmed. It accepted the difference by two types of attitudes: one of them toward the brand and the other toward eating a hamburger. Also, it showed the gap between the beta indicators with 0.250 to predict the purchase intention. The attitude toward the brand got first place in the hypotheses. Based on the previous study, the theory and empirical research suggested that attitude toward the brand will positively influence the intention to buy. After the results, it confirmed the positive influence and on the same road with other studies. In this case, it corroborated with the results of Hwang, Yoon and Park (2011) [29] which mentioned that the affective responses positively influence brand attitudes and purchase intention. The attitude toward eating had the right place in the final model. This hypothesis was confirmed, and the values obtained help to explain, with a higher percentage, the purchase intention. Other authors affirm the importance to investigate eating behavior to get knowledge about the positive or negative predisposition to eat [23,24]. The hypotheses related to food values were an essential variable in this model, i.e., the relationship of this variable to both attitudes. At this point, it is demonstrated that the food values could be impacted in a different way to each attitude. It validated the influence of food values affecting indirectly on the purchase intention. With this information, it led to some discussion to add more food values and to get an effect indirect to purchase intention. For example, these results match to Lang and Lemmerer (2019) [53] which affirm that personal values impact on forming a food attitude. Last, the positive anticipated emotion positively influenced attitude toward the brand, attitude toward eating, and intention to buy a hamburger. The results are consistent with previous research, which assert that emotion is an irreplaceable variable to try predicting the purchase intention. Positive anticipated emotion is a significant variable, which participates in three hypotheses addressing attitude toward the brand, attitude toward eating a hamburger and purchase intention. This confirms findings in other studies [74,93,94].

Managerial implications are confirmations derived from this research. First of all, managers of fast-food restaurants have to focus on the purchase intention of consumers. The findings support that purchase intention is more influenced by attitude toward the brand than by attitude toward eating a hamburger. Subsequently, the food values do not impact very strongly, but positive anticipated emotions do. The managers need to study how powerful each emotion (contentment, excited and satisfied) is before thinking about eating something at a fast-food restaurant. Also, the best values to build into the product are taste and tradition. Hence, in this case, the managers need to investigate about preferences, tastes and culture around consumption in fast-food restaurants. In that way, they need to prefer a strategy with a focus to increase and improve the value of the brand toward the brand equity oriented into the consumer. Correspondingly, positive anticipated emotions do not have a good association directly with purchase intention. This explains that without an attitude toward eating a hamburger or the attitude toward the brand, the consumer does not perceive the intention to buy a hamburger at a fast-food restaurant.

Limitations and Future Orientations

There are limitations and suggested future lines of research. First of all, the sample should be increased to raise the level of confidence and lower the level of sampling error. Alternatively, it is recommended to add other variables related to TPB as perceived control, perceived difficulty and subjective norms on purchase intention. Finally, it is suggested to apply these surveys in other cities, products, and brands to know if there are significant differences between the samples.

5. Conclusions

The goal for this study was building a development and testing model, having one comprehensive model about the purchase intention. The study planted a model with the importance of functional and emotional aspects through their effects on two attitudes. This model is an approximation to better explain the purchase intention. The food values have a low position on attitude toward the brand and attitude toward eating a hamburger. On the other hand, anticipated positive emotions have more relevance on attitudes, especially the attitude toward the brand and to purchase intention.

The positive food values are taste and tradition in fast-food consumers. This model provides information to fast-food restaurants to pay attention to constantly evaluate the taste that has the consumers' favor and to explore insights about a different perception of taste in the hamburger. Also, the tradition is significant because it includes and preserves traditional consumption patterns, since children families and reference groups help to educate this kind of consumption. From the other view, the consumer does not care about the nutrition of the hamburger against the knowledge of the brand. This confirms the results from Barone et al. (1996) [95] that examined the cause to form incorrect conclusions about the product. In this case, the consumer does not give value to the types of fat, proteins, vitamins, and carbohydrates that the hamburgers have. This demonstrates the lack of sensitivity and knowledge of healthy and responsible consumption.

Similarly, it is also happening with the environment value where the most significant weight in the variable of food value is. The consumer does not care if the burger is produced while taking care of the environment. The problem of having production for the environment and pollution does not see some or any benefit knowing how the food was manufactured. So, the adequacy of practices in favor of the environment and eco-friendly consumption is not significantly crucial for attitude or purchase intention.

It was also shown that positive anticipated emotions form the best way to explain the purchase intention. First of all, it was verified that the anticipated negative emotions did not show any relevant data that included that variable within the model. Subsequently, the items with the greatest loadings were analyzed, and the results were positive anticipated emotions like contentment, delighted, excited, proud, satisfied, and self-assured. If the consumer is to have one of these emotions, it is probably to have a good level of attitude toward the brand and then to get a purchase intention.

For this reason, the results of the study confirm the existence of a strong relationship between attitudes toward the brand on purchase intention by way of anticipated positive emotions in the consumer of fast-food restaurant. This proves, as in previous literature, that emotions are a necessary measure of the decision-making process of the consumer [96].

Author Contributions: Conceptualization, H.H.P.-V. and M.P.M.-R.; Methodology, H.H.P.-V. and A.I.-Y.; software, H.H.P.-V. and A.I.-Y.; validation, H.H.P.-V. and A.I.-Y.; formal analysis, H.H.P.-V., M.P.M.-R., and A.I.-Y.; investigation, H.H.P.-V.; resources; H.H.P.-V.; data curation, A.I.-Y.; writing—original draft preparation, H.H.P.-V., M.P.M.-R., and A.I.-Y.; writing—review and editing, H.H.P.-V., M.P.M.-R., and A.I.-Y.; visualization, H.H.P.-V.; supervision, M.P.M.-R., and A.I.-Y.; project administration, H.H.P.-V.; funding acquisition, H.H.P.-V.

Funding: This research was funded by Universidad Popular Autónoma del Estado de Puebla (UPAEP), Sistemas de Información de Marketing: Sistemas de información, modelización y gestión para la toma de decisiones en Marketing and the APC was funded by UPAEP.

Conflicts of Interest: The authors declare no conflict of interest.

References

1. Manan, H.A. The Hierarchical Influence of Personal Values on Attitudes toward Food and Food Choices. *Procedia Econ. Financ.* **2016**, *37*, 439–446. [CrossRef]
2. Chen, M.; Lu, T. Modeling e-coupon proneness as a mediator in the extended TPB model to predict consumers' usage intentions. *Internet Res.* **2011**, *21*, 508–526. [CrossRef]
3. Yuzhanin, S.; Fisher, D. The efficacy of the theory of planned behavior for predicting intentions to choose a travel destination: A review. *Tour. Rev.* **2016**, *71*, 135–147. [CrossRef]
4. Liu, J.; Lin, S.; Feng, Y. Understanding why Chinese contractors are not willing to purchase construction insurance. *Eng. Constr. Archit. Manag.* **2018**, *25*, 257–272. [CrossRef]
5. Barahona, I.; Hernández, D.M.; Pérez-Villarreal, H.H.; del Pilar Martínez-Ruíz, M. Identifying research topics in marketing science along the past decade: A content analysis. *Scientometrics* **2018**, *117*, 293–312. [CrossRef]
6. Ruth, J.A. Promoting a Brand's Emotion Benefits: The Influence of Emotion Categorization Processes on Consumer Evaluations. *J. Consum. Psychol.* **2001**, *11*, 99–113. [CrossRef]
7. Handley, L. Brands are the vital ingredient of health drive. *Marketting Week*. 2010. Available online: https://www.marketingweek.com/brands-are-the-vital-ingredient-of-health-drive/ (accessed on 31 May 2019).
8. Ding, C.G.; Tseng, T.H. On the relationships among brand experience, hedonic emotions, and brand equity. *Eur. J. Mark.* **2015**, *49*, 994–1015. [CrossRef]
9. Wang, E.S.-T. Displayed emotions to patronage intention: Consumer response to contact personnel performance. *Serv. Ind. J.* **2009**, *29*, 317–329. [CrossRef]
10. Goldsmith, R.E.; Freiden, J.; Henderson, K.V. The impact of social values on food-related attitudes. *J. Prod. Brand Manag.* **1995**, *4*, 6–14. [CrossRef]
11. Lorenz, B.A.-S.; Langen, N.; Hartmann, M.; Klink-Lehmann, J. Decomposing attitudes towards food leftovers: Implications for general attitude, intention and behavior. *Br. Food J.* **2018**, *120*, 2498–2509. [CrossRef]
12. Koenig-Lewis, N.; Palmer, A. The effects of anticipatory emotions on service satisfaction and behavioral intention. *J. Serv. Mark.* **2014**, *28*, 437–451. [CrossRef]
13. Zhao, X.; Deng, S.; Zhou, Y. The impact of reference effects on online purchase intention of agricultural products: The moderating role of consumers' food safety consciousness. *Internet Res.* **2017**, *27*, 233–255. [CrossRef]

14. Song, J.; Qu, H. How does consumer regulatory focus impact perceived value and consumption emotions? *Int. J. Contemp. Hosp. Manag.* **2019**, *31*, 285–308. [CrossRef]
15. Zhang, H.; Sun, J.; Liu, F.; Knight, J.G. Be rational or be emotional: advertising appeals, service types and consumer responses. *Eur. J. Mark.* **2014**, *48*, 2105–2126. [CrossRef]
16. Nicolini, V.; Cassia, F.; Bellotto, M. Children perceptions of emotional and rational appeals in social advertisements. *Young Consum.* **2017**, *18*, 261–277. [CrossRef]
17. Ajzen, I. The theory of planned behavior. *Organ. Behav. Hum. Decis. Process.* **1991**, *50*, 179–211. [CrossRef]
18. Ajzen, I.; Fishbein, M. *Understanding Attitudes and Predicting Social Behavior*; Prentice-Hall: Englewood Cliffs, NJ, USA, 1980; ISBN 978-0-13-936443-3.
19. Wu, S. The relationship between consumer characteristics and attitude toward online shopping. *Mark. Intell. Plan.* **2003**, *21*, 37–44. [CrossRef]
20. Garg, N.; Wansink, B.; Inman, J.J. The Influence of Incidental affect on Consumers' Food Intake. *J. Mark.* **2007**, *71*, 194–206. [CrossRef]
21. Talih Akkaya, D.; Akyol, A.; Gölbaşı Şimşek, G. Sosyal medya reklamciliğinda tüketici algilarinin tutum, davraniş ve satin alma niyeti üzerine etkisi. *Marmmara Univ. Econ. Adm. Sci.* **2018**, *39*, 361–388. [CrossRef]
22. Chang, C. Feeling Ambivalent About Going Green. *J. Advert.* **2011**, *40*, 19–32. [CrossRef]
23. Chen, M. Attitude toward organic foods among Taiwanese as related to health consciousness, environmental attitudes, and the mediating effects of a healthy lifestyle. *Br. Food J.* **2009**, *111*, 165–178. [CrossRef]
24. Ghoochani, O.M.; Torabi, R.; Hojjati, M.; Ghanian, M.; Kitterlin, M. Factors influencing Iranian consumers' attitudes toward fast-food consumption. *Br. Food J.* **2018**, *120*, 409–423. [CrossRef]
25. Bai, L.; Wang, M.; Yang, Y.; Gong, S. Food safety in restaurants: The consumer perspective. *Int. J. Hosp. Manag.* **2019**, *77*, 139–146. [CrossRef]
26. Coricelli, C.; Foroni, F.; Osimo, S.A.; Rumiati, R.I. Implicit and explicit evaluations of foods: The natural and transformed dimension. *Food Qual. Prefer.* **2019**, *73*, 143–153. [CrossRef]
27. Rezai, G.; Teng, P.K.; Shamsudin, M.N.; Mohamed, Z.; Stanton, J.L. Effect of perceptual differences on consumer purchase intention of natural functional food. *J. Agribus. Dev. Emerg. Econ.* **2017**, *7*, 153–173. [CrossRef]
28. Diallo, M.F.; Seck, A.M. How store service quality affects attitude toward store brands in emerging countries: Effects of brand cues and the cultural context. *J. Bus. Res.* **2018**, *86*, 311–320. [CrossRef]
29. Hwang, J.; Yoon, Y.-S.; Park, N.-H. Structural effects of cognitive and affective reponses to web advertisements, website and brand attitudes, and purchase intentions: The case of casual-dining restaurants. *Int. J. Hosp. Manag.* **2011**, *30*, 897–907. [CrossRef]
30. Foroudi, P. Influence of brand signature, brand awareness, brand attitude, brand reputation on hotel industry's brand performance. *Int. J. Hosp. Manag.* **2019**, *76*, 271–285. [CrossRef]
31. Jeng, S.-P. The influences of airline brand credibility on consumer purchase intentions. *J. Air Transp. Manag.* **2016**, *55*, 1–8. [CrossRef]
32. Assael, H. *Consumer Behavior and Marketing Action*; PWS-KENT Pub.: Boston, MA, USA, 1992; ISBN 978-0-534-92552-9.
33. Zhang, Y.; Jing, L.; Bai, Q.; Shao, W.; Feng, Y.; Yin, S.; Zhang, M. Application of an integrated framework to examine Chinese consumers' purchase intention toward genetically modified food. *Food Qual. Prefer.* **2018**, *65*, 118–128. [CrossRef]
34. Phau, I.; Teah, M. Devil wears (counterfeit) Prada: a study of antecedents and outcomes of attitudes towards counterfeits of luxury brands. *J. Consum. Mark.* **2009**, *26*, 15–27. [CrossRef]
35. Jahn, S.; Tsalis, G.; Lähteenmäki, L. How attitude towards food fortification can lead to purchase intention. *Appetite* **2019**, *133*, 370–377. [CrossRef]
36. Asif, M.; Xuhui, W.; Nasiri, A.; Ayyub, S. Determinant factors influencing organic food purchase intention and the moderating role of awareness: A comparative analysis. *Food Qual. Prefer.* **2018**, *63*, 144–150. [CrossRef]
37. Yadav, R.; Pathak, G.S. Intention to purchase organic food among young consumers: Evidences from a developing nation. *Appetite* **2016**, *96*, 122–128. [CrossRef]
38. Ghali-Zinoubi, Z.; Toukabri, M. The antecedents of the consumer purchase intention: Sensitivity to price and involvement in organic product: Moderating role of product regional identity. *Trends Food Sci. Technol.* **2019**, *90*, 175–179. [CrossRef]

39. Chiu, H.-C.; Hsieh, Y.-C.; Kuo, Y.-C. How to Align your Brand Stories with Your Products. *J. Retail.* **2012**, *88*, 262–275. [CrossRef]
40. Diallo, M.F. Effects of store image and store brand price-image on store brand purchase intention: Application to an emerging market. *J. Retail. Consum. Serv.* **2012**, *19*, 360–367. [CrossRef]
41. Ghvanidze, S.; Velikova, N.; Dodd, T.; Oldewage-Theron, W. A discrete choice experiment of the impact of consumers' environmental values, ethical concerns, and health consciousness on food choices: A cross-cultural analysis. *Br. Food J.* **2017**, *119*, 863–881. [CrossRef]
42. Clarkson, C.; Mirosa, M.; Birch, J. Consumer acceptance of insects and ideal product attributes. *Br. Food J.* **2018**, *120*, 2898–2911. [CrossRef]
43. Raaijmakers, I.; Sijtsema, S.; Labrie, C.; Snoek, H. Consumer segmentation based on health-related motive orientations and fruit and vegetable consumption. *Br. Food J.* **2018**, *120*, 1749–1763. [CrossRef]
44. Ditlevsen, K.; Sandøe, P.; Lassen, J. Healthy food is nutritious, but organic food is healthy because it is pure: The negotiation of healthy food choices by Danish consumers of organic food. *Food Qual. Prefer.* **2019**, *71*, 46–53. [CrossRef]
45. Basha, M.B.; Lal, D. Indian consumers' attitudes towards purchasing organically produced foods: An empirical study. *J. Clean. Prod.* **2019**, *215*, 99–111. [CrossRef]
46. De Boer, J.; Schösler, H. Food and value motivation: Linking consumer affinities to different types of food products. *Appetite* **2016**, *103*, 95–104. [CrossRef]
47. Sprotles, G.B.; Kendall, E.L. A Methodology for Profiling Consumers' Decision-Making Styles. *J. Consum. Aff.* **1986**, *20*, 267–279. [CrossRef]
48. Hwang, J. Organic food as self-presentation: The role of psychological motivation in older consumers' purchase intention of organic food. *J. Retail. Consum. Serv.* **2016**, *28*, 281–287. [CrossRef]
49. Rana, J.; Paul, J. Consumer behavior and purchase intention for organic food: A review and research agenda. *J. Retail. Consum. Serv.* **2017**, *38*, 157–165. [CrossRef]
50. Martínez-Ruiz, M.P.; Gómez-Cantó, C.M. Key External Influences Affecting Consumers' Decisions Regarding Food. *Front. Psychol.* **2016**, *7*, 1618. [CrossRef]
51. Lee, P.Y.; Lusk, K.; Mirosa, M.; Oey, I. The role of personal values in Chinese consumers' food consumption decisions. A case study of healthy drinks. *Appetite* **2014**, *73*, 95–104. [CrossRef]
52. Tey, Y.S.; Arsil, P.; Brindal, M.; Liew, S.Y.; Teoh, C.T.; Terano, R. Personal values underlying ethnic food choice: Means-end evidence for Japanese food. *J. Ethn. Foods* **2018**, *5*, 33–39. [CrossRef]
53. Lang, M.; Lemmerer, A. How and why restaurant patrons value locally sourced foods and ingredients. *Int. J. Hosp. Manag.* **2019**, *77*, 76–88. [CrossRef]
54. Lusk, J.L. External validity of the food values scale. *Food Qual. Prefer.* **2011**, *22*, 452–462. [CrossRef]
55. Lusk, J.L.; Briggeman, B.C. Food Values. *Am. J. Agric. Econ.* **2009**, *91*, 184–196. [CrossRef]
56. Wood, S.L.; Moreau, C.P. From Fear to Loathing? How Emotion Influences the Evaluation and Early Use of Innovations. *J. Mark.* **2006**, *70*, 44–57. [CrossRef]
57. Levav, J.; Mcgraw, A.P. Emotional Accounting: How Feelings about Money Influence Consumer Choice. *J. Mark. Res.* **2009**, *46*, 66–80. [CrossRef]
58. Agrawal, N.; Duhachek, A. Emotional Compatibility and the Effectiveness of Antidrinking Messages: A Defensive Processing Perspective on Shame and Guilt. *J. Mark. Res.* **2010**, *47*, 263–273. [CrossRef]
59. Teixeira, T.; Wedel, M.; Pieters, R. Emotion-Induced Engagement in Internet Video Advertisements. *J. Mark. Res.* **2012**, *49*, 144–159. [CrossRef]
60. Berger, J.; Milkman, K.L. What Makes Online Content Viral? *J. Mark. Res.* **2012**, *49*, 192–205. [CrossRef]
61. Poor, M.; Duhachek, A.; Krishnan, H.S. How Images of Other Consumers Influence Subsequent Taste Perceptions. *J. Mark.* **2013**, *77*, 124–139. [CrossRef]
62. Hsee, C.K.; Yang, Y.; Zheng, X.; Wang, H. Lay Rationalism: Individual Differences in using Reason versus Feelings to Guide Decisions. *J. Mark. Res.* **2015**, *52*, 134–146. [CrossRef]
63. Thompson, C.J.; Rindfleisch, A.; Arsel, Z. Emotional Branding and the Strategic Value of the Doppelgänger Brand Image. *J. Mark.* **2006**, *70*, 50–64. [CrossRef]
64. Strahilevitz, M.A.; Odean, T.; Barber, B.M. Once Burned, Twice Shy: How Naive Learning, Counterfactuals, and Regret Affect the Repurchase of Stocks Previously Sold. *J. Mark. Res.* **2011**, *48*, S102–S120. [CrossRef]
65. Lee, C.J.; Andrade, E.B. Fear, Social Projection, and Financial Decision Making. *J. Mark. Res.* **2011**, *48*, S121–S129. [CrossRef]

66. Golder, P.N.; Mitra, D.; Moorman, C. What is Quality? An Integrative Framework of Processes and States. *J. Mark.* **2012**, *76*, 1–23. [CrossRef]
67. Small, D.A.; Verrochi, N.M. The Face of Need: Facial Emotion Expression on Charity Advertisements. *J. Mark. Res.* **2009**, *46*, 777–787. [CrossRef]
68. Nielsen, J.H.; Shapiro, S.A.; Mason, C.H. Emotionality and Semantic Onsets: Exploring Orienting Attention Responses in Advertising. *J. Mark. Res.* **2010**, *47*, 1138–1150. [CrossRef]
69. De Pelsmaeker, S.; Schouteten, J.J.; Gellynck, X.; Delbaere, C.; De Clercq, N.; Hegyi, A.; Kuti, T.; Depypere, F.; Dewettinck, K. Do anticipated emotions influence behavioural intention and behaviour to consume filled chocolates? *Br. Food J.* **2017**, *119*, 1983–1998. [CrossRef]
70. Wen, J.; Hu, Y.; Kim, H.J. Impact of individual cultural values on hotel guests' positive emotions and positive eWOM intention: Extending the cognitive appraisal framework. *Int. J. Contemp. Hosp. Manag.* **2018**, *30*, 1769–1787. [CrossRef]
71. Io, M.-U. Understanding the effects of multi-dimensional tourism experiences on tourists' positive emotions and satisfaction in the context of casino hotels. *Int. J. Cult. Tour. Hosp. Res.* **2017**, *11*, 142–156. [CrossRef]
72. Williams, P.; Aaker, J.L. Can Mixed Emotions Peacefully Coexist? *J. Consum. Res.* **2002**, *28*, 636–649. [CrossRef]
73. Haws, K.L.; Winterich, K.P. When Value Trumps Health in a Supersized World. *J. Mark.* **2013**, *77*, 48–64. [CrossRef]
74. Aggarwal, P.; McGill, A.L. When Brands Seem Human, Do Humans Act Like Brands? Automatic Behavioral Priming Effects of Brand Anthropomorphism. *J. Consum. Res.* **2012**, *39*, 307–323. [CrossRef]
75. Sarstedt, M.; Hair, J.F.; Ringle, C.M.; Thiele, K.O.; Gudergan, S.P. Estimation issues with PLS and CBSEM: Where the bias lies! *J. Bus. Res.* **2016**, *69*, 3998–4010. [CrossRef]
76. Shmueli, G.; Ray, S.; Velasquez Estrada, J.M.; Chatla, S.B. The elephant in the room: Predictive performance of PLS models. *J. Bus. Res.* **2016**, *69*, 4552–4564. [CrossRef]
77. Hair, J.; Hollingsworth, C.L.; Randolph, A.B.; Chong, A.Y.L. An updated and expanded assessment of PLS-SEM in information systems research. *Ind. Manag. Data Syst.* **2017**, *117*, 442–458. [CrossRef]
78. Streukens, S.; Leroi-Werelds, S. Bootstrapping and PLS-SEM: A step-by-step guide to get more out of your bootstrap results. *Eur. Manag. J.* **2016**, *34*, 618–632. [CrossRef]
79. Bagozzi, R.P.; Dholakia, U.M. Antecedents and purchase consequences of customer participation in small group brand communities. *Int. J. Res. Mark.* **2006**, *23*, 45–61. [CrossRef]
80. Becker, J.-M.; Ismail, I.R. Accounting for sampling weights in PLS path modeling: Simulations and empirical examples. *Eur. Manag. J.* **2016**, *34*, 606–617. [CrossRef]
81. Diamantopoulos, A.; Papadopoulos, N. Assessing the cross-national invariance of formative measures: Guidelines for international business researchers. *J. Int. Bus. Stud.* **2010**, *41*, 360–370. [CrossRef]
82. Jarvis, C.B.; MacKenzie, S.B.; Podsakoff, P.M. A Critical Review of Construct Indicators and Measurement Model Misspecification in Marketing and Consumer Research. *J. Consum. Res.* **2003**, *30*, 199–218. [CrossRef]
83. Hu, L.; Bentler, P.M. Fit indices in covariance structure modeling: Sensitivity to underparameterized model misspecification. *Psychol. Methods* **1998**, *3*, 424–453. [CrossRef]
84. Hu, L.; Bentler, P.M. Cutoff criteria for fit indexes in covariance structure analysis: Conventional criteria versus new alternatives. *Struct. Equ. Model. Multidiscip. J.* **1999**, *6*, 1–55. [CrossRef]
85. Bentler, P.M.; Bonett, D.G. Significance tests and goodness of fit in the analysis of covariance structures. *Psychol. Bull.* **1980**, *88*, 588–606. [CrossRef]
86. Hair Rolph, E.A., Jr.; Barry, J.B.; William, C.B. *Multivariate Data Analysis: A Global Perspective*, 7th ed.; Pearson Education: Upper Saddle River, NJ, USA, 2010; ISBN 978-0-13-515309-3.
87. Werts, C.E.; Linn, R.L.; Jöreskog, K.G. Intraclass Reliability Estimates: Testing Structural Assumptions. *Educ. Psychol. Meas.* **1974**, *34*, 25–33. [CrossRef]
88. Hair, J.F. (Ed.) *A Primer on Partial Least Squares Structural Equation Modeling (PLS-SEM)*, 2nd ed.; Sage: Los Angeles, CA, USA, 2017; ISBN 978-1-4833-7744-5.
89. Fornell, C.; Larcker, D.F. Evaluating Structural Equation Models with Unobservable Variables and Measurement Error. *J. Mark. Res.* **1981**, *18*, 39. [CrossRef]
90. Huang, C.-C.; Wang, Y.-M.; Wu, T.-W.; Wang, P.-A. An Empirical Analysis of the Antecedents and Performance Consequences of Using the Moodle Platform. *Int. J. Inf. Educ. Technol.* **2013**, *3*, 217–221. [CrossRef]

91. Hair, F.J.; Sarstedt, M.; Hopkins, L.; Kuppelwieser, G.V. Partial least squares structural equation modeling (PLS-SEM): An emerging tool in business research. *Eur. Bus. Rev.* **2014**, *26*, 106–121. [CrossRef]
92. Esposito Vinzi, V.; Chin, W.W.; Henseler, J.; Wang, H. (Eds.) *Handbook of Partial Least Squares: Concepts, Methods and Applications*; Springer: Berlin/Heidelberg, Germany, 2010; ISBN 978-3-540-32825-4.
93. Evers, C.; Adriaanse, M.; de Ridder, D.T.D.; de Witt Huberts, J.C. Good mood food. Positive emotion as a neglected trigger for food intake. *Appetite* **2013**, *68*, 1–7. [CrossRef]
94. Jiang, Y.; King, J.M.; Prinyawiwatkul, W. A review of measurement and relationships between food, eating behavior and emotion. *Trends Food Sci. Technol.* **2014**, *36*, 15–28. [CrossRef]
95. Barone, M.J.; Rose, R.L.; Manning, K.C.; Miniard, P.W. Another Look at the Impact of Reference Information on Consumer Impressions of Nutrition Information. *J. Public Policy Mark.* **1996**, *15*, 55–62. [CrossRef]
96. Bagozzi, R.P.; Dholakia, U.M.; Basuroy, S. How effortful decisions get enacted: the motivating role of decision processes, desires, and anticipated emotions. *J. Behav. Decis. Mak.* **2003**, *16*, 273–295. [CrossRef]

© 2019 by the authors. Licensee MDPI, Basel, Switzerland. This article is an open access article distributed under the terms and conditions of the Creative Commons Attribution (CC BY) license (http://creativecommons.org/licenses/by/4.0/).

Article

Perception of the Attributes of Sherry Wine and Its Consumption in Young People in the South of Spain

Serafín J. Cruces-Montes [1,2,*], **Ana Merchán-Clavellino** [1,2,*], **Antonio Romero-Moreno** [1,2] and **Alberto Paramio** [1,2]

[1] Department of Psychology, Faculty of Education Sciences, University of Cádiz, 11519 Puerto Real, Spain; antoniofrancisco.romero@uca.es (A.R.-M.); alberto.paramio@uca.es (A.P.)
[2] INDESS (University Institute for Sustainable Social Development), University of Cádiz, 11406 Jerez de la Frontera, Spain
* Correspondence: serafin.cruces@uca.es (S.J.C.-M.); ana.merchan@uca.es (A.M.-C.); Tel.: +34-956-037124 (S.J.C.-M.); +34-956-016754 (A.M.-C.)

Received: 29 February 2020; Accepted: 25 March 2020; Published: 2 April 2020

Abstract: The wine with the designation of origin "Jerez-Xerez-Sherry" is one of the most produced in Spain and with a greater volume of exports abroad. This study analyzes the preferences of Sherry Wine and its different varieties, based on gender and knowledge and interest in the world of wine. Similarly, the influence of the attributes of Sherry Wine on its choice and consumption is investigated. For this purpose, 1502 participants (1407 wine consumers) were recruited; among the consumers, 58.5% are women, and 74.3% have little knowledge of wine (Mean age 22.6; SD = 3.07; range 18–30). Data collection was done through an online survey. The results reveal that among the types of wines from Sherry, the Fino and the Manzanilla are the most chosen. The young people who have the highest consumption of wine are those who have the most prior knowledge of wine. Also, these young people attribute their choice of wine to intrinsic factors, and even women and connoisseurs are more important in this type of dimension. But the importance of the attributes differs according to the types of wines (Fino/Cream—flavor, Palo Cortado/Pedro Ximénez—color, Amontillado/Manzanilla—price and Oloroso—prizes). These findings will allow establishing measures for their promotion, as well as for the design and specific sales strategies for each type of wine.

Keywords: consumer behaviour; wine attribute; sherry wine; gender

1. Introduction

The latest data from the International Organization of Vine and Wine (OIV) show that the consumption of wine in 2018 totalled 246 MHL [1]. Of the quantities consumed, Spain was the largest exporter, with statistics representing 19.4% of the global market, that is, with a volume of 20.9 MHL of exports and 34.3 MHL of production [2]. In this way, Spain has the largest land area of vineyards, with a total of 969 MHA [1].

Of wines produced in Spain, Sherry Wine (SW) is more significantly produced in the south of Spain (region of Cádiz), framed in the vast "Sherry Wine Region" vineyards. Weather conditions and a particular production system, such as the dynamic system "soleras" and "criaderas" [3] play a crucial role in the nature of these wines. According to Regulatory Council of Denomination of Origin "Jerez-Xérès-Sherry", "Manzanilla-Sanlúcar de Barrameda" and "Vinagre de Jerez" (RCDO) in the Sherry Wine Region there are 63 wineries dedicated to the breeding and processing of Sherry Wine, and these wines are the product with the oldest designation of origin in Spain [4].

The SW is based on three types of grape; the "Palomino Fino" grape (the basis of the total production), the "Pedro Ximénez" grape and the "Moscatel" grape [5,6]. These types of grape are used for the production of the so-called "Generosos" wines, characterized by being dry (with a maximum residual sugar quantity of five grams per litre), known as "Manzanilla", "Fino", "Amontillado", "Oloroso" and "Palo Cortado". Generosos Liqueur Sherry Wines, such as "Pale Cream", "Medium" and "Cream", are obtained based on the type of "generosos" wine used as a base, and the final levels of sweetness of the blend (always with a sugar content of over five grams per litre). Finally, we can find naturally sweet Sherry Wines, produced according to the variety of grape used: "Moscatel" and "Pedro Ximénez" [4].

In general, 81.3% of the Spanish population between the age of 15 and 64 has consumed alcohol in the last year, with wine being the second most popluar choice, with a 26.1% preference over other alcoholic beverages such as beer, tall drinks, strong liquors, vermouth, and fruit liqueur, according to the latest data of 2019 [7]. However, if we focus on ages between 18 and 30 years, the consumption of alcohol in the last year increased by almost ten percent, even though, this increase is not observed in the preference for wine [7]. However, in 2019, the Spanish Wine Market Observatory (OEMV) [8] reported that wine consumption grew by 7.2% in Spain, due to changes in wine distribution and a wine tourism boom.

For this reason, studies on the factors that determine the purchase and choice of wine have increased, especially those that analyze the influence of consumer attitudes and the relevance of consumption contexts. However, few studies have addressed the incidence of the characteristics of the wine, both intrinsic (taste, aroma, graduation, etc.) and extrinsic (brand, labelling, bottling, price, etc.), but we can even find fewer studies that focused their population study on the youth segment [9]. Thus, as Silva, Figueiredo, Hogg, and Sottomayor [10] suggested, research has focused primarily on quantitative studies on trends in wine consumption in adults, and when they have focused on the youth group, they have only focused on issues related to consumer abuse [11–14]. Nevertheless, some knowledge of the elements that motivate the non-abusive consumption of wine among young people will help wine producers have a better idea of how future consumers will react, as well as to better understand their expectations [15].

In this sense, research on the preferences of young people for the attributes of wine has concluded that characteristics such as price, taste and brand value are reasons related to their choice [16–18]. In the case of young people, the price of wine is one of the main reasons that can lead to the choice of cheaper alcoholic beverages [19–21], and the taste of wine is frequently indicated as the main reason for aversion among young non-consumers [10]. Therefore, as Capitello, Agnoli, and Begalli [22] pointed out, when it comes to reaching young consumers, marketing approaches should be specially adapted to them, promoting communication for educational purposes, acknowledging intrinsic and sensorial signals of wine, such as aroma and flavor, among others. Promoting knowledge and interest in the world of wine has proven effective in adults, increasing the amount of wine purchases [23,24].

Similarly, aesthetic aspects, such as packaging and labelling, are also important attributes that explain the choice of this product among young people [10,25]. Elliot and Barth [26] found that the wine choices that young people make (defined as Millennials by the authors) are fundamentally influenced by extrinsic type factors (bottling, labelling, and design) rather than by the characteristics of the product itself (producer, country of origin, type of wine, graduation, quality or solera). But as young people get older and gain experience drinking wine, their opinions and references regarding extrinsic factors may change to intrinsic factors. In addition, they express a desire to develop skills and knowledge about wine in the future, which denotes a purpose of wanting to learn about, understand and appreciate wine for its sensory qualities [10]. Thus, knowing the reasons of consumption would facilitate the realization of specific promotions to better target different age groups and different genders. As of today, it is not clear whether men and women drink wine for the same reasons [27]. In this sense, women seem to make less abusive use of wine than men and are more sensitive to sustainable wine, even among millennials [14,28–30].

In short, young consumers evaluate wine as a multifaceted category [31], so that, due to the complexity of this product, novice consumers often find it difficult to appreciate its quality, which can affect the decision and choice processes [32,33]. Young people, although they have limited experience, can assess wines using specific characteristics such as origin, harvest, label, brand and grape variety [34,35]. Thus, as previously mentioned, it would be desirable to promote greater dissemination and publicity of the wine addressed to this group, using aspects such as attention to value for money, flavor, innovative packaging and environmental emphasis [18], among others. In transmitting such information, it would be interesting to use internet-based channels and social networks, since they are sources mainly used by young people [36]. By always encouraging responsible consumption, it will allow us to appreciate wine as an important nutritional, cultural and economic elements, which can be beneficial for health when consumed in moderation [37,38]. In summary, as Tealgle, Mueller, and Lockshin [39] indicate, although young millennials are certainly neophytes in terms of participation and subjective knowledge of wine, they are learning quickly.

Therefore, the present study focuses on analyzing the current behaviour of the Sherry Wine consumer, and its varieties, in a large sample of young people between 18 and 30 years old. It is intended to investigate the importance attached to the different attributes of Sherry Wine, and especially to its types of wine. Also, taking into account the current interest in the segmentation of the wine consumer, the exploration is proposed according to demographic aspects such as gender and behaviour, based on knowledge and interest in the world of wine. In conclusion, knowing the consumer profile of this type of wine will help Spanish wineries to direct commercial aspects, by developing and adapting their wines to the new behaviours of these young users.

2. Materials and Methods

The sample consisted of 1502 participants, community members of the University of Cádiz (94.2% undergraduate and master students, teaching and administrative staff). Of all those who participated in the study, 1407 consumed SW at least once a year. Among the consumers, 58.5% are women and 74.3% are considered to have little knowledge regarding wine (mean age 22.6; SD = 3.07; range 18–30). These participants were divided to analyze the differences in the consumption and the perception of the importance of wine attributes by gender and by knowledge and interest in the Sherry Wine. Participation in this study was voluntary and confidential. The study was conducted in compliance with the Declaration of Helsinki of 1975, and all participants signed the informed consent. All students completed the online self-report questionnaires and the criteria for joining the analysis of this study was to be in the 18–30 age range.

The authors prepared a survey. The survey was sent to the community of the University of Cádiz through professional emails. The survey was divided into three parts: data of gender and knowledge and interest about the SW, frequency of SW consumption and importance of intrinsic and extrinsic attributes. The intrinsic attributes were composed of Flavor, Aroma, Color, Alcoholic Content and Ecological characteristics; and the extrinsic attributes by Price, Labels, Prizes, Brand and Bottling.

Frequencies and basic descriptive statistics of the questionnaire variables were analyzed. As the principle of normality in the variables was not fulfilled, non-parametric analyses of independent samples were carried out to verify if there were significant differences between the groups (U Mann-Whitney). In addition, multiple linear regressions were carried out to develop the predictive models of consumption in each type of wine.

Data analysis and processing were performed with the IBM Statistical Package for the Social Sciences (SPSS) v25 software (IBM Corporation, Armonk, NY, USA). The results were considered significant with a $p < 0.05$.

3. Results

The results on the sample of 1502 young adults show a relatively low-sporadic consumption in general. In total, 17.4% of the participants declared that they only consume sherry once a year and 33.2% consume wine once every three months. Daily consumers make up only 2.4% of the total sample, and 6.3% said they never drink Sherry Wines. Table 1 shows the frequencies of consumption according to the types of wines of "The Sherry Wine Region".

Table 1. Frequencies of consumption of the types of Sherry Wines.

Consumption	Fino		Manzanilla		Oloroso		Cream		Amontillado		Palo Cortado		Pedro Ximénez	
	n	%	n	%	n	%	n	%	n	%	n	%	n	%
Never	331	22	348	23.2	591	39.3	701	46.7	833	55.5	971	64.6	361	24.0
Once a year	513	34.2	544	36.2	356	23.7	300	20.0	306	20.4	261	17.4	440	29.3
Once every three months	351	23.4	374	24.9	316	21.0	259	17.2	202	13.4	163	10.9	368	24.5
Once a month	203	13.5	163	10.9	170	11.3	136	9.1	109	7.3	73	4.9	226	15.0
Once a week	90	6.0	64	4.3	63	4.2	94	6.3	48	3.2	29	1.9	93	6.2
Daily	14	0.9	9	0.6	6	0.4	12	0.8	4	0.3	5	0.3	14	0.9

Next, in Table 2, the descriptive statistics of Sherry Wine consumption are presented, both for the total sample and the segmentation variables of the study, such as gender and knowledge and interest in the world of wine.

Table 2. Descriptive analyzes (means and standard deviations) and statistics (Mann–Whitney U Test) of Sherry Wine consumption for the general sample, between genders and between knowledge and interest in the world of wine.

	n	Overall		Gender				U	Knowledge and Interest				U
				Female		Male			No		Yes		
		M	SD	M	SD	M	SD		M	SD	M	SD	
Sherry Wines	1407	2.51	1.07	2.49	1.06	2.53	1.08	234956.5	2.35	1.02	2.94	1.08	131864.5 **
Fino	1171	1.92	1.01	1.92	1.03	1.94	0.99	164103.5	1.8	0.95	2.25	1.1	105501.0 **
Manzanilla	1154	1.8	0.93	1.78	0.92	1.84	0.95	158175.5	1.69	0.85	2.11	1.07	101954.0 **
Oloroso	911	1.95	0.96	1.95	0.97	1.96	0.94	101150.5	1.82	0.9	2.26	1.01	66486.0 **
Cream	801	2.07	1.07	2.09	1.05	2.05	1.09	75458.5	1.98	1.01	2.25	1.16	62819.0 **
Amontillado	669	1.87	0.97	1.89	0.96	1.84	0.99	53444.5	1.72	0.86	2.13	1.1	41109.5 **
Palo Cortado	531	1.78	0.94	1.78	0.9	1.79	0.99	34768.0	1.68	0.87	1.95	1.03	28893.0 **
Pedro Ximénez	1141	2.01	1.01	2	1	2.03	1.03	155901.5	1.92	0.98	2.26	1.06	105030.0 **

Notes: ** $p < 0.001$; SD, Standard Deviation; M, Mean.

Statistical analyses showed no significant differences between men and women regarding the consumption of wine, neither for consumption in general nor in its different types. However, we find differences between those who have a previous interest and knowledge about the world of Sherry Wine and those who do not, both for consumption in general and for different types (see Table 2).

Regarding the importance of intrinsic and extrinsic factors when choosing Sherry Wine in consumers, significant differences are observed ($Z = -10.052$; $p = 0.000$), so that inherent factors are more important than extrinsic (see Figure 1).

The same applies to each gender (Men: $Z = -4.905$; $p = 0.000$ and Women: $Z = -8.978$; $p = 0.000$) and those who have knowledge or not about the world of wine (Yes knowledge $Z = -5.839$; $p = 0.000$ and No knowledge: $Z = -8.179$; $p = 0.000$). There are also differences between genders in the different factors, assessing both types of attributes with a higher level of importance for women compared to men (Intrinsic: $U = 199768.5$; $p = 0.000$ and Extrinsic: $U = 220930.5$; $p = 0.010$). On the other hand, the values increase significantly in both factors for drinkers who have previous knowledge with respect to those who do not have any (Intrinsic: $U = 154773.5$; $p = 0.000$ and Extrinsic: $U = 164854$; $p = 0.010$).

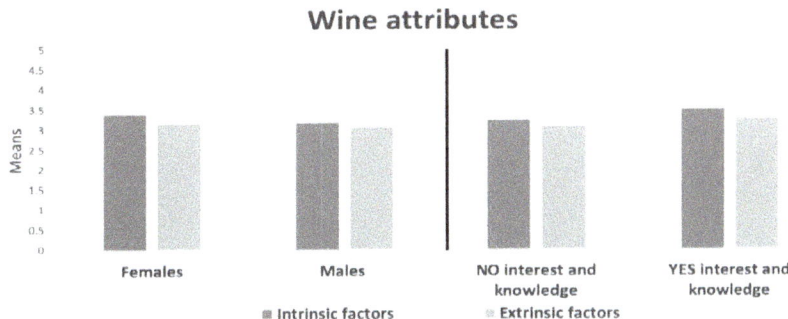

Figure 1. Mean of importance intrinsic and extrinsic attributes, genders, knowledge, and interest in the world of wine.

Of all the attributes selected for analysis, described in Table 3, Flavor, Aroma, Alcoholic Content, Ecological Characterisitcs, Price and Bottling showed significant differences concerning gender ($p < .05$), with women granting greater importance to these attributes than men. However, concerning prior knowledge, except for the Ecological attribute, significant differences appear in the level of importance related to the attributes, reflecting a higher level of importance on the part of the participants with prior knowledge and interest in wine.

Table 3. Descriptive analyzes (means and standard deviations) and statistics (Mann–Whitney U Test) of the perception of the importance of wine attributes for the general sample, between genders and between knowledge and interest in the world of wine.

Atttribute	Knowledge and Interest				U	Gender				U	Overall	
	No		Yes			Female		Male				
	M	SD	M	SD		M	SD	M	SD		M	SD
Flavor	4.35	0.99	4.51	0.83	227941.5 **	4.44	0.93	4.33	1	287122.5	4.4	0.96
Aroma	3.62	1.09	4.03	0.94	258008.5 **	3.79	1.06	3.62	1.07	294134.5 **	3.72	1.07
Color	2.82	1.16	3.16	1.13	245216 **	2.94	1.15	2.85	1.16	279168.5	2.9	1.16
Alcohol Content	2.76	1.18	2.92	1.12	226350 **	2.93	1.17	2.62	1.13	305622 **	2.8	1.17
Ecological	2.67	1.26	2.82	1.27	223515.5 *	2.84	1.26	2.52	1.23	306622.5 **	2.71	1.26
Price	3.66	1.19	3.59	1.1	196607.5	3.71	1.15	3.55	1.18	295356.5 **	3.65	1.17
Labels	3.1	1.29	3.43	1.2	241097.5 **	3.21	1.28	3.14	1.28	281317	3.18	1.28
Prizes	2.47	1.18	2.81	1.2	244473 **	2.56	1.19	2.56	1.21	271509.5	2.56	1.2
Brand	3.01	1.22	3.24	1.15	233318. **	3.11	1.2	3.01	1.21	283031.5	3.07	1.21
Bottling	3.03	1.25	3.25	1.13	231961.5 **	3.18	1.22	2.96	1.21	294728.5 **	3.09	1.22

Note: ** $p < 0.001$; * $p < 0.05$.

Various regression models were made on the general consumption of Sherry and for each type, using the input variables: gender, knowledge and interest in wine, importance for taste, for aroma, for color, for alcoholic content, for its ecological character, for the price, for its label, for its prizes, for the brand and bottling. These models are shown in Table 4. In the table, we can see the attributes that significantly predict the consumption of wine in general, and in each of its types.

Table 4. Multiple linear regression analysis that predicts variables of the Sherry Wine consumption due to the importance of its attributes.

	R^2	F	Predictor Variables	Beta	t
Sherry Wine	0.196	29.510 **	Flavor	0.165	4.832 **
			Aroma	0.178	5.231 **
			Color	0.091	3.066 **
			Price	−0.136	−4.599 **
			Prizes	0.068	2.112 *
			Brand	0.095	3.062 **
			Knowledge and interest	0.169	6.887 **
Fino	0.107	12.71 **	Flavor	0.148	3.779 **
			Color	0.082	2.403 *
			Price	−0.100	−2.971 **
			Prizes	0.103	2.721 **
			Brand	0.070	1.967 *
			Knowledge and interest	0.143	5.055 **
Manzanilla	0.085	9.98 **	Aroma	0.124	3.121 **
			Price	−0.124	−3.531 **
			Brand	0.082	2.245 *
			Knowledge and interest	0.146	5.055 **
Amontillado	0.097	6.99 **	Flavor	0.150	2.916 **
			Color	0.138	2.972 **
			Price	−0.151	−3.504 **
			Bottling	−0.100	−2.181 *
			Knowledge and interest	0.168	4.487 **
Oloroso	0.096	9.061 **	Flavor	0.101	2.213 *
			Aroma	0.109	2.385 *
			Price	−0.115	−3.006 **
			Premios	0.110	2.592 *
			Knowledge and interest	0.166	5.116 **
Cream	0.083	6.997 **	Flavor	0.202	4.276 **
			Color	0.156	3.592 **
			Price	−0.135	−3.341 **
			Brand	0.110	2.501 *
			Knowledge and interest	0.078	2.238 *
Palo cortado	0.069	4.266 **	Color	0.140	2.655 **
			Price	−0.130	−2.635 **
			Prizes	0.119	2.029 *
			Knowledge and interest	0.101	2.362 *
Pedro Ximénez	0.071	8.3 **	Color	0.128	3.628 **
			Price	−0.091	−2.596 *
			Prizes	0.103	2.670 **
			Knowledge and interest	0.110	3.769 **

Note: ** $p < 0.001$; * $p < 0.05$.

4. Discussion

This study tries to analyze in a sample of young people the current behavior of the SW consumer, and its varieties. In general, the results confirm that 93.7% of the proportion consumes SW, thereby corroborating the data in the Spanish population, where young people drink alcohol with percentages close to 90% [7]. The latest surveys [7] also informed us that wine is the second drink of choice, with a 26.1% preference over other beverages. Although we cannot confirm this option, we observe that the frequency of consumption is not very high, as the young population's daily consumption only reaches

2.4%. Moreover, wine is a drink only chosen sporadically, as the highest percentage of consumption is once every three months among young people.

Regarding the consumption of the SW variety, our data show that, in order of preference, they choose Fino and Manzanilla, with very similar consumption percentages (77.96% and 76.83%, respectively). The data also confirm that Manzanilla is the best-selling wine, with 23% of the total, followed by Fino with 21.3% [40]. However, although sales of Pedro Ximénez or sweet wines represent the lowest percentages according to the Regulatory Council (see Figure 2) [40], we observe that it is the third most consumed type of wine. This disagreement may be due to the increase in sales that has been found since 2018 or due to the fact that the Spanish prefer to buy Pedro Ximénez over other wines [40]. Ultimately, the Amontillado, the Oloroso and the Palo Cortado barely represent 4% of total sales, confirming that they are the least consumed wines in the young population.

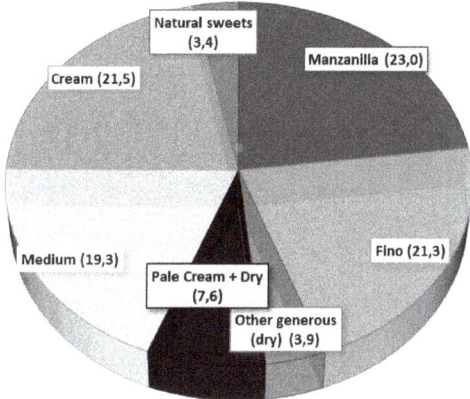

Figure 2. Percentage of sales of Sherry Wine, by types [40].

In general, few studies have shown trends or distribution of wine consumption in young people, and even less, of SW. When they have, they have dealt with issues related to consumer abuse [11–14]. It is not yet clearly established whether men and women drink wine on the same occasions [27]. This situation turned out to repeat itself in our population since we do not find significant differences between genders in wine consumption. On the other hand, other studies have shown that men drink slightly more wine than women and these differences worsen after 35 years [29–41]. We do not find such differences in our study as our population is between 18 and 30 years, and those differences in consumption are not yet observed. Also, these differences are reversed depending on the type of wine, so that men drink more red wines and women consume white wine [42]. It has also been found that these slight differences between gender diminish with the growing experience in wine [42]. In this way, it is observed how knowledge and prior interest in the world of wine plays an essential role in its consumption. Our results show that people who have more experience with wine consume more Sherry Wine, in all its varieties. Purchase data form other studies corroborate that those who visited wineries helped increase the purchase percentages by 13% [23,24].

As a result of the multifaceted and complex nature that young people attribute to the choice of wine [31,43], it was necessary to increase knowledge about the importance given to the different attributes for the consumption of SW, and especially for their types. Also, with the current interest in defining consumer segmentation, demographic aspects such as gender and those based on knowledge and interest in the world of wine were investigated. Thus, some studies have shown how young people's wine choices are fundamentally influenced by extrinsic type factors (bottling, labelling, and design) rather than by the characteristics of the product itself (producer, country of origin, type of wine, graduation, quality or solera) [15,26]. Even women give greater importance to the external signals of the wine than to the internal ones, according to Bruwer and McCutcheon [42].

However, our results present a preference for attributing their choices of Sherry Wine consumption more to intrinsic or product factors than to extrinsic factors. Therefore, these data are not consistent with the previous literature. To explain this, we must take into account that the study population is from a wine region and according to specific authors we could consider them as quality consumers; that is, consumers with high involvement and great reflection in their decision process. In summary, they need more senior level signals for their choice of purchase, such as intrinsic factors [43–46].

Initially, we expected to find these differences and this trend in women and those with higher prior knowledge, since women have more capacity to capture the subtleties and smells of wine [47] and because the so-called "connoisseurs" need more information; that is to say, to search information before its purchase, using the opinion of the experts by reading wine magazines and books. In short, they are more involved in the decision process before making a purchase, and will, therefore, be guided by higher marks [44–46,48]. Concerning the search for information, Millennials have demonstrated active participation in activities related to wine, such as the search for emotional, experimental and educational value [15].

Next, we considered investigating which attributes between intrinsic and extrinsic have higher predictive power and show significant associations with the different types of SW. In this way, our results will help Spanish wineries to direct the commercial aspects, by developing and adapting their wines to the most outstanding elements in the population.

After reviewing the different regression models, both gender and etiquette are unimportant variables when predicting the consumption of SW, so we are in line with several studies that demonstrate this low importance [42,46]. However, being knowledgeable or having experiences related to wine is a good predictor for the consumption of SW, although observing varieties, both for Cream, for the array of Palo Cortado and Pedro Ximénez do not present a strong association as in the rest of wines. Based on these results, it would be interesting to investigate whether the amounts of sugar can explain the trend detected. While, in general, our data are in line with other studies, as mentioned above, prior knowledge and interest in wine predict its consumption and purchase intention [23,24].

It should be noted that young people perceive specific characteristics such as aroma, flavor, price, brand, color, and prizes as essential factors for their consumption of SW, and it is in line with the most chosen attributes in different types of populations. For example, taste and smell is an indicator of "commitment" to the product, price is the best attribute in younger consumers, and the brand is another important factor because it relates to the consumer expectations that the associated images transmit in advertising [9,34,35,46,49]. Next, regarding the types of wine, it has been found that Fino and Cream are mostly consumed for flavor, Palo Cortado and Pedro Ximénez are mostly consumed for their color, Amontillado and Manzanilla for their price and finally Oloroso is more consumed for the prizes received.

Notice that the models described predict 19.6% of the consumption of SW, and that the percentages of the models with the analyzed variables vary from 7.1% of the predictive power for the consumption of Pedro Ximénez up to 10% of Fino consumers, contributions with values to highlight and that may have a great interest in the wine sector. In addition, taking into account the fact that young consumers evaluate wine according to a multitude of factors [31], for example, the newer ones have more difficulty in knowing its quality and that it may affect their choices [32,33].

With these results, Spanish wineries can be helped to direct their efforts toward certain commercial aspects, by developing and adapting their wines to the new behaviors of these young consumers, while creating a specialized marketing campaign for the variety of wines presented by the sherry frame. We believe that this study places value and places its focus on the development of wine tourism and its landscapes worldwide and that it is of vital importance for the 2020-2024 Strategic Plan, between the OIV and the World Tourism Organization, since it has been shown that boosting wine and wine distribution increases wine consumption [8]. The limitations of this study open opportunities for future research; for example, more extensive and random samples, adding additional questions to the current survey and incorporating more detailed information on psychosocial aspects.

5. Conclusions

The results of this preliminary study suggest that there is a relationship between prior knowledge of and interest in wine culture and wine consumption in young adults. Despite being very focused in the wine region of Jerez, this research provided us with a way to delve into the psychosocial aspects of a product whose complexity and variety is further of the organoleptic and chemical elements, conventional approaches in wine research. Considering the limitations, our results show that wine consumption by young people is low, and consumers' gender is not a determining factor in consumption and the perceptions of its intrinsic and extrinsic attributes. Even so, the consumption of wine is recognized to different dimensions: Fino and Cream for its flavor, Palo Cortado and Pedro Ximénez for its color, Amontillado and the Manzanilla for its price and finally Oloroso are more consumed by the awards received. For future research, we recommend a more extensive and random sample, adding additional questions to the current survey and incorporating more detailed information on psychosocial aspects. Emphasizing knowledge of the culture of wine and involving local wineries of the denomination of origin area, since the awareness of these aspects is lower, will probably achieve a better product promotion and better specific marketing strategies, attending to the most important factors linked to each of the types of wine.

Author Contributions: Conceptualization, methodology, and formal analysis, S.J.C.-M.; A.P.; A.M.-C. and A.R.-M.; investigation and data curation, S.J.C.-M. and A.P.; writing—original draft preparation S.J.C.-M.; A.P.; A.M.-C. and A.R.-M.; writing—review and editing, S.J.C.-M. and A.P.; visualization, A.M.-C. and A.R.-M.; supervision S.J.C.-M. and A.P.; project administration, S.J.C.-M.; funding acquisition, S.J.C.-M. All authors have read and agreed to the published version of the manuscript.

Funding: The University of Cádiz funded this research, grant number PR2017-039 of Plan Propio Project and was supported by the Institute of Research and Development Social and Sustainability (INDESS).

Conflicts of Interest: The authors declare no conflict of interest.

References

1. International Organization of Vine and Wine (OIV). *State of the Vitiviniculture World Market*; International Organization of Vine and Wine: Paris, France, 2019.
2. International Organization of Vine and Wine (OIV). *State of Conditions report*; International Organization of Vine and Wine: Paris, France, 2019.
3. Roldán, A.; Palacios, V.; Caro, I.; Pérez, L. Evolution of resveratrol and piceid contents during the industrial winemaking process of sherry wine. *J. Agric. Food Chem.* **2010**, *58*, 4268–4273. [CrossRef]
4. Regulatory Council of Denomination of Origin "Jerez-Xérès-Sherry"—"Manzanilla-Sanlúcar de Barrameda"—"Vinagre de Jerez" (RCDO). Available online: https://www.sherry.wine/es/marco-de-jerez/el-consejo-regulador (accessed on 22 February 2020).
5. Ferreira, I.M.; Pérez-Palacios, M.T. Chapter 1—Anthocyanic compounds and antioxidant capacity in fortified wines. In *Processing and Impact on Antioxidants in Beverages*; Preedy, V., Ed.; Academic Press: San Diego, CA, USA, 2014; pp. 3–14. ISBN 978-0-12-404738-9.
6. Marcq, P.; Schieberle, P. Characterization of the key aroma compounds in a commercial amontillado sherry wine by means of the sensomics approach. *J. Agric. Food Chem.* **2015**, *63*, 4761–4770. [CrossRef]
7. Observatorio Español sobre Drogas Informe 2019. *Alcohol, Tabaco y Drogas Ilegales en España*; Ministerio de Sanidad, Consumo y Bienestar Social: Madrid, Spain, 2019.
8. Observatorio Español del Mercado del Vino (OEMV). *Consumo de Vino en España*; Observatorio Español del Mercado del Vino: Madrid, Spain, 2019.
9. Lockshin, L.; Corsi, A.M. Consumer behaviour for wine 2.0: A review since 2003 and future directions. *Wine Econ. Policy* **2012**, *1*, 2–23. [CrossRef]
10. Silva, A.P.; Figueiredo, I.; Hogg, T.; Sottomayor, M. Young adults and wine consumption a qualitative application of the theory of planned behavior. *Br. Food J.* **2014**, *116*, 832–848. [CrossRef]

11. Collins, M.A.; Neafsey, E.J.; Wang, K.; Achille, N.J.; Mitchell, R.M.; Sivaswamy, S. Moderate ethanol preconditioning of rat brain cultures engenders neuroprotection against dementia-inducing neuroinflammatory proteins: Possible signaling mechanisms. *Mol. Neurobiol.* **2010**, *41*, 420–425. [CrossRef] [PubMed]
12. Johnston, K.L.; White, K. Binge-drinking in female university students: A theory of planned behaviour perspective. *Youth Stud. Aust.* **2004**, *23*, 22–30.
13. Norman, P.; Bennett, P.; Lewis, H. Understanding binge drinking among young people: An application of the theory of planned behaviour. *Health Educ. Res.* **1998**, *13*, 163–169. [CrossRef]
14. Ferretti, F.; Pozza, A.; Harri, P.; Francalanci, C.; Gualtieri, G.; Coluccia, A. Drinking wine to "get high": The influence of awareness of the negative effects among young adults. *Addict. Behav. Rep.* **2018**, *8*, 56–61. [CrossRef]
15. Spielmann, N.; Babin, B.J.; Verghote, C. A personality-based measure of the wine consumption experience for millennial consumers. *Int. J. Wine Bus. Res.* **2016**, *28*, 228–245. [CrossRef]
16. Hall, J.; Binney, W.; O'Mahony, G.G. Age related motivational segmentation of wine consumption in a hospitality setting. *Int. J. Wine Mark.* **2004**, *16*, 29–44. [CrossRef]
17. Quester, P.G.; Smart, J. The influence of consumption situation and product involvement over consumers' use of product attribute. *J. Consum. Mark.* **1998**, *15*, 220–238. [CrossRef]
18. Thach, E.C.; Olsen, J.E. Market segment analysis to target young adult wine drinkers. *Agribusiness* **2006**, *22*, 307–322. [CrossRef]
19. Treloar, P.; Hall, C.M.; Mitchell, R. Wine Tourism and the Generation Y Market: Any Possibilities. In Proceedings of the 14th International Research Conference of the Council for Australian University Tourism and Hospitality Education, Queensland, Australia, 10–13 February 2004.
20. Mehta, R.; Bhanja, N. Consumer preferences for wine attributes in an emerging market. *Int. J. Retail Distrib. Manag.* **2018**, *46*, 34–48. [CrossRef]
21. Stergiou, D.P. An importance-performance analysis of young people's response to a wine tourism situation in Greece. *J. Wine Res.* **2018**, *29*, 229–242. [CrossRef]
22. Capitello, R.; Agnoli, L.; Begalli, D. Determinants of consumer behaviour in novice markets: The case of wine. *J. Res. Mark. Entrep.* **2015**, *17*, 110–126. [CrossRef]
23. Mitchell, R.; Hall, C.M. The post-visit consumer behaviour of New Zealand winery visitors. *J. Wine Res.* **2004**, *15*, 39–49. [CrossRef]
24. García, J.R.; Rodríguez, Á.V.; López-Guzmán, T. Segmentación del perfil de enoturista en la ruta del vino del marco de jerez-xérès-sherry. *TURyDES* **2012**, *5*, 1–14.
25. Vannevel, M.; Vink, N.; Brand, J.; Panzeri, V. Marketing Pinotage to South African student millennials. *Int. J. Wine Bus. Res.* **2018**, *30*, 331–342. [CrossRef]
26. Elliot, S.; Barth, J.J. Wine label design and personality preferences of millennials. *J. Prod. Brand Manag.* **2012**, *21*, 183–191. [CrossRef]
27. Thach, L. Time for wine? Identifying differences in wine-drinking occasions for male and female wine consumers. *J. Wine Res.* **2012**, *23*, 134–154. [CrossRef]
28. Pomarici, E.; Vecchio, R. Millennial generation attitudes to sustainable wine: An exploratory study on Italian consumers. *J. Clean. Prod.* **2014**, *66*, 537–545. [CrossRef]
29. Schulte, M.T.; Ramo, D.; Brown, S.A. Gender differences in factors influencing alcohol use and drinking progression among adolescents. *Clin. Psychol. Rev.* **2009**, *29*, 535–547. [CrossRef] [PubMed]
30. Vecchio, R. Determinants of willingness-to-pay for sustainable wine: Evidence from experimental auctions. *Wine Econ. Policy* **2013**, *2*, 85–92. [CrossRef]
31. Agnoli, L.; Begalli, D.; Capitello, R. Generation Y's perception of wine and consumption situations in a traditional wine-producing region. *Int. J. Wine Bus. Res.* **2011**, *23*, 176–192. [CrossRef]
32. D'Alessandro, S.; Pecotich, A. Evaluation of wine by expert and novice consumers in the presence of variations in quality, brand and country of origin cues. *Food Qual. Prefer.* **2013**, *28*, 287–303. [CrossRef]
33. LaTour, K.A.; LaTour, M.S.; Feinstein, A.H. The Effects of perceptual and conceptual training on novice wine drinkers' development. *Cornell Hosp. Q.* **2011**, *52*, 445–457. [CrossRef]
34. De Magistris, T.; Groot, E.; Gracia, A.; Albisu, L.M. Do Millennial generation's wine preferences of the "New World" differ from the "Old World". *Int. J. Wine Bus. Res.* **2011**, *23*, 145–160. [CrossRef]

35. Henley, C.D.; Fowler, D.C.; Yuan, J.; Stout, B.L.; Goh, B.K. Label design: Impact on millennials' perceptions of wine. *Int. J. Wine Bus. Res.* **2011**, *23*, 7–20. [CrossRef]
36. Bauman, M.J.; Velikova, N.; Dodd, T.; Blankenship, T. Generational differences in risk perception and situational uses of wine information sources. *Int. J. Wine Bus. Res.* **2019**. ahead-of-print. [CrossRef]
37. Covas, M.I.; Gambert, P.; Fitó, M.; de la Torre, R. Wine and oxidative stress: Up-to-date evidence of the effects of moderate wine consumption on oxidative damage in humans. *Atherosclerosis* **2010**, *208*, 297–304. [CrossRef] [PubMed]
38. Walzem, R.L. Wine and health: State of proofs and research needs. *Inflammopharmacology* **2008**, *16*, 265–271. [CrossRef] [PubMed]
39. Teagle, J.; Mueller, S.; Lockshin, L. How Do Millennials' Wine Attitudes and Behaviour Differ from Other Generations? In Proceedings of the 5th International Academy of Wine Business Research Conference, Auckland, New Zealand, 8–10 February 2010.
40. Regulatory Council of Denomination of Origin (RCDO). *Memoria de Actividades*; Regulatory Council of Denomination of Origin: Jerez de la Frontera, Spain, 2018.
41. Bruwer, J.; Saliba, A.; Miller, B. Consumer behaviour and sensory preference differences: Implications for wine product marketing. *J. Consum. Mark.* **2011**, *28*, 5–18. [CrossRef]
42. Bruwer, J.; McCutcheon, E. Marketing implications from a behaviourism perspective of consumption dynamics and socio-demographics of wine consumers. *Asia Pac. J. Mark. Logist.* **2017**, *29*, 519–537. [CrossRef]
43. Lockshin, L.; Hall, J. *Consumer Purchasing Behaviour for Wine: What We Know and Where We Are Going Prof Larry Lockshin*; Wine Marketing Research Group, University of South Australia: Adelaide, SA, Australia, 2003.
44. Hollebeek, L.D.; Jaeger, S.R.; Brodie, R.J.; Balemi, A. The influence of involvement on purchase intention for new world wine. *Food Qual. Prefer.* **2007**, *18*, 1033–1049. [CrossRef]
45. Lockshin, L.; Albisu, L.M. Co-editors' introduction to the special issue. *Agribusiness* **2006**, *22*, 301–306. [CrossRef]
46. Guíñez, N.; Cornejo, E. Caracterización de los hábitos de compra y consumo de vino en la ciudad de Chillán, Chile. *RAN Rev. Acad. Neg.* **2016**, *2*, 73–84.
47. Wenzel, K. Women purchase wine based on taste. *Tribune-Review*, 4 May 2005.
48. Chaney, I. External search effort for wine. *Int. J. Wine Mark.* **2000**, *12*, 5–15. [CrossRef]
49. Pomarici, E.; Lerro, M.; Chrysochou, P.; Vecchio, R.; Krystallis, A. One size does (obviously not) fit all: Using product attributes for wine market segmentation. *Wine Econ. Policy* **2017**, *6*, 98–106. [CrossRef]

 © 2020 by the authors. Licensee MDPI, Basel, Switzerland. This article is an open access article distributed under the terms and conditions of the Creative Commons Attribution (CC BY) license (http://creativecommons.org/licenses/by/4.0/).

Article

Impulsivity, Emotional Intelligence, and Alcohol Consumption in Young People: A Mediation Analysis

Ana Merchán-Clavellino [1,2,*], María Pilar Salguero-Alcañiz [3], Rocío Guil [1,2] and Jose Ramón Alameda-Bailén [3]

[1] Department of Psychology, Faculty of Education Sciences, University of Cádiz, 11519 Puerto Real, Spain; rocio.guil@uca.es
[2] INDESS (Research Universitary Institute for Sustainable Social Development), University of Cádiz, 11406 Jerez de la Frontera, Spain
[3] Basic Psychology Area, Department of Clinical and Experimental Psychology, University of Huelva, 21007 Huelva, Spain; pilar.salguero@dpsi.uhu.es (M.P.S.-A.); alameda@uhu.es (J.R.A.-B.)
* Correspondence: ana.merchan@uca.es; Tel.: +34-956016754

Received: 7 November 2019; Accepted: 3 January 2020; Published: 8 January 2020

Abstract: Alcohol consumption in young people is a public health problem. Due to the harmful consequences and the large population using alcoholic substances, it would be important to determine the biological, psychological, and social factors associated with alcohol use and abuse. The main object of this study is to explore which components of impulsivity, according to the main theoretical models, have predictive power regarding alcohol consumption in young people. A secondary objective is to determine if emotional intelligence has a mediating role between the components of impulsivity and alcohol consumption, and thus specifically contribute to the knowledge about the mediation processes between those variables that are involved in the initiation and maintenance of alcohol consumption. For this purpose, 384 participants were recruited (83.1% females, $n = 319$), with mean age of 20.46 years ($SD = 1.90$; range 18–25). All participants were alcohol consumers at the beginning of the study. Data collection was conducted via online survey; impulsivity was evaluated by several questionnaires (Sensation Seeking Scale Form V, Barratt Impulsivity Scales 11, and Sensitivity to Punishment and Sensitivity to Reward), and emotional intelligence was evaluated by the Trait Meta-Mood Scale. The results reveal that the dimension of disinhibition (a dimension of the sensation search scale) significantly has the highest predictive value on alcohol consumption. Moreover, our data show that the total effect and direct effect of disinhibition on frequency of alcohol consumption were both significant. The mediating role of emotional intelligence in this process was also significant. These findings show which variables should be considered to prevent alcohol consumption in young people.

Keywords: alcohol; impulsivity; emotional intelligence; sensation seeking

1. Introduction

Alcohol consumption in young people is a public health problem, as recognized by the World Health Organization (WHO) [1]. Around the world, 26.5% of young people between 15–19 years old consume alcohol, representing 155 million adolescents, with the highest consumption rates currently in Europe, specifically 43.8% [1,2].

Therefore, the future impact on the health of young people is enormous, in such a way that it would imply the increase of possible diseases, such as certain types of cancer, cardiovascular dysfunction, and liver problems [3] associated with premature deaths [1]. Due to the harmful consequences and the large population that uses these substances, different disciplines, including psychology, have joined forces to determine the biological, psychological, and social factors that are associated with alcohol use and abuse.

From a psychological point of view, evidence indicates that personality variables are clearly associated with alcohol consumption. Indeed, numerous works have related different patterns of alcohol consumption with different personality traits [4–7]. Considering the great variety of personality traits, the purpose of the present study is to explore which personality traits, specifically impulsive traits, have a greater predictive power on alcohol consumption in young people.

Additionally, alcohol consumption has been linked to impulsivity. Previous research has consistently demonstrated the relationship between impulsivity and alcohol consumption in young people, showing that greater impulsivity is associated with higher alcohol consumption [8–12]. However, there is no consensus on how impulsivity could be defined and measured [11,13]. Different models and theories have proposed different conceptualizations [14–17], but the concept that impulsivity is a multidimensional construct is nowadays the most accepted [18]. Thus, it seems necessary to investigate which of the characteristics or dimensions of impulsivity have a greater impact on alcohol consumption.

Different studies are based on the main theoretical models of impulsivity and their relationship with alcohol and other substance abuse. For example, based on the personality model of the five factors, Shin et al. (2012) [19] investigated the potential of the four sub-traits of impulsivity (urgency, lack of premeditation, lack of perseverance, and search for sensations) to influence different patterns of alcohol consumption (frequency, alcohol-related problems, excessive consumption, and alcohol use disorders). These authors concluded that the search for sensations and urgency are consistently related to all alcohol consumption patterns. Particularly, they found that people with high urgency and search for sensations have the highest levels of alcohol consumption, as well as problems related to alcohol consumption. They also found that the lack of premeditation is associated with alcohol consumption, but not with alcohol-related problems. Therefore, different dimensions of impulsivity could have different effects on alcohol consumption patterns. Likewise, Aluja et al. (2019) [20], in a sample of men, studied the effects of personality traits in drinkers, but in this case based on the personality models of Eysenck, Gray, and Zuckerman. They showed that the impulsive-inhibited personality factor is related to alcohol consumption, as well as to alcohol-related problems. Therefore, greater impulsivity and disinhibition could be associated with greater alcohol consumption.

Overall, it seems that impulsive personality traits could be optimal predictors of different alcohol consumption patterns. We hypothesize that the dimension of disinhibition could be considered the impulsiveness trait with the greatest predictive value over alcohol use in young people, according to Aluja et al. [20] who found that the impulse-disinhibition factor was strongly related to alcohol.

However, alcohol use is a multifactorial factor and, in addition, should be considered the indissoluble union between cognition and emotion [21]. Therefore, we hypothesize that emotional processes may act as mediators in the relation of the different aspects of impulsivity and alcohol consumption in young people.

Specifically, the concept that could reflect this union is emotional intelligence (EI). This is also supported by previous studies that have linked this construct with the use of several substances. Currently, the most accepted definition considers the EI as "the ability to perceive, evaluate and express emotions accurately, the ability to access and/or generate feelings when they facilitate thinking; the ability to understand emotions and emotional knowledge, and the ability to regulate emotions by promoting emotional and intellectual growth" [22] (p. 5). With respect to the measurement process, one of the most used questionnaires is the Trait Meta-Mood Scale (TMMS-24), which measures the level of emotional self-efficacy [23], a thorough ability to identify one's emotions and those of others and know how to express them (emotional attention), to understand emotions (emotional clarity), and to handle emotions (emotional repair).

Considering this background, the relationship between EI and alcohol consumption has also been analyzed in this study. EI has been shown to correlate negatively with alcohol and tobacco consumption in adolescents. Therefore, young people showing adequate EI can interpret the emotions of others and detect unwanted group pressure, revealing that EI is able to generate greater resistance to alcohol and tobacco consumption [24,25]. EI is also related to the use of other substances, such as cannabis [26], which suggests that a low EI is not only predictive of alcohol consumption but also of the abuse of other drugs [27–30].

In addition, some studies confirmed the relationship between EI and impulsivity. According to some results, a low EI, that is, a poor reasoning capacity on one's own or another's mood, could provoke more impulsive responses to situations of threat or frustration. Therefore, improving emotional clarity (understanding of emotions) and emotional repair or regulation (ability to handle emotions) components could improve impulsive behavior [31].

To our knowledge, there are no data on the relationship between EI, impulsivity, and alcohol consumption, although the influence of these variables has certainly been described regarding cannabis use. Particularly, it has been showed that impulsive young people tend to abuse cannabis more often, and EI appears to be related to consumption, since young people focused on their own emotions and lacking adequate mechanisms to control them are prone to the excessive consumption of cannabis as a coping mechanism [32].

In summary, it can be argued that both impulsivity and EI are related to alcohol consumption. Therefore, EI, considered as the ability to process emotional information for adaptive purposes, could be a mediating variable regarding the effects of impulsivity on alcohol consumption.

Thus, the objectives of this study are: (i) to explore what components of impulsivity, according to the main theoretical models (proposed by authors such as Zuckerman, Barrat and Gray) [14–17] have predictive value over alcohol consumption in young people, and (ii) to analyze if EI (attention, clarity and emotional repair) has a mediating effect between the components of impulsivity and alcohol consumption. Our hypothesis is that greater impulsiveness will be associated with lower levels of EI, that is, an inadequate attention level, which implies a poor compression of emotions, and therefore an inadequate capacity to regulate them, which, in turn, implies greater alcohol consumption, both in frequency and quantity (see Figure 1 for a representation of these interactions).

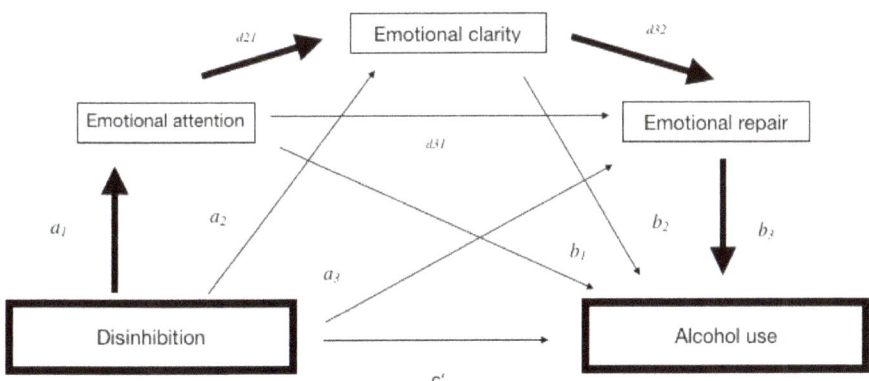

Figure 1. Representation of the indirect effects for serial mediation. **Notes:** direct effect (c'); total indirect effect (a) represents the association between the predictors DIS and three mediators (a_1, a_2, and a_3); total indirect effect (b) refers to the role of the three mediators in the use of alcohol (b_1, b_2, and b_3); total indirect effect (d) refers to the relationship of the three mediators with each other (d_{21}, d_{32}, and d_{31}).

In summary, this study could have an impact on global public policies, since they could reveal some psychological determinants of abuse behavior in young people. More interesting, the results could help to clarify the processes that arise between variables that initiate and maintain the use of drugs, providing a view to designing prevention programs that can be developed through personalized profiles.

2. Materials and Methods

2.1. Participants

The sample consists of 384 Spanish university students (83.1% females, $n = 319$) with a mean age of 20.46 years ($SD = 1.90$; minimum = 18; maximum = 25). All participants were consumers of alcohol, and reported an average consumption in the last year of 48.33 times ($SD = 44.76$; minimum = 1; maximum = 360) and an average amount of consumption of 3.43 units ($SD = 1.64$; minimum = 0.5; maximum = 10) on the day of consumption.

2.2. Procedure

Participation in this study was voluntary and confidential. The study was conducted in compliance with the Declaration of Helsinki of 1975, and all participants signed the informed consent. All students completed the online self-report questionnaires and their participation was rewarded with course credits.

2.3. Instruments

The following questionnaires were used for the evaluation of impulsivity:

Sensation Seeking Scale (SSS-V) [14]. A Spanish adapted version consisting of 42 items of forced-choice was used. This version assesses four aspects of sensation seeking: Thrill and Adventure Seeking (TAS), Experience Seeking (ES), Disinhibition (DIS) and Boredom Susceptibility (BS). In our sample, a total alpha of 0.8 was obtained, and for each subscale the following alpha values were observed: TAS = 0.8; ES = 0.5; DIS = 0.7; BS = 0.5.

Barratt Impulsivity Scales 11 (BIS-11) [33]. The Spanish version of Oquendo, Baca-García, Graver, Morales, Montalbán, and Mann (2001) [34] scale was used. This version consists of 30 Likert 1-4 scale items and covers the three dimensions of impulsivity proposed by Barratt: Cognitive (CI), Motor (MI), and Non-planning (NPI). The reliability of the scale is adequate, showing a total alpha of 0.6, 0.4 for the subscale CI, 0.6 for the MI, and 0.6 for the NPI subscales.

The Sensitivity to Punishment and Sensitivity to Reward Questionnaire (SPSRQ) [35]. This is a Spanish version to evaluate the behavioral inhibition system (BIS) and the behavioral approach system (BAS) [36]. This version consists of 48 dichotomous items (Yes, No) and is divided into two scales: Sensitivity to Punishment (SP), which consists of 24 items considered measures of BIS, and Sensitivity to Reward (SR) as a measure of BAS. The reliability of the scale is adequate, with the SP scale showing an alpha of 0.83 and the SR scale showing an alpha of 0.76 [37]. In our sample of young people, Cronbach's alphas are similar, since the SP scale shows an alpha of 0.8, and the SR scale has an alpha of 0.7.

On the other hand, the Spanish version [38] of the Trait Meta-Mood Scale (TMMS-24) [23] was used for the evaluation of Emotional Intelligence. This questionnaire assesses the perception or beliefs about one's emotional abilities. It contains 24 items, rated on a 1–5 Likert scale. TMMS-24 is divided into three dimensions, each consisting of 8 elements: emotional attention (ability to identify one's emotions and those of others and know how to express them), emotional clarity (understanding of emotions) and emotional repair or regulation (ability to handle emotions). The reliability and validity indexes reported are adequate [38]. In our sample the alpha value was 0.8 for the total scale, 0.8 for the attention dimension, 0.9 for clarity, and 0.8 for emotional repair.

Finally, an ad hoc questionnaire was applied which included items about sex (man and woman), age, and alcohol consumption in the last year, where the frequency of alcohol consumption was recorded by the days of consumption in a year, and where the consumption amount was measured through the number of drinks in one day of consumption.

2.4. Statistical Analysis

All analyses were carried out using the SPSS package (version 20.0; IBM, Chicago, IL, USA). Descriptive statistics and the Student's t-test were used to determine sex differences as described in the preliminary analyses. In addition, Pearson correlations were calculated for all study variables, including age. To verify the predictive value of personality models on over alcohol consumption (frequency and quantity), multiple regression models were performed including sex as control variable. From the predictive models, the mediation analyses were performed with the PROCESS macro [39]. We used model 6 to examine the direct and indirect effects of impulsivity on alcohol consumption (frequency). Mediation analyses were completed using EI as mediator. To verify which of the indirect effects was the most influencial, we conducted specific contrasts for indirect effects. As a criterion of statistical significance, we used the 95% confidence interval (CI) generated by the bias-corrected bootstrap method set to 10,000 reiterations.

3. Results

3.1. Preliminary Analyses

The descriptive statistics of each study variable are presented, both for the total sample and separately for men and women (Table 1). Analyses of the differences between sex are also included.

Table 1. Descriptive statistics and sex difference (Student's t-test) for personality trait and emotional intelligence.

		Females		Males		Overall		t	gl	p
		M	SD	M	SD	M	SD			
	Alcohol Frequency	46.39	42.25	57.85	54.84	48.33	44.76	−1.592	80.184	0.115
	Amount of Alcohol	3.35	1.53	3.86	2.06	3.43	1.64	−1.911	78.966	0.060
	Thrill and Adventure Seeking	5.52	2.96	6.94	2.74	5.76	2.97	−3.568	382	0.000 **
SSS-V	Experience Seeking	6.34	1.76	6.55	1.99	6.37	1.80	−0.893	382	0.373
	Disinhibition	4.35	2.08	5.74	2.59	4.58	2.23	−4.073	81.603	0.000 **
	Boredom Susceptibility	3.57	1.96	3.60	1.93	3.57	1.96	−0.122	382	0.903
	Cognitive	13.97	4.11	15.51	4.79	14.23	4.27	−2.672	382	0.008 **
BIS-11	Motor	15.51	6.23	15.57	6.13	15.52	6.21	−0.065	382	0.948
	Non-planning	14.27	5.93	16.54	7.09	14.65	6.20	−2.714	382	0.007 **
SPSRQ	Sensitivity to Punishment	11.32	4.92	10.23	5.43	11.14	5.02	1.602	382	0.11
	Sensitivity to Reward	9.58	4.16	11.32	4.33	9.87	4.23	−3.065	382	0.002 **
	Emotional Attention	29.18	5.24	28.54	5.00	29.07	5.20	0.9	382	0.369
TMMS-24	Emotional Clarity	28.83	5.39	29.25	4.99	28.90	5.32	−0.569	382	0.57
	Emotional Repair	29.16	5.82	30.17	4.53	29.33	5.63	−1.560	111.846	0.122

Notes: ** $p < 0.001$. $N = 384$. Abbreviations: M = Means, SD = Standard Deviations. SSS-V, Sensation Seeking Scale; TMMS-24, Trait Meta-Mood Scale; BIS-11, Barratt Impulsivity Scales 11; SPSRQ, Sensitivity to Punishment and Sensitivity to Reward Questionnaire.

Significant differences in the factor impulsivity were observed using the above-mentioned questionnaires. According to the SSS-V, men obtained significantly higher scores in the TAS and DIS dimensions. The results obtained in the BIS-11 scale are congruent, showing that the scores of men were significantly higher than those of females in the CI and NPI dimensions. Based on the Gray model (SPSRQ), male scores were significantly higher than those of women in SR, but not in SP. With respect to emotional intelligence, there are no differences between men and females in any of the three dimensions assessed by the TMMS-24.

Table 2 shows the Pearson correlations between the main variables of the study. The results indicate a relationship between impulsivity and alcohol consumption, with different variations depending on the instrument used in the impulsivity evaluation. Specifically, the SSS-V shows positive correlations with alcohol consumption for the dimensions TAS, ES, and DIS. The results of the BIS 11 also reveal significant positive correlations between both non-planning and motor impulsiveness. Likewise, the results of the SPSRQ show a significant correlation between the sensitivity to reward and alcohol consumption.

Regarding the variable EI (Table 2), we found a significant negative correlation between alcohol consumption and emotional attention. We also observed that emotional dimensions correlate positively each other, that is, attention with clarity and clarity with emotional repair.

To explore what dimensions of impulsivity could best predict alcohol consumption, based on the significant correlations observed, multiple linear regression analyses were conducted as described above. The variable sex was included in both analyses as a control variable.

Table 3 shows the results of multiple regression analyses; model 1 has all subscales of impulsivity and emotional intelligence, model 2 has all subscales and sex, model 3 includes only the significant subscales, and model 4 includes significant subscales and sex. We conducted analyses for the frequency of alcohol consumption and for the amount of alcohol consumed.

All the models revealed significant effects ($p = 0.000$) with interval adjusted R^2 from 0.118 to 0.132 and of all impulsivity subscales, only DIS was associated with the frequency of alcohol consumption ($p < 0.01$). Regarding the amount of alcohol consumed, the analyses showed significant effect ($p = 0.000$), with adjusted R^2 from 0.072 to 0.091. In congruence with the previous model, the results show that disinhibition is the only variable significantly associated with the amount of alcohol consumed ($p < 0.01$).

3.2. Mediation Analyses

In the present study, DIS was considered the first variable (predictor, X) and the frequency of alcohol consumption was the measured result (Y). Emotional attention (M1), emotional clarity (M2), and emotional repair (M3) were considered mediating variables. In the second model (according to the amount of alcohol consumed), the mediation of indirect effects was not considered relevant to be analyzed because no correlations between the amount of consumption and any of the dimensions of emotional intelligence were found.

As illustrated in Figure 1, total effect (c) refers to the relationship between disinhibition and alcohol, in terms of Frequency, without controlling for the mediators; direct effect (c') refers to the relationship between DIS and Frequency, after controlling for the mediators; total indirect effect (a) represents the association between the predictors DIS and three mediators (a_1, a_2, and a_3); and total indirect effect (b) refers to the role of the three mediators in the frequency of consumption (b_1, b_2, and b_3). Total indirect effect (d) refers to the relationship of the three mediators with each other (d_{21}, d_{32}, and d_{31}), and specific indirect effect (a_1b_1, a_2b_2, and/or a_3b_3) refers to the role of a specific mediator in the relationship between DIS and frequency.

The model that evaluates the possible mediation of EI (attention, clarity, and repair) in the relationship between DIS and frequency is shown in Table 4. In the first regression, DIS accounted for 9.71% of the unique variance in frequency ($R^2 = 0.0971$, $F = 41.06$, $p < 0.01$). However, 12.39% of the total amount of variance was accounted for by the global model, which included DIS and the three proposed EI mediators ($R^2 = 0.1205$, $F = 12.98$, $p < 0.01$).

The values provided in Table 4 show that the total effect (c) and the direct effect (c') of DIS on Frequency were both significant. According to the regression coefficient, based on the fact that the 95% CI of the point estimate does not contain zero—which is evidence of the mediation of indirect effects, we obtained one specific indirect effect through the emotional clarity relationships (Ind5 = a_2b_2), in which less DIS was associated with greater emotional clarity which was, in turn, associated with higher frequency of alcohol consumption. Therefore, it can be argued that EI, through clarity, mediates the relationship between impulsivity (disinhibition) and the frequency of alcohol consumption (Figure 2).

Table 2. Pearson correlations between alcohol, personality trait, emotional intelligence, and age.

	1	2	3	4	5	6	7	8	9	10	11	12	13	14
1 Alcohol Frequency	-													
2 Amount of alcohol	0.260 **													
3 Thrill and Adventure Seeking	0.162 **	0.129 *												
4 Experience Seeking	0.180 **	0.172 **	0.376 **											
5 Disinhibition	0.312 **	0.262 **	0.356 **	0.492 **										
6 Boredom Susceptibility	0.070	0.095	0.195 **	0.181 **	0.290 **									
7 Cognitive	0.085	0.087	0.076	0.272 **	0.315 **	0.229 **								
8 Motor	0.117 *	0.114 *	0.119 **	0.259 **	0.313 **	0.314 **	0.493 **							
9 No planning	0.147 **	0.142 **	0.226 **	0.291 **	0.301 **	0.331 **	0.392 **	0.356 **						
10 Sensitivity to Punishment	−0.086	−0.082	−0.126 *	−0.151 **	−0.045	−0.034	0.051	−0.084	−0.112 *					
11 Sensitivity to Reward	0.186 **	0.131 **	0.189 **	0.237 **	0.508 **	0.353 **	0.289 **	0.388 **	0.183 **	0.008				
12 Emotional Attention	−0.01 *	−0.042	−0.037	−0.001	0.009	−0.059	0.035	0.014	−0.028	0.238 **	0.064			
13 Emotional Clarity	0.029	0.010	0.023	−0.105 *	−0.182 **	−0.219 **	−0.208 **	−0.182 **	−0.083	−0.319 **	−0.183 **	0.116 *		
14 Emotional Repair	−0.012	−0.043	0.250 **	0.053	0.030	−0.102 *	−0.056	0.011	0.012	−0.339 **	−0.025	0.017	0.274 **	
15 Age	−0.059	0.056	0.003	0.097	0.065	−0.056	−0.006	−0.034	−0.050	−0.050	−0.038	0.005	0.125 *	−0.023

Notes: * $p < 0.05$; ** $p < 0.001$. $N = 384$.

Table 3. Linear multiple regression analyses predicting alcohol variables.

Alcohol Frequency

	Model 1		Model 2		Model 3		Model 4	
R	0.363		0.363		0.343		0.344	
R^2	0.132		0.132		0.118		0.118	
F-value	4.692 **		4.320 **		16.939 **		12.685 **	
Predictor variables	Emotional Attention	Emotional Clarity	Emotional Attention	Emotional Clarity	Emotional Attention	Emotional Clarity	Emotional Attention	Emotional Clarity
Beta	−0.114	0.11	−0.114	0.11	−0.116	0.102	−0.116	0.102
t	−2.209 *	1.959 *	−2.202 *	1.953 *	−2.398 *	2.077 *	−2.378 *	2.049 *
Predictor variables		DIS		DIS		DIS		DIS
Beta		0.273		0.273		0.273		0.331
t		4.199 **		4.123 **		4.123 **		6.489 **

Amount of Alcohol

	Model 1		Model 2		Model 3		Model 4	
R	0.301		0.306		0.262		0.268	
R^2	0.091		0.093		0.069		0.072	
F-value	3.077 **		2.931 **		28.173 **		14.797 **	
Predictor variables	DIS		DIS		DIS		DIS	
Beta	0.229		0.217		0.267		0.248	
t	3.446 **		3.213 **		5.308 **		4.887 **	

Notes: ** $p < 0.001$; * $p < 0.05$. $N = 384$. Predictors: model 1 = all subscales of impulsivity and emotional intelligence; model 2 = all subscales and sex; model 3 = significant subscales of model 2; model 4 = model 3 and sex.

Table 4. Path coefficients; total effect; direct effect; indirect effect; specific indirect effects and 95% bias-corrected confidence interval predicting frequency alcohol scores ($N = 384$).

Path	Coefficient	SE	BootLLCI	BootULCI	t	p
Total effect (c)	6.255	0.9762	4.336	8.175	6.408	0.000
Direct effect (c')	6.738	0.987	4.796	8.680	6.822	0.000
a_1	0.0215	0.1193	−0.2131	0.256	0.1798	0.857
a_2	−0.4368	0.1194	−0.6716	−0.202	−36.576	0.000
a_3	0.2089	0.1263	−0.0394	0.4573	1.654	0.098
b_1	−1.009	0.4179	−1.831	−0.1882	−2.416	0.016
b_2	0.9897	0.4328	0.1387	1.841	2.287	0.022
b_3	−0.4153	0.3997	−1.201	0.3706	−1.039	0.299
d_{21}	0.1204	0.0512	0.0197	0.2211	2.351	0.019
d_{31}	−0.0188	0.0536	−0.1242	0.0867	−0.35	0.726
d_{32}	0.3078	0.0533	0.2031	0.4126	5.779	0.000
Indirect effects	**Effect**	**SE**	**BootLLCI**	**BootULCI**		
Total indirect effect	−0.4825	0.2643	−1.048	−0.0021		
Ind2: a_2b_2	−0.4323	0.2293	−0.9312	−0.0417		

Notes: Abbreviations: BootLLCI, bootstrapping lower limit confidence interval; BootULCI, bootstrapping upper limit confidence interval; SE, standard error. Model: 6. Y: Alcohol Frequency. X: Disinhibition. M1: Emotional attention. M2: Emotional clarity. M3: Emotional repair. $N = 384$.

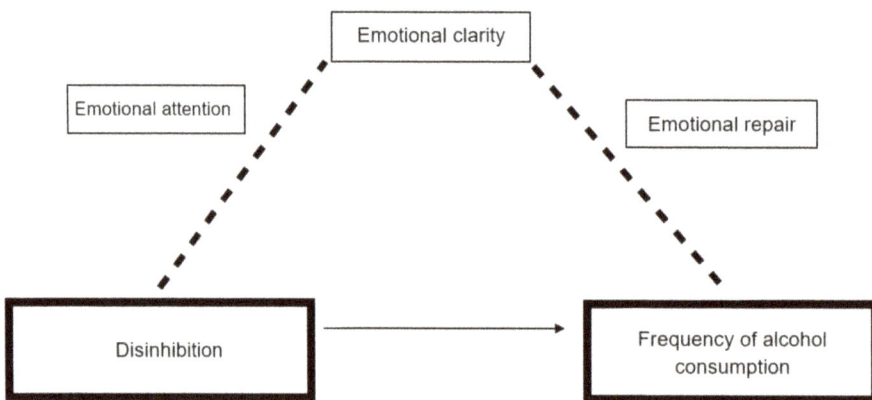

Figure 2. Illustration of mediation model between disinhibition and frequency of alcohol consumption.

4. Discussion

The first objective of this study was to determine which component of impulsivity shows a greater impact on alcohol consumption in young people. Three impulsiveness measures were used for this purpose, according to several main models based on: (a) SSS-V-Zuckerman [14], (b) BIS-11-Barrat [15,33], and (c) SPSRQ-Reinforcement Sensitivity Theory-Gray [16,36].

Our results show significant differences in the impulsivity variable between females and males, as revealed by different questionnaires (SSS-V, BIS-11, and SPSRQ), with higher scores observed in males. These results are congruent with previous studies that reveal higher impulsiveness scores (and sensation seeking) in men compared to women [40,41].

On the other hand, our results show correlations between the different dimensions of impulsivity and alcohol consumption. The results of the SSS-V scale indicate that alcohol consumption correlates with the search for sensations, emotions, adventures, search for experiences and disinhibition subscales. These results confirm the previously described association between impulsivity and alcohol consumption in adolescence [42]. Specifically, the search for sensations has been strongly associated with the frequency of consumption [20,43–45], although this variable is also relevant in other aspects of alcohol consumption, such as excessive alcohol consumption and alcohol-related problems [20].

Similarly, and according to the model proposed by Barrat in 1985 [15], alcohol consumption correlates with non-planning impulsivity, but not with the dimensions of cognitive and motor impulsiveness. These results are discordant with recent works [42] that report alcohol consumption is associated with total, motor, and cognitive impulsiveness.

However, the impulsivity results observed in the present study, considered as sensitivity to punishment and reward, are congruent with previous studies, since the sensitivity to reward, but not the sensitivity to punishment, seems to be related to alcohol consumption [21,31].

In short, according to our results and other studies, it can be concluded that the impulsive-disinhibited personality factor is strongly related to alcohol consumption. Interestingly, some dimensions of impulsivity are differentially related to different variables of alcohol consumption. Thus, for example, impulsivity seems to be more associated to alcohol-related problems, whereas sensation seeking is more related to a non-problematic use of alcohol [21].

Our results also indicate that not all dimensions of EI have the same relation to alcohol consumption. On the one hand, a negative correlation between emotional attention and the frequency of alcohol consumption, but not the amount of consumption, is observed. We did not found correlations between clarity and emotional repair regarding alcohol consumption.

These results differ partially from those described in previous works, in which emotional attention was shown to positively and directly correlate with alcohol consumption, and the emotional repair showed a negative correlation with alcohol consumption [30]. Thus, young people reporting not consuming alcohol consider that they pay less attention to their emotions and report a greater perceived ability to manage their emotional states, while young alcohol consumers show less emotional repair than non-consumers.

Data reported by Trinidad and Johnson in 2002 [25] seems to differ slightly different from our results. These authors observed significant correlations between emotional clarity and alcohol consumption. Other studies have not found significant relationships between emotional attention and the clarity and emotional reparation factors, although high clarity scores have correlated significantly with emotional reparation [24].

In general, the results of previous research show a negative and significant correlation between EI and alcohol consumption [27,28], indicating that a low EI is the best predictor of alcohol consumption. This relationship is based on the assumption that a high EI allows the person to have self-control and emotional management skills, which involve positive coping and better decision-making, which decreases the probability of consuming alcohol.

Taking into account impulsivity and EI, our results are congruent with others studies, showing that young people with low levels of EI tend to be more impulsive and have a worse handling of their emotions, a fact that can increase the risk of consumption, while young people with good emotional skills show lower substance use [25,30,46].

Our second objective was to determine if EI (attention, clarity and emotional repair) has a serial mediating effect on the relationship between the components of impulsivity and alcohol consumption. This potential effect was deduced from the hypothesis that greater impulsivity is associated with lower levels of emotional intelligence which, in turn, implies greater alcohol consumption, both in frequency and quantity. In this sense, the results of the mediation analyses show that disinhibition has a significant direct effect on the frequency of alcohol consumption, and also has an indirect effect, through emotional clarity, which in turn affects the frequency of consumption. These results partially differ from the initial hypothesis, since greater impulsivity is associated with lower levels of emotional clarity, which in turn implies lower alcohol consumption, but only regarding the frequency of consumption.

Therefore, EI seems to mediate the relationship between disinhibition and the frequency of alcohol consumption, thus confirming that EI may mediate the effects of impulsivity on substance use. These results are congruent with previous works showing that EI can explain and modulate the consumption of substances such as alcohol [47–50]. Thus, young people with lower levels of disinhibition, i.e., less impulsive, are expected to consume alcohol less frequently. But this relationship is affected by the understanding of young people of their own emotional states. In fact, if young people have emotional clarity and understand their own emotional states, more alcohol consumption becomes more likely, and it could be argued that in less disinhibited people alcohol consumption is a maladaptive mechanism to suffering or emotional states.

The uses of self-reporting measures is a limitation of this study. In general the levels of honesty may be compromised using self-reports. This applies particularly when assessing risky, sensitive or highly stigmatized behaviors such as drug use. Therefore, students might have insufficiently recorded the amount of alcohol consumption [51], although the validity in the alcohol use register may be considered high because we used closed questions [52].

5. Conclusions

To conclude, our results suggest that the impulsive-uninhibited personality factor is strongly related to alcohol consumption, but this relationship is mediated by EI. Overall, these results could be of great interest for the prevention of alcohol consumption in young people, considering that the skills attributed to EI are susceptible to improvement through learning. Therefore, we can assume that training young people in skills involved in emotional intelligence could provide strategies to protect themselves against harmful alcohol consumption.

Author Contributions: Conceptualization, A.M.-C., M.P.S.-A.; Data curation, A.M.-C., J.R.A.-B.; Formal Analysis, A.M.-C., R.G.; Investigation, A.M.-C., R.G., and J.R.A.-B.; Methodology, A.M.-C., M.P.S.-A., and R.G.; Writing—original draft preparation, A.M.-C., M.P.S.-A., and J.R.A.-B.; Writing—review and editing, A.M.-C., M.P.S.-A., R.G., and J.R.A.-B. All authors have read and agreed to the published version of the manuscript.

Funding: This publication and research has been totally granted by INDESS (Research Universitary Institute for Sustainable Social Development), University of Cádiz, Spain.

Conflicts of Interest: The authors declare that there are no conflicts of interest in this research article.

References

1. World Health Organization (WHO). *Global Status Report on Alcohol and Health 2018*; World Health Organization (WHO): Geneva, Switzerland, 2018.
2. Observatorio Europeo de las Drogas y las Toxicomanías (EMCDDA). *Informe Europeo Sobre Drogas 2018. Tendencias Y Novedades*; Oficina de Publicaciones de la Unión Europea: Luxembourg, 2018.
3. Rehm, J.; Mathers, C.; Popova, S.; Thavorncharoensap, M.; Teerawattananon, Y.; Patra, J. Global burden of disease and injury and economic cost attributable to alcohol use and alcohol-use disorders. *Lancet* **2009**, *373*, 2223–2233. [CrossRef]
4. Adan, A.; Forero, D.A.; Navarro, J.F. Personality Traits Related to Binge Drinking: A Systematic Review. *Front. Psychiatry* **2017**, *8*, 134. [CrossRef] [PubMed]
5. Luchetti, M.; Sutin, A.R.; Delitala, A.; Stephan, Y.; Fiorillo, E.; Marongiu, M.; Masala, M.; Schlessinger, D.; Terracciano, A. Personality traits and facets linked with self-reported alcohol consumption and biomarkers of liver health. *Addict. Behav.* **2018**, *82*, 135–141. [CrossRef] [PubMed]
6. Mezquita, L.; Camacho, L.; Ibáñez, M.I.; Villa, H.; Moya-Higueras, J.; Ortet, G. Five-Factor Model and alcohol outcomes: Mediating and moderating role of alcohol expectancies. *Personal. Individ. Differ.* **2015**, *74*, 29–34. [CrossRef]
7. Dick, D.M.; Smith, G.; Olausson, P.; Mitchell, S.H.; Leeman, R.F.; O'Malley, S.S.; Sher, K. Understanding the construct of impulsivity and its relationship to alcohol use disorders. *Addict. Biol.* **2010**, *15*, 217–226. [CrossRef]
8. Adams, Z.W.; Kaiser, A.J.; Lynam, D.R.; Charnigo, R.J.; Milich, R. Drinking motives as mediators of the impulsivity-substance use relation: Pathways for negative urgency, lack of premeditation, and sensation seeking. *Addict. Behav.* **2012**, *37*, 848–855. [CrossRef]

9. Evren, C.; Dalbudak, E. Relationship of Personality Trait Impulsivity with Clinical Variables in Male Alcohol-Dependent Inpatients. *Klin. Psikofarmakol. Bul. Istanb.* **2009**, *19*, 15–23.
10. James, L.M.; Taylor, J. Impulsivity and negative emotionality associated with substance use problems and Cluster B personality in college students. *Addict. Behav.* **2007**, *32*, 714–727. [CrossRef]
11. MacKillop, J.; Mattson, R.E.; Anderson MacKillop, E.J.; Castelda, B.A.; Donovick, P.J. Multidimensional Assessment of Impulsivity in Undergraduate Hazardous Drinkers and Controls. *J. Stud. Alcohol Drugs* **2007**, *68*, 785–788. [CrossRef]
12. Magid, V.; MacLean, M.G.; Colder, C.R. Differentiating between sensation seeking and impulsivity through their mediated relations with alcohol use and problems. *Addict. Behav.* **2007**, *32*, 2046–2061. [CrossRef]
13. Lejuez, C.W.; Magidson, J.F.; Mitchell, S.H.; Sinha, R.; Stevens, M.C.; De Wit, H. Behavioral and biological indicators of impulsivity in the development of alcohol use, problems, and disorders. *Alcohol. Clin. Exp. Res.* **2010**, *34*, 1334–1345. [CrossRef] [PubMed]
14. Behavioral Expressions and Biosocial Bases of Sensation Seeking. Available online: https://www.cambridge.org/cn/academic/subjects/life-sciences/animal-behaviour/behavioral-expressions-and-biosocial-bases-sensation-seeking?format=HB&isbn=9780521432009 (accessed on 8 September 1994).
15. Barratt, E.S. Impulsiveness subtraits: Arousal and information processing. In *Motivation, Emotion and Personality*; Spence, J.T., Izard, C.E., Eds.; North Holland Elsevier Science Publishers: New York, NY, USA, 1985; pp. 137–146.
16. The Psychology of Fear and Stress. Available online: https://books.google.com.hk/books?hl=zh-CN&lr=&id=nww5AAAAIAAJ&oi=fnd&pg=PR6&dq=The+Psychology+of+Fear+and+Stress%3B&ots=roCw7tXewX&sig=tW8zVJryaix7axpXZTo8dtSXU9A&redir_esc=y&hl=zh-CN&sourceid=cndr#v=onepage&q=The%20Psychology%20of%20Fear%20and%20Stress%3B&f=false (accessed on 8 January 1987).
17. Gray, J.A. A Critique of Eysenck's Theory of Personality. In *A Model for Personality*; Eysenck, H.J., Ed.; Springer: New York, NY, USA, 1981; pp. 246–276.
18. Squillace, M.; Picón Janeiro, J.; Schmidt, V. El concepto de impulsividad y su ubicación en las teorías psicobiológicas de la personalidad. *Rev. Neuropsicol. Latinoam.* **2011**, *3*, 8–18. [CrossRef]
19. Shin, S.H.; Hong, H.G.; Jeon, S.-M. Personality and alcohol use: The role of impulsivity. *Addict. Behav.* **2012**, *37*, 102–107. [CrossRef] [PubMed]
20. Aluja, A.; Lucas, I.; Blanch, A.; Blanco, E. Personality and disinhibitory psychopathology in alcohol consumption: A study from the biological-factorial personality models of Eysenck, Gray and Zuckerman. *Personal. Individ. Differ.* **2019**, *142*, 159–165. [CrossRef]
21. Extremera Pacheco, N.; Fernández Berrocal, P. Inteligencia emocional percibida y diferencias individuales en el meta-conocimiento de los estados emocionales: Una revisión de los estudios con el TMMS. *Ansiedad y estrés* **2005**, *11*, 101–122.
22. Mayer, J.D.; Salovey, P. What is emotional intelligence? In *Emotional Development and Emotional Intelligence: Educational Implications*, 2nd ed.; Salovey, P., Sluyter, D.J., Eds.; Basic: New York, NY, USA, 1997; pp. 3–31.
23. Salovey, P.; Mayer, J.D.; Goldman, S.L.; Turvey, C.; Palfai, T.P. Emotional attention, clarity, and repair: Exploring emotional intelligence using the Trait Meta-Mood Scale. In *Emotion, Disclosure, and Health*; Pennebaker, J.W., Ed.; American Psychological Assn.: Washington, DC, USA, 1995; pp. 125–154.
24. Claros, E.; Sharma, M. The relationship between emotional intelligence and abuse of alcohol, marijuana, and tobacco among college students. *J. Alcohol Drug Educ.* **2012**, *56*, 8–37.
25. Trinidad, D.R.; Johnson, C.A. The association between emotional intelligence and early adolescent tobacco and alcohol use. *Personal. Individ. Differ.* **2002**, *32*, 95–105. [CrossRef]
26. Nehra, D.K.; Sharma, V.; Mush-taq, H.; Sharma, N.R.; Sharma, M.; Nehra, S. Emotional intelligence and self esteem in cannabis abusers. *J. Indian Acad. Appl. Psychol.* **2012**, *38*, 385–393.
27. Kun, B.; Demetrovics, Z. Emotional intelligence and addictions: A systematic review. *Subst Use Misuse* **2010**, *45*, 1131–1160. [CrossRef]
28. Resurrección, D.M.; Salguero, J.M.; Ruiz-Aranda, D. Emotional intelligence and psychological maladjustment in adolescence: A systematic review. *J. Adolesc.* **2014**, *37*, 461–472. [CrossRef]
29. Riley, H.; Schutte, N.S. Low emotional intelligence as a predictor of substance-use problems. *J. Drug Educ.* **2003**, *33*, 391–398. [CrossRef] [PubMed]
30. Ruiz-Aranda, D.; Fernandez-Berrocal, P.; Cabello, R.; Extremera, N. Inteligencia Emocional Percibida Y Consumo De Tabaco Y Alcohol En Adolescentes. *Ansiedad y Estrés* **2006**, *12*, 223–230.

31. Coccaro, E.F.; Zagaja, C.; Chen, P.; Jacobson, K. Relationships between perceived emotional intelligence, aggression, and impulsivity in a population-based adult sample. *Psychiatry Res.* **2016**, *246*, 255–260. [CrossRef] [PubMed]
32. Limonero, J.T.; Gómez, M.J.; Fernández, J.; Tomás-Sábado, J. Influencia de la inteligencia emocional percibida y la impulsividad en el abuso de cánnabis en jóvenes. *Ansiedad y estrés* **2013**, *19*, 223–234.
33. Patton, J.H.; Stanford, M.S.; Barratt, E.S. Factor structure of the Barratt impulsiveness scale. *J. Clin Psychol* **1995**, *51*, 768–774. [CrossRef]
34. Oquendo, M.A.; Baca-García, E.; Graver, R.; Morales, M.; Montalvan, V.; Mann, J. Spanish adaptation of the Barratt Impulsiveness Scale (BIS-11). *Eur. J. psychiatry* **2001**, *15*, 147–155.
35. Torrubia, R.; Ávila, C.; Moltó, J.; Caseras, X. The Sensitivity to Punishment and Sensitivity to Reward Questionnaire (SPSRQ) as a measure of Gray's anxiety and impulsivity dimensions. *Personal. Individ. Differ.* **2001**, *31*, 837–862. [CrossRef]
36. Carver, C.S.; White, T.L. Behavioral Inhibition, Behavioral Activation, and Affective Responses to Impending Reward and Punishment: The BIS/BAS Scales. *J. Personal. Soc. Psychol.* **1994**, *67*, 319–333. [CrossRef]
37. Caseras, X.; Àvila, C.; Torrubia, R. The measurement of individual differences in Behavioural Inhibition and Behavioural Activation Systems: A comparison of personality scales. *Personal. Individ. Differ.* **2003**, *34*, 999–1013. [CrossRef]
38. Fernández-Berrocal, P.; Extremera, N.; Ramos, N. Validity and reliability of the spanish modified version of the trait meta-mood scale. *Psychol. Rep.* **2004**, *94*, 751–755. [CrossRef]
39. Hayes, A.F. *Introduction to Mediation, Moderation, and Conditional Process. Analysis. A Regression-Based Approach*, 2nd ed.; Guilford Publications: New York, NY, USA, 2017.
40. Adan, A.; Navarro, J.F.; Forero, D.A. Personality profile of binge drinking in university students is modulated by sex. A study using the Alternative Five Factor Model. *Drug Alcohol Depend.* **2016**, *165*, 120–125. [CrossRef] [PubMed]
41. Martínez-Loredo, V.; Fernández-Hermida, J.R.; de La Torre-Luque, A.; Fernández-Artamendi, S. Polydrug use trajectories and differences in impulsivity among adolescents. *Int. J. Clin. Health Psychol.* **2018**, *18*, 235–244. [CrossRef] [PubMed]
42. Charfi, N.; Smaoui, N.; Turki, M.; Maâlej, M.B.; Omri, S.; Ben, J.T.; Zouari, N.; Zouari, L.; Maâlej, M. Alcohol use in adolescents and its association with sensation seeking and impulsivity: A survey in the city of Sfax, Tunisia. *Rev. Epidemiol Sante Publique* **2019**, *67*, 13–20. [CrossRef] [PubMed]
43. Fischer, S.; Settles, R.; Collins, B.; Gunn, R.; Smith, G.T. The role of negative urgency and expectancies in problem drinking and disordered eating: Testing a model of comorbidity in pathological and at-risk samples. *Psychol. Addict. Behav.* **2012**, *26*, 112–123. [CrossRef]
44. Fischer, S.; Smith, G.T. Binge eating, problem drinking, and pathological gambling: Linking behavior to shared traits and social learning. *Personal. Individ. Differ.* **2008**, *44*, 789–800. [CrossRef]
45. Whiteside, S.P.; Lynam, D.R. Understanding the role of impulsivity and externalizing psychopathology in alcohol abuse: Application of the UPPS Impulsive Behavior Scale. *Personal. Disord. Theory Res. Treat.* **2009**, *11*, 69–79. [CrossRef]
46. Austin, E.J.; Saklofske, D.H.; Egan, V. Personality, well-being and health correlates of trait emotional intelligence. *Personal. Individ. Differ.* **2005**, *38*, 547–558. [CrossRef]
47. Canto, J.; Fernández-Berrocal, P.; Guerrero, F.; Extremera, N. Función protectora de las habilidades emocionales en las adicciones. In *Psicología Social y Problemas Sociales*; Biblioteca Nueva: Madrid, Spain, 2005; pp. 583–590.
48. Fernández, B.; Jorge, V.; Bejar, E. Función protectora de las habilidades emocionales en la prevención del consumo de tabaco y alcohol: Una propuesta de intervención. *Psicooncología* **2009**, *6*, 243–256.
49. García del Castillo, J.A.G. Del Editorial: Evaluation of drug use in perspective/La evaluación del consumo de drogas en perspectiva. *Health Addict. Salud y Drog.* **2011**, *11*, 7–15.
50. Trinidad, D.R.; Unger, J.B.; Chou, C.-P.; Anderson Johnson, C. The protective association of emotional intelligence with psychosocial smoking risk factors for adolescents. *Personal. Individ. Differ.* **2004**, *36*, 945–954. [CrossRef]

51. Harrison, L. The validity of self-reported drug use in survey research: An overview and critique of research methods. *NIDA Res. Monogr* **1997**, *167*, 17–36. [PubMed]
52. Lintonen, T.; Ahlström, S.; Metso, L. The reliability of self-reported drinking in adolescence. *Alcohol Alcohol.* **2004**, *39*, 362–368. [CrossRef] [PubMed]

© 2020 by the authors. Licensee MDPI, Basel, Switzerland. This article is an open access article distributed under the terms and conditions of the Creative Commons Attribution (CC BY) license (http://creativecommons.org/licenses/by/4.0/).

Article

Ethnic Food Consumption in Italy: The Role of Food Neophobia and Openness to Different Cultures

Giulia Mascarello *, Anna Pinto, Valentina Rizzoli, Barbara Tiozzo, Stefania Crovato and Licia Ravarotto

Health Awareness and Communication Department, Istituto Zooprofilattico Sperimentale delle Venezie, Legnaro 35020, Italy; apinto@izsvenezie.it (A.P.); vrizzoli@izsvenezie.it (V.R.); btiozzo@izsvenezie.it (B.T.); scrovato@izsvenezie.it (S.C.); lravarotto@izsvenezie.it (L.R.)
* Correspondence: gmascarello@izsvenezie.it; Tel.: +39-049-8084265

Received: 23 December 2019; Accepted: 17 January 2020; Published: 21 January 2020

Abstract: While the ethnic food market has become increasingly important in Italy, the effects of the hybridization of consumption patterns have been slowed by a consolidated culinary tradition. This study investigates the relationships among ethnic food consumption, food neophobia, and openness to different cultures with sociodemographic characteristics. A sample of 1317 Italian consumers responded to an online survey. The sociodemographic profile of the neophobic consumer appears to substantially differ from that of the consumer with an attitude of openness. Neophobic respondents are males, are older than 55 years of age, are less educated, have children, are retired, have difficulty meeting their financial responsibilities, and do not eat ethnic food. Respondents who are more open to different cultures are young adults, are highly educated, have no children, are employed, and are consumers of ethnic food. The relationship between food neophobia and openness to different cultures is confirmed to be the relationship between these variables and ethnic food consumption. The measurement of these characteristics could serve as a crucial indicator for analyzing the willingness to accept elements of novelty in an increasingly multicultural society. Additionally, consumers with the neophobic trait and who are less open to different cultures might have a less varied diet that is essential to good health.

Keywords: Italian consumers; food attitudes; psychological trait; sociodemographic variables; ethnic food

1. Introduction

Italy has a consolidated culinary tradition that has its roots in regional cuisine. This tradition may serve as a stabilizing factor in the eating habits of Italians that slows the globalization of consumption patterns [1,2]. However, Italy appears to be evolving with regard to food consumption. In recent decades, significant changes have occurred in the lifestyles and dietary habits of the Italian population, including an increase in dining out [3], the widespread presence of take-out and street food, a recreational attitude towards food particularly in young consumers [4], and increasing consumer demand in terms of food variety. Food polytheism is a term used to describe the current context of food consumption in Italy. Food polytheism refers to a subjective combination of food choices and highly complex and occasionally seemingly contradictory places of purchase and consumption [3,5–7].

1.1. Increasing of Ethnic Food Presence in Italy

The hybridization of food models is favored by different factors, including the globalization of markets and the mixture of populations through migration and the development of tourist exchanges with foreign countries [8]. In recent decades, many social, political, and economic changes have fostered the arrival of significant flows of new residents into Italy who have promoted the development of economic activities in the food and catering sectors that are strongly linked to their countries of origin. The number of foreign entrepreneurs working in the catering sector increased by 43.3% from 2010 to 2014, leading to a record number of 21,176 owners of foreign enterprises (12.9% of the total number) [9]. Therefore, ethnic foods are increasingly available on the Italian food market: Since 2007, ethnic food sales have increased by 93% [10]. In addition to introducing new flavors and ingredients, ethnic food has cultural significance because it represents the food cultures and traditions of populations from other countries whose presence in Italy is increasing. For these reasons, foods from the culinary traditions of distant countries have started to have an increasingly important presence in Italy. However, their success has been delayed relative to what has been observed in other Western countries and has been less overwhelming than what has been witnessed in the Anglo-Saxon countries [11].

1.2. Consumption of Ethnic Food: The Role of Food Neophobia and Openness to Different Cultures

Different interrelated aspects contribute to delineate consumption decisions, particularly regarding unfamiliar foods. They can be contextual (e.g., cultural or social), related to individual cognition/perception/sensation (e.g., the fear of negative consequences of eating a particular food or finding a certain type of food disgusting), or related to individual traits [12,13]. The willingness to try non-traditional ethnic foods seems to be significantly predicted by a trait known as food neophobia [14,15], which is defined as a "reluctance to eat and/or avoidance of novel foods" [16]. Several instruments have been developed to measure food neophobia as a behavior involving the rejection of foods in a particular situation and as a personal trait related to the propensity to avoid novel foods that remains constant over time and across different contexts [12]. The Food Neophobia Scale (FNS) developed by Pliner and Hobden [16] is considered a reliable and valid instrument for measuring neophobia as a personality characteristic in adults [17].

The study of this psychological trait is important because it can affect the acceptance of new foods [18] and influence consumers' daily food choices [19,20]. Studies on children and adults suggest that food neophobia can affect the consumption of healthy foods (i.e., fruit and vegetables) [21,22] and the willingness to try healthy alternatives (e.g., meat substitutes) [23]. Additionally, neophilic individuals consume a broader variety of food [20,24,25] and have a diet higher in nutritional quality [26] than neophobes. Thus, neophobic individuals may be more exposed to nutritional risks or suffer from specific risks related to an unvaried diet.

As many studies have highlighted, sociodemographic variables are key determinants of food choices and perceptions [27–29]. Food preferences and acceptance seem to be associated with food exposure [30]. Education, occupation, and income influence the chances of exposure because they can favor a habit of dining out and knowledge of different cultures and gastronomic traditions. The association between these variables and food neophobia has been observed in several studies [31,32]. The influence of age [33–38] and place of residence [27] has also been observed. Therefore, individuals who are more exposed to different cultures should be less neophobic. The relationship between food neophobia and general neophobia was assessed by Pliner and Hobden [16]. Openness to different cultures seems to influence the acceptance of and willingness to try new foods. Studying this attitude in relation to food neophobia could contribute interesting information in the development of a general approach that could influence the propensity to try foods from other countries. Several survey items have been proposed by Verbeke and Poquiviqui López [39] to study the attitudes of Belgians towards Latin American ethnic foods in an approach based on the dimensions of ethnic identity defined by Laroche et al. [40].

Few studies have focused on these issues in reference to the Italian context. A number of studies have focused on Italians' attitudes towards Eastern European foods [15], on the relation between neophobia and odor identification [41] and food preferences [42–44], and on the role of neophobia in determining food preferences [13]. A measure of neophobia designed for Italian primary school children has also been validated [45]. Focusing on aspects that have been shown to influence food choices is particularly interesting in a context like the Italian one, which is characterized by a deep-rooted food culture and at the same time by increasingly multicultural conditions and consequently by food polytheism.

1.3. Aims

In light of the above specificities of the Italian context and of the impacts of neophobia on food preferences, this study has two objectives:

- To analyze the relationships between ethnic food consumption, the psychological trait of food neophobia, and openness to different cultures in Italy; and
- To identify the sociodemographic characteristics of food neophobic consumers and of consumers who are open to different cultures.

2. Materials and Methods

2.1. Data Collection

Data were collected through a national survey conducted via the computer-assisted web interviewing method (CAWI) [46] between 8 September and 25 September 2014 by the Demetra opinioni.net firm. The sample was selected using a method that considered the stratification of the Italian population by gender and geographical area as of 31 December 2013 as determined by the Italian National Institute of Statistics (ISTAT). A sample of 1317 Italian consumers responded to a questionnaire sent to 2871 consumers for a response rate of 45.8%. The complete questionnaire includes 45 questions.

A set of questions was designed to investigate ethnic food consumption habits and risk perceptions. An overview of the consumption of ethnic food in Italy and an analysis of perceptions of risk associated with this type of food are provided in a previous article [47]. Ethnic food/products were defined as "food coming from a foreign country with gastronomic and cultural traditions different from Italian ones" [48]. In this article, several aspects are reported to frame ethnic food consumption in Italy: Whether respondents have ever eaten ethnic food in Italy (response options: Yes and no) and the ways in which respondents come into contact with ethnic cuisine (response options: Through relatives and friends, through travel, by myself, through the mass media, and other).

Food neophobia was measured with 10 items [16], and openness to different cultures was measured with 7 items [39], with response options expressed on a 1–10 Likert scale of "strongly disagree" to "strongly agree" (see Table 1 and Table 3 for response options). The original FNS was administered with a 7-point response scale. In this study, a 10-point scale was used to ensure consistency between the two measurements and the other rating scales of the questionnaire (different scales were also used by Demattè et al. [41] and Meiselman et al. [31]). Ritchey et al. [49] demonstrated through his study that excluding 2 or 4 items from the FNS improves the instrument when applied in several countries. However, we decided to maintain the original 10 items since we applied the FNS to the Italian context alone.

Personal information investigated through the questionnaire included the following: Gender, age, educational qualifications, the presence of children, occupation, location, size of the city of residence, and how well the interviewee's income meets his or her financial responsibilities (see Table 2 and Table 4 for response options).

Table 1. Mean values and standard deviations of FNS (Food Neophobia Scale) items and varimax rotated factor loadings.

Item	Mean	SD	Factor 1 [b]	Factor 2 [b]
I am constantly sampling new and different food (R) [a]	5.4	2.6	**0.828**	−0.046
I don't trust new foods	6.9	2.3	−0.211	**0.770**
If I don't know what is in a food, I won't try it	5.3	2.8	0.032	**0.723**
I like foods from different countries (R)	4.9	2.3	**0.878**	−0.028
Ethnic food looks too weird to eat	6.5	2.4	−0.098	**0.752**
At dinner parties, I will try a new food (R)	4.4	2.7	**0.858**	−0.063
I am afraid to eat things I have never had before	6.5	2.5	−0.213	**0.794**
I am very particular about the foods I will eat	4.3	2.3	0.151	**0.472**
I will eat almost anything (R)	5.8	2.8	**0.703**	−0.037
I like to try new ethnic restaurants (R)	5.1	2.7	**0.873**	−0.086
% variance explained			38	23.3

[a] R = Reversed items; [b] Loadings that are higher on either factor are shown in bold.

Table 2. Food neophobia scores by sociodemographic variables.

Variables	N	Mean (± SD)	Range	F	p-Value
Gender					
Male	629	51.98 (± 14.37)	14–100	4.246	0.040
Female	688	50.31 (± 15.06)	10–100		
Age					
18–34	297	48.51 (± 15.27)	10–98	10.070	0.000
35–54	487	50.50 (± 14.94)	14–100		
>55	533	53.11 (± 14.02)	14–98		
Location					
Northwestern Italy	346	50.07 (± 15.03)	10–100		
Northeastern Italy	252	52.15 (± 15.71)	10–100	1.098	0.349
Central Italy	256	51.62 (± 16.38)	14–98		
Southern Italy and islands [a]	463	51.02 (± 12.94)	14–94		
Size of city of residence					
<30,000	512	52.36 (± 15.24)	10–100		
30,001–100,000	365	50.46 (± 13.91)	15–98	2.548	0.054
100,001–250,000	160	51.32 (± 14.35)	10–93		
>250,000	280	49.54 (± 15.01)	14–100		
Educational qualifications					
Elementary/lower secondary school diploma	130	54.14 (± 14.36)	14–98		
Vocational qualification	70	52.93 (± 15.12)	22–92		
Upper secondary school diploma	607	51.94 (± 14.29)	14–100	4.679	0.000
Higher education diploma	52	53.48 (± 12.99)	24–85		
Degree	387	48.61 (± 15.16)	10–100		
Postgraduate qualification	72	48.52 (± 15.94)	20–100		
Children					
Yes	804	51.99 (± 14.38)	14–100	7.451	0.006
No	513	49.72 (± 15.23)	10–100		
Occupation					
Student/looking for first job	155	48.99 (± 14.48)	14–98		
Homemaker	154	53.20 (± 13.48)	18–91		
Retired	244	55.37 (± 13.47)	14–98	11.129	0.000
Unemployed	138	53.36 (± 13.89)	19–94		
Employed	626	48.95 (± 15.31)	10–100		
Meeting financial responsibilities					
Very easy	121	46.94 (± 16.06)	10–100		
Quite easy	498	50.96 (± 14.33)	14–100	8.336	0.000
With some difficulty	545	50.87 (± 14.91)	14–100		
With much difficulty	153	55.70 (± 13.64)	14–100		
Ethnic food consumption					
Yes	1116	49.15 (± 14.26)	10–100	141.289	0.000
No	201	61.92 (± 12.63)	19–100		

[a] Islands include Sicily and Sardinia.

2.2. Data Analysis

Descriptive statistics were applied to all variables (the sociodemographic information listed above and whether ethnic food was consumed or not) to develop a general understanding of ethnic food consumption in the Italian context. The two scales were studied over two steps. Cronbach's alpha coefficient was used to assess the internal consistency of the scales while a principal component analysis (PCA) (the maximum likelihood method with varimax rotation) was used to investigate the factor structure. The skewness and kurtosis of the two scales' distributions were also analyzed. Two indices were constructed to measure the levels of food neophobia and openness to different cultures. The two indices were calculated by summing scores allocated to the 10 statements from the FNS (range 10–100) and to the 7 statements from the openness to different cultures scale (ODCS) (range 7–70). To calculate the FNS index, the positive items were reversed [16]. An analysis of variance (ANOVA) facilitated the study of differences in the levels of food neophobia and in the openness to different cultures on the basis of social information. Based on the FNS index, the respondents were divided into three groups: Neophilic (low scores), neutral (medium scores), and neophobic (high scores). One standard deviation from the mean was used as the cut-off point. This classification has been used in previous studies and is considered an effective method [14,15,32,50]. The subjects were also divided using the same method in relation to the ODCS index. Three groups were identified: Those less (low scores), moderately (medium scores), and highly (high scores) open to different cultures. The relation between the two indices was studied by means of the Pearson correlation index. Different levels of food neophobia in relation to attitudes towards different cultures were analyzed by cross tabulation. A Chi-square test was used to verify the dependence relationship between the two variables identifying the FNS and ODCS groups. Data were processed using the SPSS (Statistical Package for Social Science) software (version 20.0) for Windows (SPSS Inc. Chicago, Illinois). The level of statistical significance was set at 5% ($\alpha = 0.05$).

3. Results

3.1. Characteristics of the Sample

The sample was 52.2% female and 47.8% male (in the Italian population, 51.5% were female and 48.5% male). Regarding regions of residence, the majority of respondents (35.2%) lived in southern Italy or in Sicily or Sardinia followed by those living in northwestern Italy (26.3%), those living in central Italy (19.4%), and those living in northeastern Italy (19.1%) (in the Italian population, 34.5% lived in southern Italy or in Sicily or Sardinia, 26.5% in northwestern Italy, 19.8% in central Italy, and 19.2% in northeastern Italy). In total, 22.5% of the respondents were between 18 and 34 years of age, 37% were between 35 and 54 years of age, and 40.5% were more than 55 years of age (in the Italian population over 18 years old, people in the three age classes were respectively 22.3%, 37.2%, and 40.8%). Of the respondents, 84.7% declared that they had eaten ethnic food in Italy. The majority of those who had consumed this food in Italy had come into contact with ethnic cuisine through relatives and friends (50.4%) while nearly one in four had been exposed to ethnic cuisine through their travels (24.5%), approximately one in five had been exposed to this cuisine by themselves (22.3%), and others had been exposed through the mass media (2.3%) or through other means (0.5%).

3.2. Food Neophobia

The internal consistency of the FNS was assessed from Cronbach's alpha ($\alpha = 0.789$). The factor structure was evaluated by means of a PCA. The scale items loaded primarily on two components, explaining 38% and 23.3% of the variance (Table 1). The first component loaded the regular items and is related to the levels of interest in trying new and ethnic foods while the second component loaded the reversed items and seems to be related to concerns regarding trying new foods. The mean FNS score of the Italian sample analyzed here was recorded as 51.1 (SD = 14.7, range 10–100). The FNS distribution had a skewness value of 0.08 and a kurtosis value of 0.31.

The investigation of levels of food neophobia observed in relation to the consumption of ethnic food and sociodemographic variables and the results of the analysis of variance conducted are presented in Table 2. The F-test results are statistically significant with regard to the following variables: Gender ($p = 0.040$), age ($p = 0.000$), educational qualifications ($p = 0.000$), the presence of children ($p = 0.006$), occupation ($p = 0.000$), meeting financial responsibilities ($p = 0.000$), and ethnic food consumption ($p = 0.000$). Levels of food neophobia were found to be higher in those who do not eat ethnic food, in males, in those older than 55 years of age, in those with no more than an elementary/lower secondary school education, in those who have children, in retirees, and in those who are experiencing many challenges in meeting their financial needs.

3.3. Openness to Different Cultures

The internal consistency of the ODCS was assessed by Cronbach's alpha ($\alpha = 0.883$). A PCA was used to evaluate the factor structure. The first and second principal components were found to explain 60% and 16% of the variance, respectively (Table 3). The first factor pertains to levels of comfort with social interactions with non-Italians while the second factor refers to language and mass media use. The mean ODCS value was recorded as 39.6 (SD = 13.9, range 7–70). The ODCS distribution generated a skewness value of 0.00 and a kurtosis value of −0.33.

Table 3. Mean values and standard deviations of ODCS (Openess to Different Cultures Scale) items and varimax rotated factor loadings.

Item	Mean	SD	Factor 1 [a]	Factor 2 [a]
1. I am very comfortable dealing with non-Italians	6.6	2.2	**0.879**	0.184
2. I like to go to places where I can be among non-Italians	6.1	2.4	**0.881**	0.261
3. I like to participate in activities of non-Italians	5.9	2.3	**0.883**	0.295
4. Some of my friends are non-Italians	6.3	2.7	**0.632**	0.353
5. I often read foreign newspapers or magazines	4.4	2.8	0.293	**0.850**
6. I often watch foreign television	4.4	2.9	0.223	**0.890**
7. I like to study foreign languages	5.9	2.7	0.258	**0.749**
% variance explained			60	16

[a] Loadings that are higher on either factor are shown in bold.

The results of the analysis of variance conducted are reported in Table 4. The F-test produced statistically significant results for the following variables: Age ($p = 0.000$), city size ($p = 0.002$), location ($p = 0.000$), educational qualifications ($p = 0.000$), the presence of children ($p = 0.034$), occupation ($p = 0.000$), and ethnic food consumption ($p = 0.000$). More openness to different cultures was observed in those who eat ethnic food, in young adults (18–34 years of age), in those living in larger cities, in those living southern Italy or on the islands, in those with a postgraduate education, in those who are childless, and in those who are employed.

Table 4. Attitudes towards different cultures based on sociodemographic variables.

Variables	N	Mean (± SD)	Range	F	p-Value
Gender					
Male	629	38.80 (± 13.70)	7–70	3.644	0.056
Female	688	40.26 (± 13.99)	7–70		
Age					
18–34	297	41.83 (± 13.86)	7–70	13.610	0.000
35–54	487	40.75 (± 13.92)	7–70		
>55	533	37.22 (± 13.49)	7–70		

Table 4. Cont.

Variables	N	Mean (± SD)	Range	F	p-Value
Location				7.649	0.000
Northwestern Italy	346	38.65 (± 13.30)	7–70		
Northeastern Italy	252	37.72 (± 13.72)	7–70		
Central Italy	256	38.23 (± 14.47)	7–70		
Southern Italy and islands [a]	463	42.00 (± 13.72)	7–70		
Size of city of residence				4.851	0.002
<30,000	512	37.80 (± 13.30)	7–70		
30,001–100,000	365	40.26 (± 13.31)	7–70		
100,001–250,000	160	41.37 (± 16.24)	7–70		
>250,000	280	40.87 (± 13.84)	7–70		
Educational qualifications				12.253	0.000
Elementary/lower secondary school diploma	130	35.48 (± 13.98)	7–66		
Vocational qualification	70	35.47 (± 14.56)	7–70		
Upper secondary school diploma	607	38.23 (± 13.18)	7–70		
Higher education diploma	52	38.32 (± 13.17)	10–70		
Degree	387	42.78 (± 13.56)	7–70		
Postgraduate qualification	72	45.81 (± 15.41)	7–70		
Children				4.498	0.034
Yes	804	38.92 (± 14.09)	7–70		
No	513	40.58 (± 13.45)	7–70		
Occupation				8.840	0.000
Student/looking for first job	155	40.50 (± 12.47)	7–70		
Homemaker	154	37.05 (± 13.78)	7–70		
Retired	244	35.78 (± 13.12)	7–66		
Unemployed	138	39.87 (± 13.57)	9–70		
Employed	626	41.36 (± 14.22)	7–70		
Meeting financial responsibilities				2.480	0.060
Very easy	121	40.71 (± 13.92)	7–70		
Quite easy	498	39.79 (± 13.18)	7–70		
With some difficulty	545	39.89 (± 14.31)	7–70		
With much difficulty	153	36.78 (± 14.21)	7–70		
Ethnic food consumption				70.514	0.000
Yes	1116	40.89 (± 13.59)	7–70		
No	201	32.21 (± 13.03)	7–70		

[a] Islands include Sicily and Sardinia.

3.4. Correlations between the FNS and ODCS Indices

The Pearson correlation coefficient calculated between the FNS and ODCS indices was measured as 0.312 ($p = 0.000$), indicating a positive but weak correlation between the two variables. For the FNS index, the subjects were divided into three groups using one standard deviation from the mean as a cut-off point: Neophilic (17%, score 10–36.4), neutral (69.2%, score 36.5–65.8), and neophobic (13.8%, score 65.9–100). In the same way, three groups were defined using an ODCS index, representing low (15.5%, score 7–25.7), moderate (67.3%, score 25.8–53.5), and high (17.2%, score 53.6–70) levels of openness to different cultures. The bivariate analysis performed on the two variables reveals that among food neophobic subjects, more than four times the number of individuals exhibit less openness than individuals exhibiting more openness. Additionally, only one of seven of those who are neophilic show lower levels of openness rather than higher levels of openness (Figure 1).

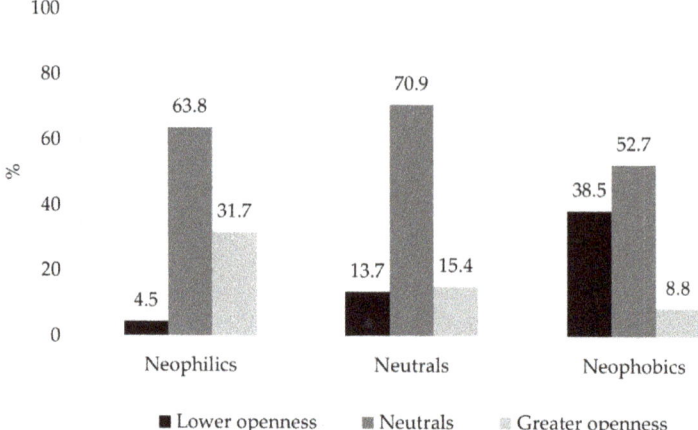

Figure 1. Bivariate analysis of attitudes towards different cultures and of food neophobic groups.

4. Discussion

The ethnic food market is an important business in Italy. The consumption of ethnic products is widespread [47], and this trend is growing [9,10]. However, ethnic food is far from being part of everyday Italian life.

The FNS and ODCS indices tested with the Italian sample present a high internal reliability coefficient. Our PCA shows that the two scales are not unidimensional and principally load on two factors. The components identified by the FNS separate the regular and reversed items, reflecting the different dimensions measured. These results are consistent with those of previous studies [41,50]. The two components identified by the ODCS recognize the dimensions measured, social interactions, as well as language and mass media use, echoing the findings of Verbeke and Poquiviqui Lopez [39].

The Italian sample seems to be slightly neophobic considering that the mean FNS index value is slightly higher than the midpoint of the scale. When we compare this result to the most recent FNS analysis of the Italian context, the samples analyzed by Monteleone [13] and Proserpio [42] seem to be less neophobic than ours and find a midpoint lower than the mean value. Although scales adopting different formats are difficult to compare, several studies suggest that a scale with more response options might produce slightly lower scores [51]. In our study, the 1–10 scale used produced higher scores, which may be attributable to the different sampling and data collection methods applied in the analyzed studies. The data presented in this work were collected from online questionnaires of panels of Italian consumers while in the two studies listed above, participants were recruited on a voluntary basis and completed the questionnaire during experimental sessions.

At the international level, samples showing lower levels of neophobia have been found in other studies [14,16,32,33] while a mean value higher than the midpoint of the scale used has been reported for Lebanese students [50]. A comparison of FNS mean scores of various countries could prove useful in providing an overview of food neophobia levels worldwide. However, generalizations and statistical comparisons are difficult to apply because the scale is sensitive to contexts, as highlighted by previous studies [49].

The mean value of the ODCS index is instead higher than the midpoint value of the scale, suggesting a quite open sample. In analyzing the sociodemographic characteristics, we found that the description of the neophobic consumer appears to differ substantially from that of the consumer with an attitude of openness. The definition of the characteristics of consumers in relation to unfamiliar foods and different cultures deserves special attention for two main reasons. First, it fosters a comprehension of a growing phenomenon. That is, the increasing prevalence of ethnic food not only reflects the proliferation of social change but also has important implications for the food market. Second, the group of neophobic consumers exhibiting less openness to different cultures might have a less varied diet (e.g., Arvola et al. [18] and Schickenberg et al. [23]). The tendency to avoid foods that are different from those usually consumed reduces one's willingness to try healthy alternatives to known foods [23]. This tendency also reduces one's willingness to eat certain basic foods, such as vegetable salads and fish [52]. A diet that includes as many different foods as possible is essential to health because it ensures nutritional quality and prevents chemical accumulation due to constant exposure to the same substances [53]. The neophobic trait is recognized as a barrier to diet modification [35] and has a negative influence on diet quality [54] while the willingness to accept different food alternatives can be an indicator of the ability to make positive changes in eating habits.

The results of this study show that men are more neophobic than women. These findings are consistent with other studies [13,32,52]. However, the effect of gender on neophobia remains less clear and varies widely across studies on different regions [31]. According to the data presented here, gender does not influence openness to different cultures. Instead, age seems to play an important role. The results of this study show that levels of food neophobia increase with age, which has already been proven by other studies [13,31–33,52]. Openness to different cultures instead declines with age and is characterized as an attitude held by younger age groups. Other studies [52] have highlighted that these results may seem counterintuitive given that with age, an individual should experience more exposure to a broader variety of foods and therefore develop more knowledge of different foods. These factors can promote the acceptance and willingness to try different alternatives. However, such acceptance and willingness could be attributed to a more exploratory and playful attitude even towards food, which can characterize young people, and which can promote curiosity and contact with new foods. Several studies of the Italian context have emphasized that it is precisely young people who adhere to food styles that differ from those of the Mediterranean diet [55] and who are more open to the consumption of ethnic food [56]. These attitudes of young people are probably favored by socialization due to the incremental likelihood of one coming into contact with different cultures relative to the past. In the Italian context, which is characterized by a culinary tradition in which food changes occur slowly, another highly interesting aspect concerns the importance of relationships to the acceptance of a new food. The majority of those reporting consuming ethnic food in Italy reported that they had come into contact with ethnic cuisine through relatives and friends. Italy has a strong gastronomic tradition, and the idea of food is linked to the idea of social relations and sharing, not only among Italians. A study recently conducted in Italy has highlighted how food appears as an element of contact and sharing between natives and migrants. Approximately two out of five immigrants interviewed stated that they have cooked their traditional dishes and have taught their recipes to Italian friends and acquaintances [9]. The social and convivial importance of food and eating practices, which traditionally characterize Italy [2], is recognizable also in Italian consumers' relationship with ethnic food. Furthermore, the presence of people of different origins and traditions than the Italian ones becomes an opportunity for culinary knowledge and experimentation.

Education, occupation, and income are considered variables that define the socioeconomic status of a person and that may affect opportunities to be exposed to different foods and cultures [27]. The impact of these variables on neophobia has revealed by other studies, whose results are confirmed by the findings of this study: Consumers who are more neophobic are less educated [31,32,52], of lower socioeconomic status [31,52], and, according to the data presented here, are retired. Conversely, consumers exhibiting an attitude of openness towards different cultures are highly educated and employed. Financial status does not emerge as a significant differentiating variable.

In addition, the place of residence (urban vs. rural) was tested as a variable that could affect exposure to new products and to a multicultural environment. This hypothesis has been confirmed by other studies [27,31,32]. However, in this study, being an inhabitant of a large or small city or of a specific area of Italy was not found to affect food neophobia. This result could be related to unique features of the Italian Peninsula that, given its geographic position, is characterized by migratory flows throughout. Otherwise, an openness to different cultures seems to characterize residents of southern

Italy and of the islands and of medium-sized cities (100,000–250,000 residents). The relationship between food neophobia, openness to different cultures, and urban living remains an aspect that deserves further study.

The variable "having children" has a significant impact on both food neophobia and openness to different cultures. The most food neophobic individuals declared that they have children while those with more open attitudes were childless. This variable was analyzed because being a parent and the presence of children in the family could result in a more protective attitude and more mistrust of novelty [29,57].

Recent studies have found that the frequency with which ethnic food is consumed is significantly correlated with levels of food neophobia [39,50] and with degrees of openness to other cultures [39]. Our analysis of this aspect in the Italian context presents similar results. Those reporting never having consumed ethnic food in Italy presented a higher FNS index and a lower ODCS index than those declaring that they had consumed such foods. The results of this study confirm the relationship between food neophobia and openness to different cultures as highlighted by other research [14,39].

This study emphasizes a relationship between the psychological trait of neophobia and attitudes towards different cultures, confirming food's symbolic and cultural value. The studied aspects are immediately evident for ethnic food. These measures have become a crucial indicator of peoples' levels of willingness to accept elements of novelty in an increasingly globalized and multicultural society. This study analyzed these aspects across a nationwide sample of consumers in Italy. On the one hand, this paper extends the existing literature by providing additional empirical evidence for the Italian context, which has rarely been studied from this point of view. On the other hand, we present an apparently counterintuitive result demonstrating a tendency for young people to be less neophobic and more open to different cultures. This tendency must be studied in more depth in consideration of further social and societal variables. In fact, even if the rooted culinary Italian tradition may seem to be a deterrent to openness to new foods, the very importance attributed to food can serve as an element that encourages sociality, which seemed to emerge from this work.

The acceptance or rejection of a new food involves a complex psychological mechanism that is influenced not only by personal traits but also by specific behaviors and cultural aspects. While the importance of focusing on personality traits and on food neophobia in particular has been demonstrated in several papers, a comprehensive study of these aspects is required to develop a broader account of the phenomenon in Italy as well as to compare it across different contexts. Contact with different cultures through other people, the mass media, travel, and language studies can affect openness to and acceptance of novelty and diversity [40]. The fact that these aspects were not measured in our survey may represent a limitation of the study. Future research should therefore investigate in more depth the actual impact of these aspects in modifying consumers' attitudes.

Another limitation of the study is due to the representativeness of the sample. As described in the method section, only gender and geographical area were used in the quota sampling. However the age of the sample was also consistent with that observed in the Italian population over 18 years old. Nevertheless, other sociodemographic variables (i.e., the size of the city of residence, the educational qualification, etc.) that would have made it possible to have a sample more closely related to the Italian population were not considered in the quota sampling,

5. Conclusions

This study investigated the relation between food neophobia and openness to different cultures and the consumption of ethnic foods together with sociodemographic variables. The main results show that participants with higher levels of food neophobia do not consume ethnic food while those exhibiting higher levels of openness to different cultures consume it. Moreover, neophobic participants tend to be less open to different cultures. Some sociodemographic variables associated with food neophobia (i.e., gender, age, educational qualifications, the presence of children, occupation, and how well the interviewee's income meets his or her financial needs) and with an openness to different cultures (i.e., age, location, size of the city of residence, the presence of children, and educational qualifications) were identified. The results of this study may prove useful for those concerned with nutrition as a means to protect public health and who are tasked with designing interventions in nutritional education and communication strategies that address the traits of consumer groups who are reluctant to adopt new proposals. Considering the relation between familiarity with food and a food's place of origin for its acceptance [52] as well as the importance of cultural and social identification [58], communication activities can be crucial in fostering an awareness of different foods and in promoting a varied and diversified diet.

Author Contributions: Conceptualization, G.M., B.T., S.C. and L.R.; Data curation, A.P.; Formal analysis, A.P.; Funding acquisition, L.R.; Methodology, G.M., A.P., S.C. and L.R.; Project administration, G.M. and S.C.; Supervision, L.R.; Writing—original draft, G.M. and A.P.; Writing—review and editing, G.M., A.P., V.R., B.T., S.C. and L.R. All authors have read and agreed to the published version of the manuscript.

Funding: This study was funded by the Italian Ministry of Health as part of the RC IZSVe 17/2012, research project promoted by the Istituto Zooprofilattico Sperimentale delle Venezie (www.izsvenezie.it).

Acknowledgments: The authors would like to thank Demetra opinioni.net for administering and disseminating the online questionnaire and the Italian consumers who participated in the survey.

Conflicts of Interest: The authors have no conflicts of interest to declare. The funders had no role in the design of the study; in the collection, analysis, or interpretation of data; in the writing of the manuscript; or in the decision made to publish the results.

References

1. Fonte, M. Food systems, consumption models and risk perception in late modernity. *Int. J. Sociol. Agric. Food* **2002**, *10*, 13–21.
2. Monteleone, E.; Dinnella, C. Italian meals. In *Meals in Science and Practice*; Meiselman, H.L., Ed.; Woodhead Publishing Limited: Cambridge, UK, 2009; pp. 359–376.
3. Fondazione Censis; Coldiretti. Primo Rapporto Sulle Abitudini Alimentari Degli Italiani. 2010. Available online: http://www.largoconsumo.info/102011/DOCAbitudinialimentaricensiscoldiretti-1011.pdf (accessed on 16 June 2011).
4. Belletti, G.; Marescotti, A. Le nuove tendenze dei consumi alimentari. In *I Prodotti Agroalimentari Di Qualità: Organizzazione Del Sistema Delle Imprese*; Berni, P., Begalli, D., Eds.; Il Mulino: Bologna, Italy, 1996; pp. 133–152.
5. Cersosimo, D. *I Consumi Alimentari. Evoluzione Strutturale, Nuove Tendenze, Risposte Alla Crisi*; Gruppo 2013; Ed. Tellus: Rome, Italy, 2011; Available online: http://www.progettareineuropa.com/wp-content/uploads/2016/07/I-consumi-alimentari.pdf (accessed on 2 November 2017).
6. Sbraga, L.; Erba, G.R. La Crisi Nel Piatto: Come Cambiano i Consumi Degli Italiani. 2012. Available online: http://www.fipe.it/files/ricerche/2012/25-02-12_la_crisi_nel_piatto.pdf (accessed on 16 August 2019).
7. Battaglini, E. *Il Gusto Riflessivo. Verso Una Sociologia Della Produzione e Del Consumo Alimentare*; Bonanno Ed: Roma, Italy, 2007; pp. 1–334.
8. Poulain, J.-P. *Alimentazione, Cultura e Società*; Il Mulino: Bologna, Italy, 2008; pp. 1–232.
9. Fondazione Censis. Ricette Italiane Di Integrazione. Abitudini Alimentari Ed Avventure Imprenditoriali Di Italiani e Migranti. 2015. Available online: http://www.integrazionemigranti.gov.it/Documenti-e-ricerche/Rapporto_finale_CENSIS.pdf (accessed on 11 May 2016).
10. Russo, A. Rapporto Coop. 2015. Available online: http://www.italiani.coop/rapporto-coop-2015-consumi-e-distribuzione/ (accessed on 11 May 2016).
11. Ambrosini, M. Il cibo che nutre l'incontro. Immigrazione, innovazione, ricambio nel settore alimentare. In *XXIV Rapporto Immigrazione 2014*; Ufficio Ricerca e Documentazione della Fondazione Migrantes, dell'Ufficio Immigrazione di Caritas Italiana, Eds.; Tau Editrice Srl: Perugia, Italy, 2014; pp. 258–274.
12. Pliner, P.; Salvy, S. Food neophobia in humans. In *The Psychology of Food Choice*; Shepherd, R., Raats, M., Eds.; Cabi: Oxfordshire, UK, 2006; pp. 75–92.
13. Monteleone, E.; Spinelli, S.; Dinnella, C.; Endrizzi, I.; Laureati, M.; Pagliarini, E.; Sinesio, F.; Gasperi, F.; Torri, L.; Aprea, E.; et al. Exploring influences on food choice in a large population sample: The Italian Taste project. *Food Qual. Prefer.* **2017**, *59*, 123–140. [CrossRef]

14. Choe, J.Y.; Cho, M.S. Food neophobia and willingness to try non-traditional foods for Koreans. *Food Qual. Prefer.* **2011**, *22*, 671–677. [CrossRef]
15. D'Antuono, F.L.; Bignami, C. Perception of typical Ukrainian foods among an Italian population. *Food Qual. Prefer.* **2012**, *25*, 1–8. [CrossRef]
16. Pliner, P.; Hobden, K. Development of a Scale to Measure the Trait of Food Neophobia in Humans. *Appetite* **1992**, *19*, 105–120. [CrossRef]
17. Damsbo-Svendsen, M.; Frøst, M.B.; Olsen, A. A review of instruments developed to measure food neophobia. *Appetite* **2017**, *113*, 358–367. [CrossRef] [PubMed]
18. Arvola, A.; Lähteenmäki, L.; Tuorila, H. Predicting the intent to purchase unfamiliar and familiar cheeses: The effects of attitudes, expected liking and food neophobia. *Appetite* **1999**, *32*, 113–126. [CrossRef] [PubMed]
19. Eertmans, A.; Victoir, A.; Vansant, G.; Van den Bergh, O. Food-related personality traits, food choice motives and food intake: Mediator and moderator relationships. *Food Qual. Prefer.* **2005**, *16*, 714–726. [CrossRef]
20. Koivisto, U.K.; Sjödén, P.O. Food and general neophobia in Swedish families: Parent-child comparisons and relationships with serving specific foods. *Appetite* **1996**, *26*, 107–118. [CrossRef]
21. MacNicol, S.A.M.; Murray, S.M.; Austin, E.J. Relationships between personality, attitudes and dietary behaviour in a group of Scottish adolescents. *Personal. Individ. Differ.* **2003**, *35*, 1753–1764. [CrossRef]
22. Mustonen, S.; Oerlemans, P.; Tuorila, H. Familiarity with and affective responses to foods in 8-11-year-old children. The role of food neophobia and parental education. *Appetite* **2012**, *58*, 777–780. [CrossRef] [PubMed]
23. Schickenberg, B.; van Assema, P.; Brug, J.; de Vries, N.K. Are the Dutch acquainted with and willing to try healthful food products? The role of food neophobia. *Public Health Nutr.* **2008**, *11*, 493–500. [CrossRef] [PubMed]
24. Falciglia, G.A.; Couch, S.C.; Gribble, L.S.; Pabst, S.M.; Frank, R. Food neophobia in childhood affects dietary variety. *J. Am. Diet. Assoc.* **2000**, *100*, 1474–1481. [CrossRef]
25. Dovey, T.M.; Staples, P.A.; Gibson, E.L.; Halford, J.C.G. Food neophobia and "picky/fussy" eating in children: A review. *Appetite* **2008**, *50*, 181–193. [CrossRef] [PubMed]
26. Knaapila, A.J.; Sandell, M.A.; Vaarno, J.; Hoppu, U.; Puolimatka, T.; Kaljonen, A.; Lagström, H. Food neophobia associates with lower dietary quality and higher BMI in Finnish adults. *Public Health Nutr.* **2015**, *18*, 2161–2171. [CrossRef]
27. Flight, I.; Leppard, P.; Cox, D.N. Food neophobia and associations with cultural diversity and socio-economic status amongst rural and urban Australian adolescents. *Appetite* **2003**, *41*, 51–59. [CrossRef]
28. Mascarello, G.; Pinto, A.; Parise, N.; Crovato, S.; Ravarotto, L. The perception of food quality. Profiling Italian consumers. *Appetite* **2015**, *89*, 175–182. [CrossRef]
29. Verbeke, W.; Vackier, I. Individual determinants of fish consumption: Application of the theory of planned behaviour. *Appetite* **2005**, *44*, 67–82. [CrossRef]
30. Pliner, P.; Pelchat, M.L.; Grabski, M. Reduction of Food Neophobia in humans by exposure to novel foods. *Appetite* **1993**, *20*, 111–123. [CrossRef] [PubMed]
31. Meiselman, H.L.; King, S.C.; Gillette, M. The demographics of neophobia in a large commercial US sample. *Food Qual. Prefer.* **2010**, *21*, 893–897. [CrossRef]
32. Tuorila, H.; Lähteenmäki, L.; Pohjalainen, L.; Lotti, L. Food neophobia among the Finns and related responses to familiar and unfamiliar foods. *Food Qual. Prefer.* **2001**, *12*, 29–37. [CrossRef]
33. Fernández-Ruiz, V.; Claret, A.; Chaya, C. Testing a Spanish-version of the Food Neophobia Scale. *Food Qual. Prefer.* **2013**, *28*, 222–225. [CrossRef]
34. Henriques, A.S.; King, S.C.; Meiselman, H.L. Consumer segmentation based on food neophobia and its application to product development. *Food Qual. Prefer.* **2009**, *20*, 83–91. [CrossRef]
35. Jaeger, S.R.; Rasmussen, M.A.; Prescott, J. Relationships between food neophobia and food intake and preferences: Findings from a sample of New Zealand adults. *Appetite* **2017**, *116*, 410–422. [CrossRef] [PubMed]
36. Soucier, V.D.; Doma, K.M.; Farrell, E.L.; Leith-Bailey, E.R.; Duncan, A.M. An examination of food neophobia in older adults. *Food Qual. Prefer.* **2019**, *72*, 143–146. [CrossRef]
37. Tan, H.S.G.; Fischer, A.R.H.; Tinchan, P.; Stieger, M.; Steenbekkers, L.P.A.; van Trijp, H.C.M. Insects as food: Exploring cultural exposure and individual experience as determinants of acceptance. *Food Qual. Prefer.* **2015**, *42*, 78–89. [CrossRef]

38. Van den Heuvel, E.; Newbury, A.; Appleton, K.M. The psychology of nutrition with advancing age: Focus on food neophobia. *Nutrients* **2019**, *11*, 151. [CrossRef]
39. Verbeke, W.; Poquiviqui López, G. Ethnic food attitudes and behaviour among Belgians and Hispanics living in Belgium. *Br. Food J.* **2005**, *107*, 823–840. [CrossRef]
40. Laroche, M.; Kim, C.; Tomiuk, M.A. Italian ethnic identity and its relative impact on the consumption of convenience and traditional foods. *Br. Food J.* **1999**, *101*, 201–228. [CrossRef]
41. Dematté, M.L.; Endrizzi, I.; Biasioli, F.; Corollaro, M.L.; Pojer, N.; Zampini, M.; Aprea, E.; Gasperi, F. Food neophobia and its relation with olfactory ability in common odour identification. *Appetite* **2013**, *68*, 112–117. [CrossRef]
42. Proserpio, C.; Laureati, M.; Bertoli, S.; Battezzati, A.; Pagliarini, E. Determinants of obesity in Italian adults: The role of taste sensitivity, food liking, and food neophobia. *Chem. Senses* **2016**, *41*, 169–176. [CrossRef]
43. Proserpio, C.; Laureati, M.; Invitti, C.; Pagliarini, E. Reduced taste responsiveness and increased food neophobia characterize obese adults. *Food Qual. Prefer.* **2018**, *63*, 73–79. [CrossRef]
44. Laureati, M.; Spinelli, S.; Monteleone, E.; Dinnella, C.; Prescott, J.; Cattaneo, C.; Proserpio, C.; De Toffoli, A.; Gasperi, F.; Endrizzi, I.; et al. Associations between food neophobia and responsiveness to "warning" chemosensory sensations in food products in a large population sample. *Food Qual. Prefer.* **2018**, *68*, 113–124. [CrossRef]
45. Laureati, M.; Bergamaschi, V.; Pagliarini, E. Assessing childhood food neophobia: Validation of a scale in Italian primary school children. *Food Qual. Prefer.* **2015**, *40*, 8–15. [CrossRef]
46. Adams, K.; Brace, I. *An Introduction to Market & Social Research: Planning & Using Research Tools & Techniques*; Kogan Page Ltd.: London, UK, 2006.
47. Mascarello, G.; Pinto, A.; Marcolin, S.; Crovato, S.; Ravarotto, L. Ethnic food consumption: Habits and risk perception in Italy. *J. Food Saf.* **2017**, *37*, 1–9. [CrossRef]
48. Marletta, L.; Turrini, A.; Camilli, E.; Spadoni, F.; Carnovale, E.; Scardella, P.; Piombo, L.; Spada, R. Alimenti etnici, un fenomeno in espansione in Europa: Studio in un Progetto europeo. *Riv. Sci. dell'Aliment.* **2006**, *35*, 9–15.
49. Ritchey, P.N.; Frank, R.A.; Hursti, U.K.; Tuorila, H. Validation and cross-national comparison of the food neophobia scale (FNS) using confirmatory factor analysis. *Appetite* **2003**, *40*, 163–173. [CrossRef]
50. Olabi, A.; Najm, N.E.O.; Baghdadi, O.K.; Morton, J.M. Food neophobia levels of Lebanese and American college students. *Food Qual. Prefer.* **2009**, *20*, 353–362. [CrossRef]
51. Dawes, J. Do data characteristics change according to the number of scale points used? An experiment using 5-point, 7-point and 10-point scales. *Int. J. Mark. Res.* **2008**, *50*, 61–77. [CrossRef]
52. Siegrist, M.; Hartmann, C.; Keller, C. Antecedents of food neophobia and its association with eating behavior and food choices. *Food Qual. Prefer.* **2013**, *30*, 293–298. [CrossRef]
53. Eskola, M.; Elliott, C.T.; Hajšlová, J.; Steiner, D.; Krska, R. Towards a dietary-exposome assessment of chemicals in food: An update on the chronic health risks for the European consumer. *Crit. Rev. Food Sci. Nutr.* **2019**, 1–22. [CrossRef] [PubMed]
54. Ucar, E.M.; Kizil, M. Effect of food neophobia on diet quality. *Clin. Nutr.* **2018**, *37*, S120. [CrossRef]
55. Mari, S.; Capozza, D.; Falvo, R.; Hichy, Z. Dieta mediterranea versus dieta Tradizionale: La scelta di uno stile alimentare. *Ric. Psicol.* **2007**, *3*, 35–66.
56. Cavazza, N.; Fischler, C. Rappresentazioni del rapporto fra alimentazione e salute in diverse fasi della vita: Norme e funzioni di un cibo che fa bene. *Psicol. Della Salut.* **2003**, *2*, 49–62.
57. Verbeke, W.; Ward, R.W.; Viaene, J. Probit analysis of fresh meat consumption in Belgium: Exploring BSE and television communication impact. *Agribusiness* **2000**, *16*, 215–234. [CrossRef]
58. Barrena, R.; Sánchez, M. Neophobia, personal consumer values and novel food acceptance. *Food Qual. Prefer.* **2013**, *27*, 72–84. [CrossRef]

© 2020 by the authors. Licensee MDPI, Basel, Switzerland. This article is an open access article distributed under the terms and conditions of the Creative Commons Attribution (CC BY) license (http://creativecommons.org/licenses/by/4.0/).

Article

An Analysis of Public Opinions Regarding Take-Away Food Safety: A 2015–2018 Case Study on Sina Weibo

Cen Song [1], Chunyu Guo [1], Kyle Hunt [2] and Jun Zhuang [2,*]

[1] School of Economics and Management, China University of Petroleum, Beijing 102249, China; songcen22@126.com (C.S.); 13121188206@163.com (C.G.)
[2] Department of Industrial and System Engineering, University at Buffalo, Buffalo, NY 14260, USA; kylehunt@buffalo.edu
* Correspondence: jzhuang@buffalo.edu

Received: 1 April 2020; Accepted: 13 April 2020; Published: 18 April 2020

Abstract: Take-away food (also referred to as "take-out" food in different regions of the world) is a very convenient and popular dining choice for millions of people. In this article, we collect online textual data regarding "take-away food safety" from Sina Weibo between 2015 and 2018 using the Octopus Collector. After the posts from Sina Weibo were preprocessed, users' emotions and opinions were analyzed using natural language processing. To our knowledge, little work has studied public opinions regarding take-away food safety. This paper fills this gap by using latent Dirichlet allocation (LDA) and *k*-means to extract and cluster topics from the posts, allowing for the users' emotions and related opinions to be mined and analyzed. The results of this research are as follows: (1) data analysis showed that the degree of topics have increased over the years, and there are a variety of topics about take-away food safety; (2) emotional analysis showed that 93.8% of the posts were positive; and (3) topic analysis showed that the topic of public discussion is diverse and rich. Our analysis of public opinion on take-away food safety generates insights for government and industry stakeholders to promote the healthy and vigorous development of the food industry.

Keywords: food safety; take-away food; online public opinion; emotional analysis; topic analysis; natural language processing

1. Introduction

Food safety issues, such as melamine-contaminated milk powder, heavy metal-contaminated foods, additives which can lead to food poisoning, unhealthy preservatives, and fake foods, pose a great threat to public health [1]. Food scandals have been widely reported and have resulted in social influences [2]. Food safety has become an increasingly important concern in the domestic food market in China over the years, where there is a serious discredit of the food safety systems and official control. Increasing incidents related to food safety have caused consumers to pay more attention to the related quality issues. To some extent, it has led to an overall discredit of the Chinese food market [3].

With an increased consumer demand for convenient services, which results from a more mobile and fast-paced world, many catering industries are beginning to provide take-away food catering services (also referred to as food delivery in some parts of the world). Take-away is very popular among young consumers, such as students and office workers, as it can meet their time-sensitive dining demands. With the rapid development of Internet commerce, the take-away food catering industry is exploding in both consumer demand and revenue, causing great concerns for food safety. Furthermore, various problems with the take-away industry have introduced widespread public concern, such as the case when China Central Television (CCTV) exposed the ordering chaos of Ele.me in 2016 [4].

The issue of food safety supervision in the take-away food industry has received increasing attention. Responding to the frequent occurrence of such phenomena, government agencies have issued laws and regulations for the online food industry (including take-away food) to strengthen the measures that are needed to ensure food safety.

At present, the chaos in the take-away catering industry has subsided. However, the food safety issue has not been fundamentally rectified, including problems associated with the preparation process and sanitary conditions surrounding take-away foods. Whenever an incident occurs, it leads to a series of hot discussions on online platforms such as Sina Weibo. The discussions on the safety of take-away foods are also multi-faceted, with many people focusing on hygiene and operational practices. For these complicated discussions, traditional data analysis is not enough to study the public's emotional opinions. To address this, this paper uses an automated learning process to analyze massive online content. The methodologies used throughout this paper are presented in Figure 1.

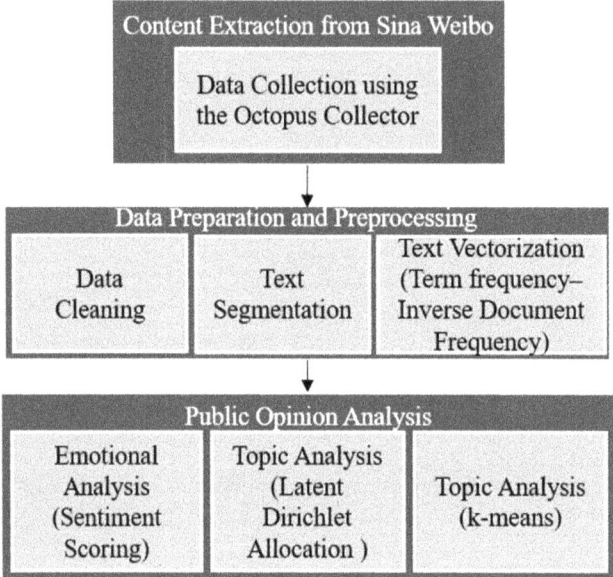

Figure 1. The research framework followed throughout this study.

Previous food safety research has focused on food suppliers [5,6], with very little emphasis on the consumer side. Research on the consumers can be deemed critical to the overall knowledge on food safety in the take-away industry, as consumers drive the demand and are the ultimate decision makers. With a lot of information consumption taking place in the online environment, it can be difficult for consumers to access information related to food processing and kitchen environments. Consumers express their related opinions and emotions on social platforms, such as Weibo.

To the best of our knowledge, research on the evolution of online public opinions relating to the safety of take-away foods is limited. The purpose of this paper is to study the microblogging remarks related to the safety of take-away foods, identify topics of concern, and extract the topic information contained in large amounts of textual data. A dictionary-based sentiment analysis method is used, and emotional trends and tendencies are studied. A public opinion analysis can help government and industry stakeholders to better understand the current situation and provide advice for better food safety regulation in the future.

2. Literature Review

2.1. Take-Away Food Research

In recent years, the selling of contaminated lunch boxes has frequently occurred, and in general, food safety issues on take-away deliveries are causing global concern. There is no systematic investigation or analysis on the pollution sources, pollution paths, and pollution laws of "secondary pollution" in the food distribution process. From the perspective of both suppliers and consumers, Han et al. [7] gave some suggestions for improving the storage quality of take-away foods, by analyzing the packaging materials for take-away, the various take-out boxes used for distribution, the health status of the distributors, the degree of contact with food, and the factors of delivery time. Yuan and Li [8] proposed an online early warning strategy for food and drug safety incidents from the perspective of improving early warning laws and organizational systems, establishing an online classification monitoring system for food and drug safety incidents, an early warning grading mechanism, and an early warning information release platform.

Scholars have conducted relevant research on the new take-away food industry. Maguire et al. [9] pointed out that take-away food is facing several challenges, such as limited kitchen space, shared cooking equipment, and the short time to complete the orders. Cobb et al. [10] found that between 2014 and 2017, the total number of take-away stores increased by 10% to nearly 58,000, while the proportion of food stores in take-away stores increased by 27%. Adams et al. [11] found through a survey of national diet and nutrition in the UK that 21% of adults and children eat take-away food at home at least once a week, and men eat take-away 5.5% more than women. Keeble et al. [12] showed that the increase in the number of take-away food stores has raised concerns about people's diet and obesity and proposed to slow down the spread of new stores through an urban planning approach. Take-away food and fast-food consumption continue to grow, which can play an important role in the development and spread of many diseases. Jaworowska et al. [13] examined the nutritional characteristics of take-away food and fast food and reported the link between take-away foods and health. Kirk et al. [14] pointed out that the acquisition and use of take-away foods may be an important determinant of subsequent unhealthy eating behaviors and obesity.

The safety of take-away foods is a social issue that is closely related to people's lives. Mahon et al. [15] used the planned behavior theory (TPB) to study the attitudes, subjective norms, perceptual control, and habits of British people on ready-to-eat food and take-away food. The results showed that attitude is the most important predictor of food intentions. Further, subjective norms had no effect on take-away foods, and habits were much more important than behavioral intentions. Turrell et al. [16] examined the relationship between individual socio-economic status, regional disadvantages, environmental characteristics of take-away foods, and consumption of take-away foods. It was shown that higher-income and more educated families were more likely to buy take-away food. Timperio et al. [17] discussed the relationship between the availability of a child-supplied take-away store and a consumer take-away store. Miura and Turrell [18] explained the role of take-away food consumption in socio-economic status and body mass index.

2.2. Public Opinion Research

Internet public opinion refers to the sum of various emotions, attitudes, and opinions held by netizens in public affairs, especially on hot and trending topics. As a typical interdisciplinary subject, online public opinion research has become the focus of experts in various fields. Savigny [19] showed that in contemporary society, public opinion is usually spread by the mass media. Sobkowicz et al. [20] mined and modeled social media online opinions, where a framework based on social media content analysis and social physics system modeling was proposed for the question of how network opinions are generated, disseminated, and gained. Wang and Zhuang [21] analyzed the content of Hurricane Sandy on Twitter and explored the dissemination of relevant crisis information by the official agencies and the public. Gu et al. [22] proposed that with the development of computer science and technology, the Internet has gradually entered all aspects of society. The popularity of various social software and the development of online media have greatly increased the speed of information transmission and have formed a network of public opinion events. Li et al. [23] designed an adaptive food safety Internet hotspot identification and collection method, that effectively realized the discovery and tracking of public opinions related to food safety. AlSumait et al. [24] introduced an online topic model, that can automatically capture the thematic patterns and identify emerging topics in online content and the related changes over time. The dynamic nature of the proposed method also provides an effective means of tracking topics over time and detecting emerging topics in real time. Tan et al. [25] argued that food safety incidents are typical public safety events and proposed a method to obtain the opinions of netizens from online posts to model food safety incidents.

3. Data Collection and Preprocessing of Sina Weibo Posts

3.1. Data Collection

This paper uses Octopus Collector to obtain a large dataset about take-away food safety from the Sina Weibo platform between 1 January 2015 and 31 December 2018 [26]. We chose this timeline as a result of the growing popularity of take-away food throughout the recent years, and also the many new food safety laws and guidelines that were issued during this period in China (e.g., Food Safety Law (2015) and Food Safety Supervision and Management Measures for Internet Catering Services (2017)). The data in this study contained Chinese postings published in Sina Weibo, and we directly translated the data into English (i.e., no software was used or needed). The keywords used to extract the Weibo posts include "take-away food", "food safety", and "food delivery". During data processing and cleaning, many posts were deleted due to lack of relevance. Some of these posts consisted of advertisements, while other posts were not related to the topic of this research and were simply noise from the data collection. Some data obtained consisted of pictures and videos, and therefore their content was not appropriate for textual analysis. Therefore, after cleaning the data using these criteria, we were left with a total of 8452 posts that were used for our analysis.

3.2. Data Preprocessing

3.2.1. Text Segmentation

Text segmentation refers to dividing a complete and continuous sentence into a set of individual words and punctuation marks, and is a common method used in natural language processing (NLP). In this paper, a word segmentation algorithm based on string matching, also known as a dictionary-based word segmentation algorithm, was used. The algorithm matches text content with the established dictionary according to certain rules in order to perform word segmentation. For example, some original content from the collected Weibo data could be "#Ele.me is unhygienic to eat#." After text segmentation we get '#', 'E', 'le', 'me', 'is', 'un', 'hygienic', 'to', 'eat', '#'. Note that the website name 'Ele.me' would be incorrectly divided into three separate parts. Therefore, we built a customized dictionary and added customized words such as 'Ele.me'. By using this customized dictionary, the phrase 'Ele.me' was treated as a complete and single word for further processing. Table 1 provides a subset of elements that were added to the customized dictionary. Based on the customized dictionary, we do not segment "food safety" as two words due to common sense; this was similar for other words and phrases.

3.2.2. Vectorization of Words

Term frequency–Inverse Document Frequency (TF-IDF), was used to measure the representativeness of words considering the times that the word appeared in a post, and the times it appeared in the corpus of all combined posts. In this paper, we used TF-IDF to construct the word vector matrix. After using TF-IDF and standardizing it, we got a sparse space vector (TF-IDF vector).

We then used the word feature vectors of each text to facilitate the subsequent text classification and clustering analyses.

Table 1. Examples of elements in the user-defined dictionary.

Customized Dictionary	Explanation
Ele.me	A professional online ordering platform in China
McDonald	The world's largest fast food chain
Food and Drug Administration	Supervise and manage food and drugs in China
315	World Consumer Rights Day
Haidilao	A famous hot pot restaurant
Meituan	Chinese local merchant e-commerce marketplace

3.3. Word Frequency Statistics

After word segmentation of all Weibo content about take-away food safety, word frequency statistics were obtained. The frequency of all words was calculated, and the top 10 words are shown in Table 2.

Table 2. The top 10 high-frequency words.

Hot Word	Frequency	Hot Word	Frequency
Take-away	26,624	Food	8920
Food safety	15,014	Order	6837
Internet	10,688	Issue	5807
Platform	9709	Meituan	5193
Catering	9099	Service	4598

Table 2 shows that the frequency of words and phrases such as take-away, food safety, Meituan, issue, catering, and other words were high. It becomes clear that consumers in the collected dataset had high interests surrounding the broad topic of take-away food safety.

4. Analysis of Online Public Opinion

4.1. Dictionary-Based Emotional Analysis of Text

4.1.1. Emotional Analysis Based on Emotional Dictionary

The emotional dictionary, Boson NLP, is based on Weibo, news, forums, and other data sources, and is used to analyze and process textual data that collected from Weibo. The NLP processing is done in Chinese and later translated into English. The Boson NLP emotion dictionary is an emotion polarity dictionary constructed automatically from millions of emotion annotation data, which includes 114,767 words in total. There are many non-emotional words in this emotional dictionary, therefore the actual number of effective emotional words is less than 114,767.

Boson NLP provides a Chinese natural language analysis cloud service that is simple to use, has powerful functionality, and reliable performance. As annotations include microblog data, the dictionary includes many network terms and informal abbreviations, and has a high coverage of non-standard text. The emotion dictionary can be used to build a social media emotion analysis engine, negative content discovery, and other applications. Unstructured data analysis can reveal the trends and correlations hidden in text, and provide strong support for business decision-making, research industry trends, and hot content analysis.

In addition, a word list of negative words (such as nothing, little, few) and a list of adverbs of degree (such as fairly, pretty, rather) are introduced into the processing and are assigned values. We calculate the emotional score of the whole text, instead of defining positive or negative by a single word. The word list of negative words and a list of adverbs of degree are introduced into the processing, and the emotional scores of the posts are obtained. If the score of a post is greater than 0, it is classified as a post with positive emotion, otherwise it is classified as a post with negative emotion. For example, a word segmentation including "Food", "Food safety", "Magic formula", "Take-away", "APP", "Qualification", "Be questioned", and "0" has an emotional score of 1.72, which means the words show positive emotion.

After emotional classification of all 8452 Weibo posts, the texts with positive emotional value were marked as 1, and the texts with negative emotional value were marked as 0. According to the statistics, there were 7930 emotionally positive posts, accounting for 93.8% of the collected data, while 522 of the posts showed negative emotion. We found that the public's comments on online take-away food safety were generally positive.

4.1.2. Emotional Time Series Analysis

Figure 2 compares the trends of discussions which have negative and positive emotions. We merge data across four months to draw each point. During these four years, the trends of positive and negative discussions on take-away food safety are similar, although the number of positive posts about food safety are far higher than the number of negative posts.

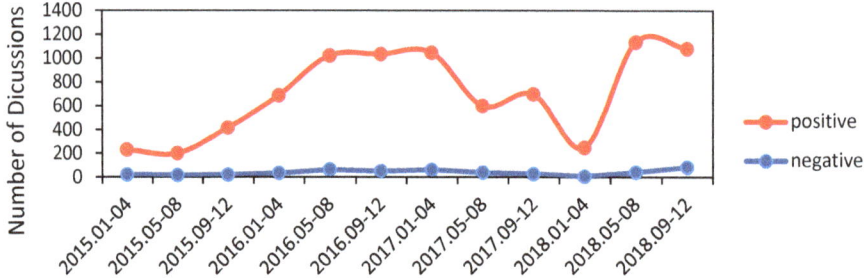

Figure 2. Overall emotional time series.

The number of positive discussions over time has shown an upward trend between January 2015 and May 2016 and between January 2018 and May 2018. It remained at a high level between May 2016 and January 2017 and between May 2018 and September 2018. While between January 2017 and January 2018, the number of positive discussions showed a downward trend. This observation may be due to the times when the FDA (Food and Drug Administration) interviewed the regional agents of Meituan and Ele.me in December 2016 and CCTV exposed black take-away workshops in March 2017. We also observe that the number of negative discussions over time had very little variation.

Table 3 summarizes some of the representative news events in the take-away catering industry between 2015 and 2018. The development of the take-away industry has always been accompanied by governance and rectification, from the new Food Safety Law in 2015, to the "Food Safety Supervision and Management Measures for Internet Catering Services," which was researched and developed by the State Food and Drug Administration in 2017. These laws have made the take-away industry more transparent and have given the public confidence in the safety of take-away food. In the comparative analysis, most of the public's emotions were positive.

Table 3. Relevant News Events.

Date	Relevant News Events
2015.12.9	The revised draft of "The new food safety law" and "The regulations on the implementation of the food safety law" has been solicited from the public.
2016.11.10	The China consumers' association reported the results of an experiential survey on online take-away ordering services in 2016, showing that food safety problems and the phenomenon of black take-away restaurants still exist.
2016.11.16	Guangzhou launched a special campaign to shut down more than 2000 online food ordering platforms.
2016.11.21	Measures on supervision and administration of food safety for online ordering in Shanxi province were promulgated.
2016.12.27	The Food and Drug Administration (FDA) interviewed Meituan take-away and the regional agents of Ele.me.
2017.3.15	China Central Television (CCTV)'s 315 gala exposes black take-away workshops.
2017.4.15	The general office of the state council issued the 2017 arrangement for key work on food safety, calling for improved judicial interpretation of criminal cases that endanger food safety, and for direct punishment of adulterated and false acts.
2017.12.19	There are more than 20,000 "sunshine catering" stores in Beijing, and 1500 take-away restaurants are broadcast live.
2017.12.27	In order to further strengthen the supervision of online catering, the State Food and Drug Administration worked out the measures for food safety supervision and administration of online catering services.
2018.9.20	Meituan listed on the 20th.
2018.9.26	Haidilao listed on the 26th.
2018.9.19	Starbucks is moving into take-away.

4.2. Topic Analysis

4.2.1. Topic Analysis Based on latent Dirichlet allocation (LDA) Model

Topic analysis was used to determine a text's topical structure, creating a representation indicating what topics were included in a text and how those topics change within the text. Topic analysis consists of two main tasks: topic identification and text segmentation.

In order to see the trend of food safety of take-away, this paper analyzed the hot words in Weibo posts over four years. Overall, the discussion around the topic of take-away food safety changed over time with the development and progression of society. Using LDA to extract topics, the top 10 hot words associated with each topic are shown in Table 4. In all, we have the following five topics by classification: Topic 1 shows the public's concern about the take-away industry; Topic 2 concerns college students, mainly reflecting the discussion and influence of this group on take-away; Topic 3 concerns the supervision and management, which shows the public's attention to the supervision mechanism of the take-away industry; Topic 4 has more objects of concern, such as platforms, journalists, consumers and so on, and demonstrates the wide range of public participation from different users' perspectives; Topic 5 focuses on the regulatory authorities, such as Food and Drug Administration, Drug Administration, Administration Bureau and so on, such that this topic reflects the public's concern with the administration and governance of the food safety industry.

Table 4. Topic distribution table.

Topic	Hot Words				
1	Catering Industry	Consumption Deliver	Ele.me Company	China Market	Internet /
2	Student Deliveryman	School Health	Canteen Work	University Worker	Campus Sanitation
3	Network License	Catering Order	Service Platform	Business Supervision	Management /
4	Meituan Meituan Take-away	Businessman Discovery	Consumption Production	Consumer Sanitation	Platform Reporter
5	Platform Baidu	Ele.me Food and drug safety	Order Catering	Meituan Food and drug administration	Network Administration

Topic extraction of Weibo posts, with respect to different emotional polarities, can be helpful to grasp the different topics that netizens in different emotional states are concerned with. The specific analysis results are shown in Tables 5 and 6.

Table 5. Distribution of topics of positive emotion.

Topic	Hot Words				
1	Student University	School China	Canteen Industry	Deliver /	Internet /
2	Meituan Order	Food and drug administration Deliveryman	Meituan Take-away Platform	Beijing Network	Drug administration Beijing
3	Network Platform	Catering Supervise	Service /	Management /	Order /
4	Consumption Kitchen	Catering Online	Consumer Sanitary	Businessman Physical store	Entity Production
5	Platform Supervise	Ele.me Meituan Take-away	Meituan Restaurant	Baidu /	Businessman /

Table 6. Distribution of topics of negative emotion.

Topic	Hot Words				
1	Student Time	School Prohibit	Canteen Classmate	University Bad	Campus Sanitation
2	Meituan Meituan Take-away	Customer Consumption	Boss Canteen	Platform Sanitation	Businessman Industry
3	Ele.me Discovery	Businessman Complain	Nausea Hospital	A Colleague	Food Vomiting

Due to the large number of positive emotional posts, this paper divided them into five topics, where each topic was described by up to 10 hot words. Table 5 shows that the topics and the focus of public concern were very similar those in Table 4, which is due to the fact that most of the posts showed positive emotion.

Due to the limited number of negative emotional posts and information, this paper could only divide the posts into three topics, and each topic was described by 10 hot words, as shown in Table 6.

Topic 1 relates to college students, and it was obvious that most people held a negative attitude towards the discussion on the delivery time of take-away and whether it could enter schools. Topic 2 show that some consumers were still worried about the take-away catering industry, and there were different worries about businesses and platforms. Topic 3 shows that there were obvious words with strong emotions such as complaint, nausea, and vomiting. It is clear that consumers may have had bad experiences with take-away, such as getting sick, causing them to show negative emotions.

4.2.2. Topic Analysis based on K-Means Clustering

k-means is an unsupervised machine learning algorithm used to cluster data into a user-defined 'k' different clusters. This algorithm was selected to analyze the vectorized textual data (which was vectorized via TF-IDF). Through many experiments and analysis, we found that it was better to divide all posts into five topics ($k = 5$), with cluster labels of 0, 1, 2, 3, and 4, respectively. Through the analysis of different topics and mining the similarities, the typical opinions and hot words in each topic are shown in Table 7.

Table 7. Clustering analysis.

Topic	Typical Weibo Post	High-Frequency Words
1 (234 items)	"Do you dare to eat black take-away?" "Baidu's own expired food ..."	Meituan, help, sorry, outdated
2 (590 items)	"Heavy sound! Deputy director of the FDA: I don't support home kitchen take-away." "The person in charge of the online catering service platform made a statement after the collective interview: management measures will be improved."	Physical store, service provider, food and drug
3 (94 items)	"Ele.me's first Corporate social responsibility (CSR) report has been released! It is also the first CSR report for the take-away industry. Food safety system upgrade, rider safety protection, support "take-away knight-errant" charity."	Righteous deeds, rider, security system
4 (1751 items)	""Internet + food ordering" is increasingly popular, but food safety risks. Beijing food and drug administration recently issued a warning online ordering consumption." "Xinhua criticized the online food delivery platform for its emphasis on expansion rather than supervision, and some shops were not fully licensed for dirty food." "Several black take-away across the country have been removed from online ordering platforms."	The third party, Food and Drug Administration, license, service
5 (5783 items)	"Many people participated in the vote launched by People's Daily online." "Online To Offline (O2O)food safety issues of food take-away have attracted wide attention and discussion." "Ele.me and Chinese people's insurance jointly launch the first food safety insurance policy "take-away insurance"!" "University bans students from ordering take-away ..."	Business, catering, food safety, network, consumer, delivery-man, deliver

Table 7 shows that hot issues that suddenly appear in society can cause a wave of extensive attention and discussion; e.g., those from black take-away of Meituan and out-of-date products in Baidu. The public often speaks out by criticizing this kind of behavior. As for some of the official policies, the public can also participate in the discussion, and show a positive attitude.

5. Discussion and Conclusions

This paper analyzed the public opinion on the issue of take-away food safety by using data mining and Boson NLP techniques. We first collected posts regarding "take-away food safety" from Sina Weibo between 2015 to 2018 using the Octopus Collector. After the posts were preprocessed, users' emotions and opinions were analyzed using natural language processing and unsupervised learning techniques. This paper fills the research gap by using latent Dirichlet allocation (LDA) and *k*-means to extract and cluster topics from the posts, allowing for the users' emotions and related opinions to be mined and analyzed.

k-means has high computing efficiency, easy operation, and good scalability for big data sets. LDA can find hidden topic information in text via unsupervised learning, and can analyze the topic distribution of the text better. The discussion around the topic of take-away food safety changed over time with various developments. Using LDA to extract topics, there were five topics by classification, which were consistent with the topics and public concerns of positive emotion. Based on *k*-means, it was better to divide all posts into five topics. We found that the results of *k*-means and LDA in terms of topics were similar, as both reflected the public's attention to the take-away industry and the regulatory mechanisms. However, LDA further demonstrated the distribution table of topics of positive and negative emotion, while there are only three topics due to the limited number of negative emotional posts and information.

Term frequency (TF) was used to show the word frequency statistics, which reflect most people's concerns better. TF-IDF tends to use less frequent words to prepare for classification. We used TF-IDF to construct the word vector matrix and then use the word feature vectors of each text to facilitate the subsequent text classification and clustering analyses.

The information was quantified and compared with the hot words that identify the focus of users and their emotional trend. Furthermore, our conclusions and suggestions for the industry and research domains are as follows:

(1) Public opinions regarding take-away food safety were studied. Based on the analysis of the relevant data obtained from Sina Weibo during 2015–2018, we conclude that there were many topics about food such as take-away, food safety, businesses, online platforms, and so on. The Online To Offline (O2O) business model perfectly combines online and offline commerce, which has been the developing trend in the take-away food industry. Whether the safety of take-away food is satisfactory or not determines follow-up development of the whole industry.

(2) Users' emotions and opinions were analyzed using natural language processing. Through the emotional analysis, the proportion of posts exhibiting positive emotions far exceeded that of negative emotions. Due to the timeliness of market supervision and the convenience offered through the services, we conclude that the take-away industry presents an overall positive environment for the consumers.

(3) Representative news events in the take-away catering industry between 2015 and 2018 were summarized. We can see that every step of the development of the take-away industry was accompanied by strict supervision and regulation. Every occurrence of this kind of regulation will cause extensive discussion on microblogging sites. These positive practices make the take-away industry more transparent and ensure the public have increased confidence in the safety of take-away food.

(4) The degree of topics increased over the years, and there were a variety of topics. As for the topic analysis, there were various discussions: some from the regulatory perspectives, some from the policies issued by the relevant departments, and others from different users, such as college students, take-away platforms, and food and drug supervision. For take-away food safety, we conclude that the focus of attention of the public is rich and diverse, therefore the potential management of public opinions should be addressed from multiple different perspectives.

(5) All posts were classed into five topics based on *k*-means clustering. It was found that, on the one hand, people usually showed a negative and bad mood for the bad public opinion events in the society. They thought that the occurrence of such events threatened their daily life, making them have great uncertainty about the future development of the take-away industry, resulting in no confidence in the healthy and safe development of the industry. Therefore, how to build people's confidence and mutual trust is particularly important in the development of the take-away industry. On the other hand, with a series of policies and measures issued by the

relevant departments of the government, great achievements have been made in the cleaning up and rectification of the take-away industry, and a good industry environment has been created. Consumers can really see and feel these changes, therefore public opinion and emotion can move forward in a good direction.

In summary, the government should monitor the public opinion on take-away food safety, pay attention to the opinions of the people, and maintain reasonable guidance and supervision. The measures taken by the Food and Drug Administration and other relevant departments to strengthen the management of take-away platforms and businesses should be continuously strengthened to ensure the health and safety of the general public.

Limitations and Future Research Directions

There are limitations of this paper, which presents some potential future research directions.

(1) In terms of data selection, this paper crawled relevant data from Sina Weibo, including some contents sent by enterprise or official users. Some of the postings are not significant for emotional analysis, and removing them could improve the accuracy of the emotional analysis.
(2) The emotion dictionary is manually controlled to improve the accuracy of emotion analysis. However, compared with the emotional analysis methods used in machine learning, this method still has some defects such as instability and lack of validation [27]. Future research directions could use deep learning algorithms for further analysis [28].
(3) This study is limited to the opinion of users who posted in China Weibo. The post data from other data source in other countries could result in different results. The geographical distribution of the authors could be further extended and analyzed in different regions in one country or different countries.

Author Contributions: Conceptualization, C.S.; Methodology, C.S.; Software, C.G.; Formal Analysis, C.G.; Data Curation, C.G.; Writing—Original Draft Preparation, C.G. and C.S.; Writing—Review and Editing, K.H. and J.Z.; Supervision, J.Z.; Funding Acquisition, C.S. All authors have read and agreed to the published version of the manuscript.

Funding: This research was funded by [National Natural Science Foundation of China] grant number [71901218] And the APC was funded by [National Natural Science Foundation of China] grant number [71901218].

Conflicts of Interest: The authors declare no conflict of interest. The sponsors had no role in the design, execution, interpretation, or writing of the study.

References

1. Haghiri, M. Consumer Choice between Food Safety and Food Quality: The Case of Farm-Raised Atlantic Salmon. *Foods* **2016**, *5*, 22. [CrossRef] [PubMed]
2. Yi, K. Food safety governance in China: Change and continuity. *Food Control* **2019**, *106*, 1–6.
3. Riccioli, F.; Moruzzo, R.; Zhang, Z.; Zhao, J.; Tang, Y.; Tinacci, L.; Boncinelli, F.; Martino, D.D.; Guidia, A. Willingness to pay in main cities of Zheijiang province (China) for quality and safety in food market. *Food Control* **2020**, *108*, 1–6. [CrossRef]
4. ShanghaiDaily. Ele.me Receives 120,000-Yuan Penalty Ticket after State TV Exposed Dirtiest Side of Food Ordering. 2016. Available online: https://archive.shine.cn/metro/society/Eleme-receives-120000yuan-penalty-ticket-after-state-TV-exposed-dirtiest-side-of-food-ordering/shdaily.shtml (accessed on 1 April 2020).
5. Song, C.; Zhuang, J. Modeling A Government-Manufacturer-Farmer Game for Food Supply Chain Risk Management. *Food Control* **2017**, *78*, 443–455. [CrossRef]
6. Song, C.; Zhuang, J. Regulating Food Risk Management—A Government–Manufacturer Game facing Endogenous Consumer Demand. *Int. Trans Oper. Res.* **2018**, *25*, 1855–1878. [CrossRef]
7. Han, F.; Liu, L.J.; Li, Y.; Fan, L. Investigation, analysis and countermeasures of food contamination in the process of online express delivery. *Logist. Eng. Manag.* **2018**, *40*, 59–61.

8. Yuan, X.L.; Li, B.Q. Study on early warning Strategy of Public opinion on Food and Drug Safety incident Network. *Chin. Mark.* **2017**, *34*, 87–88.
9. Maguire, E.R.; Burgoine, T.; Monsivais, P. Area deprivation and the food environment over time: A repeated cross-sectional study on takeaway outlet density and supermarket presence in Norfolk, UK, 1990–2008. *Health Place* **2015**, *33*, 142–147. [CrossRef]
10. Cobb, L.K.; Appel, L.J.; Franco, M.; Jones-Smith, J.C.; Nur, A.; Anderson, C.A.M. The relationship of the local food environment with obesity: A systematic review of methods, study quality, and results. *Obes. Rev.* **2015**, *23*, 1331–1344. [CrossRef]
11. Adams, J.; Goffe, L.; Brown, T.; Lake, A.A.; Summerbell, C.; White, M.; Wrieden, W.; Adamson, A.J. Frequency and socio-demographic correlates of eating meals out and take-away meals at home: Cross-sectional analysis of the UK national diet and nutrition survey, waves 1-4 (2008-12). *Int. J. Behav. Nutr. Phys. Act.* **2015**, *12*, 51. [CrossRef]
12. Keeble, M.; Burgoine, T.; White, M.; Summerbell, C.; Cummins, S.; Adams, J. How does local government use the planning system to regulate hot food takeaway outlets? A census of current practice in England using document review. *Health Place* **2019**, *57*, 171–178. [CrossRef] [PubMed]
13. Jaworowska, A.; Blackham, T.; Davies, I.G.; Steve, L. Nutritional challenges and health implications of takeaway and fast food. *Nutr. Rev.* **2013**, *71*, 310–318. [CrossRef]
14. Kirk, S.F.L.; Penney, T.L.; McHugh, T.L.F. Characterizing the obesogenic environment: The state of the evidence with directions for future research. *Obes. Rev.* **2010**, *11*, 109–117. [CrossRef] [PubMed]
15. Mahon, D.; Cowan, C.; McCarthy, M. The role of attitudes, subjective norm, perceived control and habit in the consumption of ready meals and takeaways in Great Britain. *Food Qual. Prefer.* **2006**, *17*, 474–481. [CrossRef]
16. Turrell, G.; Giskes, K. Socioeconomic disadvantage and the purchase of takeaway food: A multilevel analysis. *Appetite* **2008**, *51*, 69–81. [CrossRef] [PubMed]
17. Timperio, A.F.; Ball, K.; Roberts, R.; Andrianopoulos, N. Children's takeaway and fast-food intakes: Associations with the neighborhood food environment. *Public Health Nutr.* **2009**, *12*, 1960–1964. [CrossRef]
18. Miura, K.; Turrell, G. Reported consumption of takeaway food and its contribution to socioeconomic inequalities in body mass index. *Appetite* **2014**, *74*, 116–124. [CrossRef]
19. Savigny, H. Public opinion, political communication and the internet. *Politics* **2002**, *22*, 1–8. [CrossRef]
20. Sobkowicz, P.; Kaschesky, M.; Bouchard, G. Opinion mining in social media: Modeling, simulating, and forecasting political opinions in the web. *Gov. Inf. Q.* **2012**, *29*, 470–479. [CrossRef]
21. Wang, B.; Zhuang, J. Crisis information distribution on Twitter: A content analysis of tweets during Hurricane Sandy. *Nat. Hazards* **2017**, *89*, 161–181. [CrossRef]
22. Gu, Q.; Jia, Y.; Hao, X. Network Public Opinion Analysis and Research were Reviewe. In Proceedings of the 2015 International Conference on Mechanical Science and Engineering, Qingdao, China, 17–19 July 2015; Atlantis Press: Paris, France, 2016; pp. 1–6.
23. Li, H.; Xiao, H.; Qiu, T.; Zhou, P. Food safety warning research based on internet public opinion monitoring and tracing. In Proceedings of the Agro-Geoinformatics (Agro-Geoinformatics) 2013 Second International Conference on IEEE, Fairfax, VA, USA, 12–16 August 2013.
24. AlSumait, L.; Barbará, D.; Domeniconi, C. On-line lda: Adaptive topic models for mining text streams with applications to topic detection and tracking. In Proceedings of the 2008 Eighth IEEE International Conference on Data Mining, Pisa, Italy, 15–19 December 2008. [CrossRef]
25. Tan, Z.W.; Mao, W.J.; Zeng, W.; Li, X.C.; Xiu, G.B. Acquiring netizen group's opinions for modeling food safety events. In Proceedings of the 2012 IEEE International Conference on Intelligence and Security Informatics, Arlington, VA, USA, 11–14 June 2012. [CrossRef]
26. Zhang, H.; Rao, H.; Feng, J. Product innovation based on online review data mining: A case study of Huawei phones. *Electron. Commer. Res.* **2018**, *18*, 3–22. [CrossRef]

27. Krosnick, J. Survey research. *Annu. Rev. Psychol.* **1999**, *50*, 537–567. [CrossRef] [PubMed]
28. Oh, J.; Yun, K.; Maoz, U.; Kim, T.; Chae, J. Identifying depression in the National Health and Nutrition Examination Survey data using a deep learning algorithm. *J. Affect. Disord.* **2019**, *257*, 623–631. [CrossRef] [PubMed]

© 2020 by the authors. Licensee MDPI, Basel, Switzerland. This article is an open access article distributed under the terms and conditions of the Creative Commons Attribution (CC BY) license (http://creativecommons.org/licenses/by/4.0/).

MDPI
St. Alban-Anlage 66
4052 Basel
Switzerland
Tel. +41 61 683 77 34
Fax +41 61 302 89 18
www.mdpi.com

Foods Editorial Office
E-mail: foods@mdpi.com
www.mdpi.com/journal/foods

www.ingramcontent.com/pod-product-compliance
Lightning Source LLC
Chambersburg PA
CBHW061357010526
44107CB00012B/963